1, 2, & 3 John
Preaching Verse-by-Verse

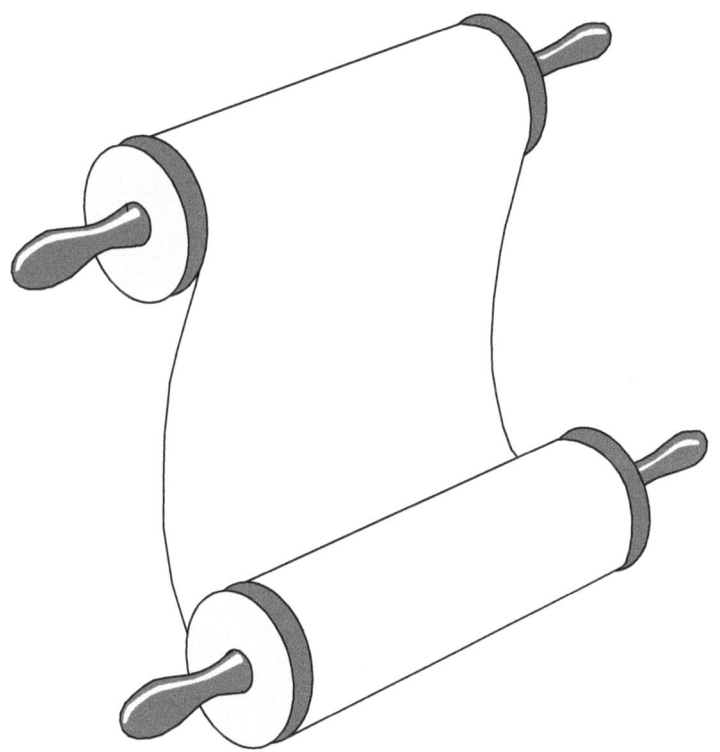

Pastor D. A. Waite, Th.D.,Ph.D.

Published by
THE BIBLE FOR TODAY PRESS
900 Park Avenue
Collingswood, New Jersey 08108 U.S.A.
Pastor D. A. Waite, Th.D., Ph.D.
Bible For Today Baptist Church
Church Phone: 856-854-4747
BFT Phone: 856-854-4452
Orders: 1-800-John 10:9
e-mail: BFT@BibleForToday.org
Website: www.BibleForToday.org
FAX: 856-854-2464

We Use and Defend
the King James Bible

Copyright, 2016
All Rights Reserved
September, 2016

BFT #4155

ISBN #978-1-56848112-8

Acknowledgments

I wish to thank and to acknowledge the assistance of the following people:

- **The Congregation** of the **Bible For Today Baptist Church**–for whom these messages were prepared, to whom they were delivered, and by whom they were published. They listened attentively and encouraged their Pastor.
- **Yvonne Sanborn Waite**–my wife, who encouraged the publication of these sermons, read the manuscript, developed the various boxes, suggested sentences to underline, and gave other helpful suggestions and comments. The boxes help the reader to see some of the more important topics that are covered in the various chapters.
- **Patricia Canter**–a friend of Mrs. Waite who volunteered to take the cassette tapes of the verse-by-verse exposition of the book of 1, 2, & 3 John and put these words into digital format to be used for this book.
- **Dr. Kirk DiVietro**–a friend for many years, one of our Dean Burgon Society faithful Vice Presidents, who is an expert on the use of computers. He has helped in various ways to make the computer work easier when performing the needed tasks.
- **Bonlyn Walls**–one of our friends who has also been an attender of our church through the Internet for many years. She has worked diligently in her proofreading by making very helpful suggestions for the improvement of this book.

Foreword

- **The Beginning.** This book is the **thirteenth** in a series of books based on my expository preaching from various books of the Bible. It is an attempt to bring to the minds of the readers two things: (1) the **meaning** of the words in the verses, and (2) the practical **application** of those words to the lives of both saved and unsaved.
- **Preached Sermons.** These were messages that I preached to our **Bible For Today Baptist Church** in Collingswood, New Jersey. They were broadcast over the radio, and over the Internet by computer streaming around the world. I took half a chapter each Sunday as the messages were preached.
- **Other Verses.** In connection with both the **meaning** and **application** of the verses in this book, there are many verses from other places in the Bible that have been quoted for further elaboration on the teachings in this book. All the verses of Scripture that were used to illustrate further truth are written out in full for easy reference.
- **A Transcription.** This entire book was typed into computer format by Patricia Canter from the tape recordings of the messages as they were preached. In addition to the words used as I preached these sermons, I have added words for clarification as needed.
- **The Audience.** The intended audience for this book is the same as the audience that listened to the messages in the first place. These studies are not meant to be overly scholarly, though there are some references to various Greek Words used. My aim and burden is to try to help genuine Christians to understand the Words of God. It is also my hope that my children, grandchildren, great grandchildren, and many others might profit from this study of 1, 2, & 3 John. There is a 25-page INDEX of words and topics.

Yours For God's Words,
D. A. Waite
Pastor D. A. Waite, Th.D., Ph.D.
Bible For Today Baptist Church

Table of Contents

Publisher's Data.................................. i
Acknowledgments. ii
Foreword.. iii
Table of Contents............................... iv
1 John Chapter One............................. 1
1 John Chapter Two............................ 51
1 John Chapter Three. 103
1 John Chapter Four. 133
1 John Chapter Five........................... 169
2 John... 199
3 John... 233
Index of Words and Phrases................... 261
About the Author.............................. 287
Order Blank Pages............................. 289
Defined King James Bible Orders............... 297

1 John
Chapter One

A Brief Background Of The Letters Of The Apostle John

These three letters by the Apostle John were written in around 90 A.D. from the Island of Patmos where he was exiled by the Roman government because he was a stalwart Christian who loved the Lord Jesus Christ with all of his heart.

While on that island, John also wrote the Gospel of John and the book of Revelation. He did not let the imprisonment and persecution by Rome and other anti-Christian forces impede his living a victorious Christian life standing up for the Lord Jesus Christ and God's Words.

1 John 1:1

"That which was from the beginning, which we have heard, which we have seen with our eyes, which we have looked upon, and our hands have handled, of the Word of life;"

John was a witness for the Lord Jesus Christ—with his ears, with his eyes, and even with his touch. That is a very important truth. In a court of law, witnesses are brought before the judge and jury in order either to establish or to refute the evidence that is being presented. The Apostle John was an excellent firsthand witness about the life, ministry, and bodily resurrection of the Lord Jesus Christ.

> **THE MEANING OF THE GREEK WORD, "THEAOMAI"**
> The Greek Word for "*looked upon*" is THEAOMAI. Some of the meanings of this Greek Word are:
> > "*1) to behold, look upon, view attentively, contemplate (often used of public shows) 1a) of important persons that are looked on with admiration; 2) to view, take a view of; 2a) in the sense of visiting, meeting with a person; 3) to learn by looking, to see with the eyes, to perceive*"

Thirteen Things About The Apostle John

Let us look at thirteen things about the Apostle John, the writer of this book, before we get into the a discussion of the verses themselves:

1. John's Call To Be Christ's Follower
- Matthew 4:18-22

"And Jesus, walking by the sea of Galilee, saw two brethren, Simon called Peter, and Andrew his brother, casting a net into the sea: for they were fishers. And he saith unto them, Follow me, and I will make you fishers of men. And they straightway left their nets, and followed him. And going on from thence, he saw other two brethren, James the son of Zebedee, and **John** his brother, in a ship with Zebedee their father, mending their nets; and **he called them**. And **they immediately left the ship and their father, and followed him**."

John is mentioned in these verses. When the Lord Jesus Christ "*called them,*" they "*immediately left the ship and their father, and followed Him.*"

- Luke 5:10

"And so *was* also James, and John, **the sons of Zebedee**, which were partners with Simon. And Jesus said unto Simon, Fear not; from henceforth thou shalt catch men."

> **THE APOSTLE JOHN RESPONDED TO CHRIST'S CALL**
> John, one of Zebedee's sons, responded to this invitation by the Lord Jesus Christ.

2. John's Commission To Preach
- Matthew 9:36-38

"But when he saw the multitudes, he was moved with compassion on them, because they fainted, and were scattered abroad, as sheep having no shepherd. Then saith he unto his disciples, The harvest truly *is* plenteous, but the labourers *are* few; Pray ye therefore the Lord of the harvest, that he will send forth labourers into his harvest."

PRAYING FOR LABORERS IN GOD'S HARVEST
The Lord Jesus Christ asked His disciples to pray for laborers in His harvest. John responded to this appeal.

- Matthew 10:1

"And when he had called unto *him* his twelve disciples, he gave them power *against* unclean spirits, to cast them out, and to heal all manner of sickness and all manner of disease."

John was one of the twelve disciples who was given this power and authority over unclean spirits and diseases.

3. John's Presence At Christ's Transfiguration

JOHN AT CHRIST'S TRANSFIGURATION
John was with the Lord Jesus Christ when He was transfigured on the Mount of Transfiguration.

- Matthew 17:1-3

"And after six days Jesus taketh Peter, James, and John his brother, and bringeth them up into an high mountain apart, And was transfigured before them: and his face did shine as the sun, and his raiment was white as the light. And, behold, there appeared unto them Moses and Elias talking with him."

CHRIST'S FACE SHOWN AS THE SUN
John saw the Lord Jesus Christ transfigured and transformed so that His face shone like the sun and His raiment was white as the light.

- Matthew 17:5-8

"While he yet spake, behold, a bright cloud overshadowed them: and behold a voice out of the cloud, which said, This is my beloved Son, in whom I am well pleased; hear ye him. And when the disciples heard *it*, they fell on their face, and were sore afraid. And Jesus came and touched them, and said, Arise, and be not afraid. And when they had lifted up their eyes, they saw no man, save Jesus only."

JOHN AND TWO OTHERS HEARD GOD'S VOICE
John was one of the three disciples who heard God's Voice on the Mount of Transfiguration and was very afraid.

4. John's Special Assignment
- Luke 22:7-9

"Then came the day of unleavened bread, when the passover must be killed. And he sent Peter and John, saying, Go and prepare us the passover, that we may eat. And they said unto him, Where wilt thou that we prepare?"

JOHN PREPARED CHRIST'S LAST PASSOVER

John was one of the two disciples who was sent to go to prepare a place for the Passover. This was the last Passover before the Lord Jesus Christ was crucified.

---

5. John's Presence At Christ's Trial
- John 18:15

And Simon Peter followed Jesus, and so did **another disciple**: that disciple was known unto the high priest, and went in with Jesus into the palace of the high priest.

"ANOTHER DISCIPLE" IS THE APOSTLE JOHN

The phrase, "*another disciple*" was a reference to the Apostle John. Both John and Peter were present at the trial of the Lord Jesus Christ.

---

6. John's Belief In Christ's Bodily Resurrection
- John 20:3-8

"Peter therefore went forth, and **that other disciple**, and came to the sepulchre. So they ran both together: and the other disciple did outrun Peter, and came first to the sepulchre. And he stooping down, *and looking in*, saw the linen clothes lying; yet went he not in. Then cometh Simon Peter following him, and went into the sepulchre, and seeth the linen clothes lie, And the napkin, that was about his head, not lying with the linen clothes, but wrapped together in a place by itself. Then went in also **that other disciple**, which came first to the sepulchre, and he saw, and believed."

JOHN SAW CHRIST'S EMPTY TOMB

Once again, "*that other disciple*" is a reference to John. John saw the empty tomb where the Lord Jesus Christ was placed. He was not there. He was raised bodily from death. The modernist apostate liberals teach that the Lord Jesus Christ rose only in spirit, not in body. This is absolutely unscriptural and wrong. It is a false teaching that must be countered by the truth. John saw the Lord

Jesus Christ's empty tomb and believed in His bodily resurrection.

7. John's Presence At The Cross
- John 19:25-27

"Now there stood by the cross of Jesus his mother, and his mother's sister, Mary the *wife* of Cleophas, and Mary Magdalene. When Jesus therefore saw his mother, and **the disciple standing by, whom he loved**, he saith unto his mother, Woman, behold thy son! Then saith he to the disciple, Behold thy mother! And from that hour **that disciple** took her unto his own *home*."

JOHN CARED FOR JESUS' MOTHER, MARY

This "**disciple**" was a reference to John himself. From that hour, at the request of His Saviour, John took care of Mary, the mother of the Lord Jesus Christ.

8. John's Return To Fishing With Peter
- John 21:2-3

"There were together Simon Peter, and Thomas called Didymus, and Nathanael of Cana in Galilee, and the *sons* of Zebedee, and two other of his disciples. Simon Peter saith unto them, I go a fishing. They say unto him, We also go with thee. They went forth, and entered into a ship immediately; and that night they caught nothing."

JOHN SHOULD NOT HAVE FOLLOWED PETER HERE

This took place after the bodily resurrection of the Lord Jesus Christ. I don't think Peter should have gone back to his fishing, nor should these six other disciples have answered his request to join him.

The Lord Jesus Christ had commissioned all of them to fish for men. They went back to fishing instead of preaching the Word. They were not successful as fishermen on this occasion.

9. John's Banishment To The Isle Of Patmos
- Revelation 1:9

"I John, who also am your brother, and companion in tribulation, and in the kingdom and patience of Jesus Christ, was in the isle that is called Patmos, for the word of God, and for the testimony of Jesus Christ."

> **JOHN WAS EXILED TO PATMOS FOR GOD'S WORDS**
> John, the apostle, was banished to the isle of Patmos. Notice the reason for his banishment. It was *"for the word of God, and for the testimony of Jesus Christ."* Church tradition teaches that he was the only one of the twelve apostles who died a natural death. He died on Patmos.

10. John's Writing Of Many Bible Books

The Apostle John was used of the Lord to write five books of the New Testament. <u>All of them were written from the isle of Patmos.</u> He wrote the Gospel of John, the epistles of 1 John, 2 John, and 3 John, and the Book of Revelation.

11. John Wrote Of Christ As The Eternal Creator

John taught clearly in his books about the Lord Jesus Christ as the Creator Who preexisted from all eternity past.

- **John 1:1**

"In the beginning was the Word, and the Word was with God, and the Word was God."

> **CHRIST'S ETERNAL DEITY**
> The Lord Jesus Christ was from the very beginning. He was Deity.

- **John 1:14-15**

"And the Word was made flesh, and dwelt among us, (and we beheld his glory, the glory as of the only begotten of the Father,) full of grace and truth. John bare witness of him, and cried, saying, This was he of whom I spake, He that cometh after me is preferred before me: for he was before me."

> **CHRIST WAS PERFECT GOD AND PERFECT MAN**
> By His miracle virgin birth, the Lord Jesus Christ was made flesh. As perfect Deity, He took upon Himself perfect Humanity. He was and is the God-Man–Perfect God and Perfect Man. He was before John and all of God's creation. <u>The Lord Jesus Christ has had eternal preexistence</u> with the other Members of the Trinity and He will maintain this relationship during all of the eternal future.

- **1 John 1:1**

"That which was from the beginning, which we have heard, which we have seen with our eyes, which we have looked upon, and our hands have handled, of the Word of life;"

THE CONTINUOUS GREEK IMPERFECT TENSE

The Lord Jesus Christ was from the beginning–from all eternity past. The words, *"That which was from the beginning,"* is a Greek imperfect tense. As such, it shows a continuous past and eternal preexistence.

- **John 8:58**

"Jesus said unto them, Verily, verily, I say unto you, Before Abraham was, I am."

CHRIST'S TITLE "I AM" SHOWS HIS ETERNAL DEITY

By His use of the Divine title, *"I Am,"* the Lord Jesus Christ declared His eternal past, present, and future existence.

- **Hebrews 1:2**

"Hath in these last days spoken unto us by *his* Son, whom he hath appointed heir of all things, by whom also he made the worlds;"

CHRIST IS THE "HEIR OF ALL THINGS"

In all eternity past, God the Father made His Son to be the *"heir of all things."*

- **Ephesians 3:9**

"And to make all *men* see what *is* the fellowship of the mystery, which from the beginning of the world hath been hid in God, who created all things **by Jesus Christ**:"

CHRIST HAD PART IN THE CREATION

The eternal Son of God had a part with the Father and the Holy Spirit in the creation of all things.

The Gnostic Critical Greek Text and all the modern versions that follow them leave out the words, *"by Jesus Christ,"* because the Gnostics did not believe the Lord Jesus Christ could create anything. He was just a sinful frail man Who was not God the Son.

- **Colossians 1:16**

"For by him were all things created, that are in heaven, and that are in earth, visible and invisible, whether *they be* thrones, or dominions, or principalities, or powers: all things were created by him, and for him:"

BY CHRIST ALL THINGS WERE CREATED

This verse offers further proof of the Lord Jesus Christ being the Creator of all things in heaven and earth.

12. John Heard And Looked Upon Christ
During the three and one-half years of ministry with the Lord Jesus Christ, **the Apostle John looked upon Him very closely and frequently.**

13. John Handled And Touched Christ
- 1 John 1:1

"That which was from the beginning, which we have heard, which we have seen with our eyes, which we have looked upon, and our hands have handled, of the Word of life;"

> **JOHN HANDLED THE LORD JESUS CHRIST**
> The Lord Jesus Christ permitted John and the other apostles to handle and touch Him.

- Luke 24:39

"Behold my hands and my feet, that it is I myself: handle me, and see; for a spirit hath not flesh and bones, as ye see me have."

> **CHRIST HAS A BODILY RESURRECTION**
> Even after His bodily resurrection, the Lord Jesus Christ encouraged His followers to touch Him to show that He had a glorified body and was not just a spirit.

- John 21:20

"Then Peter, turning about, seeth the disciple whom Jesus loved following; which also leaned on his breast at supper, and said, Lord, which is he that betrayeth thee?"

> **JOHN LEANED ON CHRIST AT THE LAST SUPPER**
> John, *"the disciple whom Jesus loved,"* leaned upon Him at the last supper.

1 John 1:2

"(For the life was manifested, and we have seen it, and bear witness, and shew unto you that eternal life, which was with the Father, and was manifested unto us;)"

Notice some of the important subjects that are mentioned in this one verse:

1. The Lord Jesus Christ Is Called The Life
First of all, the Lord Jesus Christ is called *"the life."* That is one of His titles.

- **John 1:4**
"In him was life; and the life was the light of men."
Life, <u>both physical and eternal</u>, was in the Lord Jesus Christ.
- **John 11:25**
"Jesus said unto her, I am the resurrection, and the life: he that believeth in me, though he were dead, yet shall he live:"
In this verse, <u>He is the resurrection and the life</u>. All those who genuinely believe in Him shall live for all eternity with Him in Heaven.
- **John 14:6**
"Jesus saith unto him, I am the way, the truth, and the life: no man cometh unto the Father, but by me."
<u>He is the only way that people</u> who genuinely trust in Him might come to God the Father and <u>receive everlasting life</u>.
- **Acts 3:15**
"And killed the Prince of life, whom God hath raised from the dead; whereof we are witnesses."

"THE PRINCE OF LIFE" IS A TITLE OF CHRIST

The *"Prince of life"* is one of the titles of the Lord Jesus Christ. His enemies brought death to the Prince of life, but God the Father raised Him up to life again.

- **Colossians 3:4**
"When Christ, *who is* our life, shall appear, then shall ye also appear with him in glory."
In this verse, the Lord Jesus Christ is given the title of *"our life"* when referring to genuine born-again Christians.
- **1 John 5:20**
"And we know that the Son of God is come, and hath given us an understanding, that we may know him that is true, and we are in him that is true, *even* in his Son Jesus Christ. This is the true God, and eternal life."
<u>Another title for the Lord Jesus Christ in this verse is</u> *"eternal life."*

2. Christ The Life Was Manifested

The Lord Jesus Christ was manifested, that is, made clear to all who will seek Him and His eternal life.
- **John 2:11**
"This beginning of miracles did Jesus in Cana of Galilee, and manifested forth his glory; and his disciples believed on him."

> **CHRIST'S FIRST NEW TESTAMENT MIRACLE**
> By His turning of this water into the fruit of the vine (delicious grape juice), the Lord Jesus Christ manifested His miracle-working glory. That convinced His disciples to believe in Him as they beheld this Divine miraculous power.

- **Galatians 4:4-5**
"But when the fulness of the time was come, God sent forth his Son, made of a woman, made under the law, to redeem them that were under the law, that we might receive the adoption of sons."

> **GOD SENT HIS SON AT HIS OWN PROPER TIME**
> When the proper time came, God the Father sent God the Son into this world, thus manifesting His Divine purpose. The Lord Jesus Christ was perfect God and perfect Man so that He could redeem whosoever might genuinely trust in Him as their Saviour.

- **1 Timothy 3:16**
"And without controversy great is the mystery of godliness: God was manifest in the flesh, justified in the Spirit, seen of angels, preached unto the Gentiles, believed on in the world, received up into glory."

What a miracle this was–to have "*God... manifest in the flesh.*" <u>That was God the Father's only way that He could bring the possibility of forgiveness to whoever might trust in His beloved Son.</u> This was made possible by His death on the cross for the sins of the entire world so that those who genuinely trust in Him might have everlasting and eternal life.

> **THE GNOSTIC GREEK TEXT REMOVES "GOD" HERE**
> Here again, the Gnostic Critical Greek Text and all the Bible versions that are based upon that Text have removed the most important word in that verse–the word "*God*" (THEOS). Since the Gnostic heretics do not believe that the Lord Jesus Christ was "*God*," they removed it from their Alexandrian manuscripts. When God the Son was manifested in the flesh, that was a miracle. The result was, through the miracle of His virgin birth, that this Incarnation resulted in perfect God and perfect Man being manifested. This was the only way that man's redemption from sin could be made possible.

- **1 Peter 1:18-20**
"Forasmuch as ye know that ye were not redeemed with corruptible things, *as* silver and gold, from your vain conversation *received* by tradition from your fathers; But with the precious blood of Christ, as of a lamb without blemish and without spot: Who verily was foreordained before the foundation of the world, but was manifest in these last times for you,"

> **GOD'S ETERNAL PLAN OF REDEMPTION BY BLOOD**
> **Though God's plan of salvation based on the blood sacrifice of the Lord Jesus Christ was an eternal plan in the mind of God, it was finally manifested for all to see when God's Son was incarnated and crucified for the sins of the world.**

- **1 John 3:5**
"And ye know that he was manifested to take away our sins; and in him is no sin."

The reason that the Lord Jesus Christ came down from Heaven as perfect God and perfect Man and was manifested was to take away the sins of those who genuinely trust Him as their Saviour.

- **1 John 3:8b**
". . . For this purpose the Son of God was manifested, that he might destroy the works of the devil."

Another purpose for the manifestation of the Lord Jesus Christ was to destroy the works of the devil.

3. Christ Showed What Eternal Life Is

"Eternal Life" is another title of the Lord Jesus Christ. There are many verses that mention eternal life.

- **Luke 10:25**
"And, behold, a certain lawyer stood up, and tempted him, saying, Master, what shall I do to inherit eternal life?"

This lawyer pretended to be interested in how he could obtain eternal life by asking the Lord Jesus Christ a question.

- **Luke 18:18**
"And a certain ruler asked him, saying, Good Master, what shall I do to inherit eternal life?"

A ruler asked what he had to do to gain eternal life.

- **John 3:14-15**
"And as Moses lifted up the serpent in the wilderness, even so must the Son of man be lifted up: That whosoever believeth in him should not perish, but have eternal life."

> **THE BRAZEN SERPENT--A PICTURE OF THE CROSS**
> The Lord Jesus Christ told Nicodemus that eternal life was obtained by whoever genuinely believed in and trusted the Saviour; such a person would not perish but have eternal life. The simplicity of this transaction was illustrated by Moses lifting up the brazen serpent so that those bitten by poisonous snakes might be healed and live.

Once again, the Gnostic Critical Greek Text, and every translation that follows it, had eliminated the words, *"should not perish."* Since the Gnostics believed that everyone in the world, including Satan, would be saved, they removed any thought of anyone perishing in Hell if they failed genuinely to trust in the Lord Jesus Christ.

- **John 6:68**

"Then Simon Peter answered him, Lord, to whom shall we go? thou hast the words of eternal life."

When the Lord Jesus Christ asked His apostles if they were going to leave Him as others had done, Peter said he was not going to leave Him because He alone had the *"words of eternal life."*

- **John 10:27-28**

"My sheep hear my voice, and I know them, and they follow me: And I give unto them eternal life; and they shall never perish, neither shall any *man* pluck them out of my hand."

> **ETERNAL LIFE GIVEN TO THOSE TRUSTING CHRIST**
> Those who have genuinely trusted the Lord Jesus Christ as their Saviour and Redeemer, have been given eternal life. They possess eternal life. They don't have to wait for it and hope for it. They have it immediately and will never perish.

The Armenians, the Pentecostals, the Charismatics, and all the other groups who teach that genuine Christians can lose their salvation when they sin are in error in this false teaching. *"Shall never perish"* means *"shall never perish"*! It's impossible for those who are born-again by the Spirit of God to be unborn. They may walk in the flesh, and must be restored to fellowship with the Lord, but they can never lose eternal life once they have it.

- **Romans 6:23**

"For the wages of sin *is* death; but the gift of God *is* eternal life through Jesus Christ our Lord."

1, 2, & 3 John–Preaching Verse-by-Verse

> **ETERNAL LIFE IS A GIFT FROM GOD**
> God bestows the gift of eternal life to those who exercise genuine faith in the Lord Jesus Christ. It is not through any works of their own. <u>Eternal life is a gift from God.</u>

- **1 John 5:11-13**

"And this is the record, that God hath given to us eternal life, and this life is in his Son. <u>He that hath the Son hath life; *and* he that hath not the Son of God hath not life.</u> These things have I written unto you that believe on the name of the Son of God; that ye may know that ye have eternal life, and that ye may believe on the name of the Son of God."

<u>The knowledge that a person has eternal life is very important. God wants every truly born-again Christian to know positively that they have eternal life and will not perish in Hell.</u>

- **1 John 5:20**

"And we know that the Son of God is come, and hath given us an understanding, that we may know him that is true, and we are in him that is true, *even* in his Son Jesus Christ. This is the true God, and eternal life.

<u>The Lord Jesus Christ is the *"true God, and eternal life."* This is another one of His titles.</u>

4. Christ Was With The Father

> **CHRIST WAS ETERNALLY WITH HIS FATHER**
> From all eternity past, the Lord Jesus Christ was *"with the Father"* in Heaven. The Pharisees didn't believe He was with the Father. They accused Him of being an illegitimate son of Joseph and Mary. They were wrong. He was born by the miracle of a virgin birth through the power of both God the Father and God the Holy Spirit.

- **John 8:42**

"Jesus said unto them, If God were your Father, ye would love me: for I proceeded forth and came from God; neither came I of myself, but he sent me."

<u>The Lord Jesus Christ came to this earth from God the Father. He was God manifested in the flesh.</u> The Jews thought that this was blasphemy.

- **John 13:3**

"Jesus knowing that the Father had given all things into his hands, and that he was come from God, and went to God;"

<u>The Lord Jesus Christ came from God the Father–from Heaven.</u>

- **John 16:27**

"For the Father himself loveth you, because ye have loved me, and have believed that I came out from God."

The Lord Jesus Christ "*came out from God*."

- **John 16:30b**

". . . by this we believe that thou camest forth from God."

Once again, it is stated clearly that the Lord Jesus Christ came forth "*from God*" the Father.

1 John 1:3

"That which we have seen and heard declare we unto you, that ye also may have fellowship with us: and truly our fellowship is with the Father, and with his Son Jesus Christ."

The Apostle John wanted to declare and be a witness to others about the things he had seen and heard concerning the Lord Jesus Christ.

Verses On Witness

- **John 1:6-7**

"There was a man sent from God, whose name *was* John. The same came for a **witness**, to **bear witness** of the Light, that all *men* through him might believe."

> **JOHN THE BAPTIST WAS A WITNESS TO CHRIST**
>
> John the Baptist came as a witness that the Lord Jesus Christ was the Light of the world, so that through Him, they might truly believe.

- **John 15:27**

"And ye also shall **bear witness**, because ye have been with me from the beginning."

The Lord Jesus Christ told His disciples that it was their job to bear a witness to Him.

- **Acts 4:33**

"And with great power gave the apostles **witness** of the resurrection of the Lord Jesus: and great grace was upon them all."

The apostles gave witness with great power that the Lord Jesus Christ had been raised bodily from the dead.

- **Acts 22:15**

"For thou shalt be his **witness** unto all men of what thou hast seen and heard."

1, 2, & 3 John–Preaching Verse-by-Verse

When Paul was saved by the Lord Jesus Christ, He told Paul that he would be His witness to all men of what he had seen and heard.
- **Acts 23:11**
"And the night following the Lord stood by him, and said, Be of good cheer, Paul: for as thou hast testified of me in Jerusalem, so must thou **bear witness** also at Rome."

After a strong dissension that the Pharisees had with Paul, they almost tore him into pieces. The Roman soldiers protected him. Then the Lord gave these words of comfort to Paul, telling him to be of good cheer and that he would bear witness to the Lord Jesus Christ also in Rome.
- **Acts 26:16**
"But rise, and stand upon thy feet: for I have appeared unto thee for this purpose, to make thee a minister and a **witness** both of these things which thou hast seen, and of those things in the which I will appear unto thee;"

In this verse, Paul is recounting his conversion on his way to Damascus. The Lord Jesus Christ told Paul of His purpose for saving his soul. The Lord wanted Paul to be minister who could witness the things Paul had seen and what he would see in the future.

Verses On Fellowship

FELLOWSHIP WITH BOTH THE FATHER AND SON
Paul wanted all of his readers to have fellowship with him and with God the Father and God the Son as well.

- **Psalms 94:20**
"Shall the throne of iniquity have **fellowship** with thee, which frameth mischief by a law?"

True Christians should have no dealings with the "*throne of iniquity.*" They should separate from such evil.
- **Acts 2:42**
"And they continued stedfastly in the apostles' doctrine and **fellowship**, and in breaking of bread, and in prayers."

Here is Biblical fellowship in the doctrine taught by the apostles, including breaking of bread and prayer.
- **1 Corinthians 1:9**
"God *is* faithful, by whom ye were called unto the **fellowship** of his Son Jesus Christ our Lord."

GENUINE CHRISTIANS' FELLOWSHIP WITH CHRIST
Those who are genuine Christians are called into the fellowship and communion with the Lord Jesus Christ.

- **1 Corinthians 10:20**

"But I *say*, that the things which the Gentiles sacrifice, they sacrifice to devils, and not to God: and I would not that ye should have **fellowship** with devils."

No true Christian should have any fellowship with devils or those who are in league with the devils' doctrines and teachings.

- **2 Corinthians 6:14**

"Be ye not unequally yoked together with unbelievers: for what **fellowship** hath righteousness with unrighteousness? and what communion hath light with darkness?"

RIGHTEOUS AND UNRIGHTEOUS--NO FELLOWSHIP

There is not, nor can there be, any fellowship between righteousness and unrighteousness.

- **Galatians 2:9**

"And when James, Cephas, and John, who seemed to be pillars, perceived the grace that was given unto me, they gave to me and Barnabas the **right hands of fellowship**; that we *should go* unto the heathen, and they unto the circumcision."

The right hands of fellowship were given to Paul and Barnabas by James, Cephas, and John. They agreed to work together in the ministry for the Lord Jesus Christ.

- **Ephesians 5:11**

"And have **no fellowship** with the unfruitful works of darkness, but rather reprove *them*."

REPROVE MEANS TO EXPOSE TO THE LIGHT

That Greek Word for *"reprove"* means to shine light upon and expose the unfruitful works of darkness. Have no fellowship with them. Stay away from them.

- **1 John 1:6**

"If we say that we have **fellowship** with him, and walk in darkness, we lie, and do not the truth:"

- **1 John 1:7**

"But if we walk in the light, as he is in the light, we have **fellowship** one with another, and the blood of Jesus Christ his Son cleanseth us from all sin."

WALKING IN THE LIGHT BRINGS FELLOWSHIP

If genuine Christians walk in the light of God's Words, they have fellowship with one another and with the Lord Jesus Christ Himself Who can cleanse them from all sin.

1 John 1:4

"**And these things write we unto you, that your joy may be full.**"

THE MEANING OF THE GREEK WORD, "PLEROO"

One of the purposes for John's writing this book was that the joy of true Christians might be full. The Greek Word for "*be*" is in the Greek present tense. It means that this action is continuous and unending.

The Greek Word for "*be full*" is PLEROO. Some of the meanings of this Greek Word are:

> "*1) to make full, to fill up, i.e. to fill to the full; 1a) to cause to abound, to furnish or supply liberally; 1a1) I abound, I am liberally supplied*
>
> *2) to render full, i.e. to complete; 2a) to fill to the top: so that nothing shall be wanting, to full measure, fill to the brim; 2b) to consummate: a number; 2b1) to make complete in every particular, to render perfect; 2b2) to carry through to the end, to accomplish, carry out, (some undertaking); 2c) to carry into effect, bring to realisation, realise; 2c1) of matters of duty: to perform, execute; 2c2) of sayings, promises, prophecies, to bring to pass, ratify, accomplish; 2c3) to fulfil, i.e. to cause God's will (as made known in the law) to be obeyed as it should be, and God's promises (given through the prophets) to receive fulfilment.*"

It should also be pointed out that this Greek verb for "*be full*" is in the Greek perfect tense. As such, it signifies an action that occurs in the past and continues on into both the present and the future. It refers to a continuous state of being full.

Verses On Joy

The English word "*joy*" occurs about 155 times in our King James Bible. Let's look at a few of these verses as they occur in both the Old and the New Testaments.

- **Psalms 16:11**
"Thou wilt shew me the path of life: in thy presence *is* **fulness of joy**; at thy right hand *there are* pleasures for evermore."

When genuine Christians are in Heaven, they will be in the presence of the Lord and will experience fullness of joy.

- **Psalms 51:12**
"Restore unto me the **joy of thy salvation**; and uphold me *with thy* free spirit."

DAVID RESTORED FROM ADULTERY AND MURDER

David had sinned two grievous sins–adultery and murder. He genuinely repented of both of them and asked the Lord to restore unto him the *"joy of thy salvation."* I'm sure the Lord granted David's request.

- **Nehemiah 8:10**
"Then he said unto them, Go your way, eat the fat, and drink the sweet, and send portions unto them for whom nothing is prepared: for *this* day *is* holy unto our Lord: neither be ye sorry; for the **joy of the LORD** is your strength."

THE JOY OF THE LORD GIVES STRENGTH

This gives a new source of strength. It is not found in muscles or human power. It is found in the *"joy of the LORD"* which gives strength to true Christians today, no matter how weak they might be physically.

- **Jeremiah 15:16**
"Thy words were found, and I did eat them; and thy word was unto me the **joy and rejoicing of mine heart**: for I am called by thy name, O LORD God of hosts."

The Words of God, when found and comprehended, become true *"joy and rejoicing"* in the very hearts of genuine Christians today.

- **Habakkuk 3:17-19**
"Although the fig tree shall not blossom, neither *shall* fruit *be* in the vines; the labour of the olive shall fail, and the fields shall yield no meat; the flock shall be cut off from the fold, and *there shall be* no herd in the stalls: Yet **I will rejoice in the LORD, I will joy in the God of my salvation**. The LORD God *is* my strength, and he will make my feet like hinds' *feet*, and he will make me to walk upon mine high places. To the chief singer on my stringed instruments."

1, 2, & 3 John–Preaching Verse-by-Verse

REJOICE IN THE LORD ALWAYS
No matter how difficult the surrounding circumstances, true Christians can *"rejoice in the LORD"* and can *"joy in the God of* [their] *salvation."*

- **Luke 2:10**
"And the angel said unto them, Fear not: for, behold, I bring you good tidings of **great joy**, which shall be to all people."

The angel told Mary that *"great joy"* would come to all people because of the miraculous virgin birth of the Lord Jesus Christ who came to die for the sins of the entire world so that those who genuinely trusted in Him might have eternal life.

- **Luke 15:7**
"I say unto you, that likewise **joy shall be in heaven** over one sinner that repenteth, more than over ninety and nine just persons, which need no repentance."

The Lord Jesus Christ said *"joy"* would be in heaven when one sinner changed his mind about sin and the Saviour and was born-again. This is speaking of someone who is saved and born again.

- **Luke 24:52**
"And they worshipped him, and returned to Jerusalem with **great joy**:"

Those two on the road to Emmaus who beheld the bodily-resurrected Lord Jesus Christ had *"great joy"* as they returned to Jerusalem.

- **John 15:11**
"These things have I spoken unto you, that **my joy** might remain in you, and *that* **your joy** might be full."

The Lord Jesus Christ wanted His joy to remain in His disciples and their joy to be full.

- **John 16:22**
"And ye now therefore have sorrow: but I will see you again, and **your heart shall rejoice**, and **your joy** no man taketh from you."

Though the disciples were very sad when the Lord Jesus Christ told them He was going away to heaven, He told them He would see them again. At that time, their hearts would rejoice and their joy would never be lost or removed.

- **John 16:24**
"Hitherto have ye asked nothing in my name: ask, and ye shall receive, that **your joy may be full**."

The Lord Jesus Christ told His disciples to make requests in His Name unto God the Father. When He would give them answers, their *"joy"* would be full.

- Acts 13:49-52
"And the word of the Lord was published throughout all the region. But the Jews stirred up the devout and honourable women, and the chief men of the city, and raised persecution against Paul and Barnabas, and expelled them out of their coasts. But they shook off the dust of their feet against them, and came unto Iconium. And **the disciples were filled with joy**, and with the Holy Ghost."

FILLED WITH JOY DESPITE PERSECUTIONS

In spite of all the persecution against them by the women and chief men of the city, the disciples were *"filled with joy,"* They were also filled with the power of God the Holy Spirit.

- Acts 20:24
"But none of these things move me, neither count I my life dear unto myself, so that I might **finish my course with joy**, and the ministry, which I have received of the Lord Jesus, to testify the gospel of the grace of God."

Paul was going to go to Jerusalem, though his friends urged him not to go. They told him that he would be killed there. He refused to listen to them. He wanted to finish *"with joy"* the course and calling that the Lord Jesus Christ gave to him.

- Romans 15:13
"Now the God of hope fill you with **all joy** and peace in believing, that ye may abound in hope, through the power of the Holy Ghost."

Paul prayed that the Christians in Rome might be filled with *"joy,"* peace, and hope through the power of the Holy Spirit.

- Galatians 5:22
"But the fruit of the Spirit is love, **joy**, peace, longsuffering, gentleness, goodness, faith,"

"JOY"--A FRUIT OF GOD THE HOLY SPIRIT

Joy is one of the fruits that the Holy Spirit produces in the genuine Christian. A devoted Christian who is filled and controlled by the Holy Spirit has Divine *"joy."* The unsaved world knows nothing about this joy, nor can it.

- 1 Thessalonians 1:6
"And ye became followers of us, and of the Lord, having received the word in much affliction, **with joy of the Holy Ghost**:"

> **JOY, EVEN THROUGH MUCH AFFLICTION**
> Though the Thessalonian Christians had much affliction, the Lord gave them the *"joy"* that was from the Holy Spirit.

- Hebrews 12:2

"Looking unto Jesus the author and finisher of *our* faith; who for the **joy that was set before him** endured the cross, despising the shame, and is set down at the right hand of the throne of God."

> **CHRIST ENDURED THE CROSS FOR FUTURE JOY**
> The Lord Jesus Christ endured the horrendous agony of the cross, including the taking in His own body the sins of the world. The *"joy"* that was set before Him was His knowing that there would be thousands upon thousands who would truly trust Him as their Saviour and be with Him in Heaven for all eternity to come.

- 1 Peter 1:8

"Whom having not seen, ye love; in whom, though now ye see *him* not, yet believing, **ye rejoice with joy unspeakable and full of glory**:"
The Apostle Peter was writing to genuine Christians. He said that because they have believed on Him, they can rejoice with *"joy unspeakable and full of glory."*

- 2 John 1:12

"Having many things to write unto you, I would not *write* with paper and ink: but I trust to come unto you, and speak face to face, that **our joy may be full**."

> **FULL JOY DESIRED FOR TRUE CHRISTIANS**
> John wanted to bring *"full joy"* to the Christians to whom he was writing. In bringing *"full joy"* to them, it would bring *"full joy"* to John as well.

- 3 John 1:4

"I have **no greater joy** than to hear that my children walk in truth."

> **WALKING IN TRUTH BRINGS GREAT JOY**
> John truly had *"no greater joy"* than to know that his Christian converts were walking by the Words of God in truth rather than walking in compromise with error.

- **Jude 1:24**
"Now unto him that is able to keep you from falling, and to present *you* faultless before the presence of his glory with **exceeding joy**,"
Genuine Christians–and them alone–will experience "*exceeding joy*" when they appear with their Saviour in the glories of Heaven.

1 John 1:5

"This then is the message which we have heard of him, and declare unto you, that God is light, and in him is no darkness at all."

Verses On Light

The word, "*light,*" occurs about 235 times in our King James Bible, both in the Old and the New Testaments. God is pure light. He has no darkness in Him at all. Here are some verses about "*light.*"

- **Genesis 1:3**
"And God said, Let there be **light**: and there was **light**."

DARKNESS TURNED TO LIGHT BY GOD'S CREATION

This is cosmic "*light.*" It was created by God Himself. Before this creation, darkness was upon all the face of the earth. God changed the original complete darkness into light.

"*And the earth was without form, and void; and darkness was upon the face of the deep. And the Spirit of God moved upon the face of the waters.*" (Genesis 1:2)

- **Psalms 27:1**
"The LORD *is* **my light** and my salvation; whom shall I fear? the LORD *is* the strength of my life; of whom shall I be afraid?"
When people trust in the LORD, He becomes their "*Light*" and their salvation, driving away spiritual darkness.

- **John 1:4**
"In him was life; and the life was **the light** of men."

CHRIST THE LIFE AND THE LIGHT

The Lord Jesus Christ is not only life, but also "*the light*" by Whom those who truly trust in Him might have eternal life and get out of the darkness of sin.

- **John 1:9**
"*That* was the **true Light**, which lighteth every man that cometh into the world."

"That" was talking about the Lord Jesus Christ Who alone is the perfect and "*true Light.*" He enables those who trust in Him to escape from their darkness of sin.

- **John 3:19-21**
"And this is the condemnation, that **light** is come into the world, and men loved darkness rather than light, because their deeds were evil. For every one that doeth evil hateth the light, neither cometh to the light, lest his deeds should be reproved. But he that doeth truth cometh to the light, that his deeds may be made manifest, that they are wrought in God."

All the evil and wicked people of this world hate the Lord Jesus Christ Who is the Light of the world. They would rather live in the darkness of sin and wickedness.

- **John 8:12**
"Then spake Jesus again unto them, saying, **I am the light of the world**: he that followeth me shall not walk in darkness, but shall have the **light** of life."

No other but the Lord Jesus Christ is the "*light of the world.*" He alone can dispel the darkness of the sinful nature of mankind and cause a life to walk in His light.

- **John 9:5**
"As long as I am in the world, **I am the light of the world**"

CHRIST THE ONLY LIGHT IN THIS DARK WORLD

The Lord Jesus Christ is the only Light in this dark world of sin and sadness. Later, He told His disciples "*ye are the light of the world*" (Matthew 5:14). They were to shine as lights in the darkness.

- **John 12:46**
"I am come a **light** into the world, that whosoever believeth on me should not abide in darkness."

God does not want genuine Christians to continue to abide in darkness, but to walk in the power of the light of their Saviour.

- **2 Corinthians 6:14b**
". . . and what communion hath **light** with darkness?"

There's no communion or fellowship between "*light*" and darkness. When you turn on a light in a dark room, the darkness disappears. Light and darkness cannot coexist.

Verses On Darkness

In 1 John 1:5, it also mentions "*darkness.*" In the Lord Jesus Christ there is "*no darkness at all.*" The word, "*darkness*" appears in about 142 places in our King James Bible. Here are a few of those places:

- **Genesis 1:4**
"And God saw the light, that it *was* good: and God divided the light from the **darkness**."

> **GOD SEPARATED THE LIGHT FROM THE DARKNESS**
> At the creation of this world, God "*divided the light from the darkness.*" These two things cannot coexist. In Hell, there will be no light. In Heaven, there will be no darkness.

- **Psalms 107:14**
"He brought them out of **darkness** and the shadow of death, and brake their bands in sunder."
This refers to God's deliverance of the people of Israel from over 400 years of bondage in Egypt.

- **Isaiah 5:20**
"Woe unto them that call evil good, and good evil; that put **darkness** for light, and light for **darkness**; that put bitter for sweet, and sweet for bitter!"

> **CONSTITUTIONALISTS NOW CALLED TERRORISTS**
> This is exactly what's happening today. Those who are Constitutional patriots are called terrorists. Those doing evil are called good. They've got it all mixed up.

- **Matthew 25:30**
"And cast ye the unprofitable servant into "**outer darkness**": there shall be weeping and gnashing of teeth."
This will take place at the judgment of all the nations that have rejected the Lord Jesus Christ as their Saviour. The "*outer darkness*" is the Lake of Fire and Hell.

- **Luke 22:52-53**
"Then Jesus said unto the chief priests, and captains of the temple, and the elders, which were come to him, Be ye come out, as against a thief, with swords and staves? When I was daily with you in the temple, ye stretched forth no hands against me: but this is your hour, and **the power of darkness**."
He's talking about Gethsemane, when they came after the Lord Jesus Christ to take Him for the trial and crucifixion.

- **John 8:12**
"Then spake Jesus again unto them, saying, I am the light of the world: he that followeth me shall not walk in **darkness**, but shall have the light of life."
Those who are true Christians and follow the Lord Jesus Christ should not walk in the "*darkness*" of sin and disobedience.

- **John 12:46**
"I am come a light into the world, that whosoever believeth on me should not abide in **darkness**."
If genuine Christians get into darkness, God does not want us to stay in that darkness, but to get out of it immediately.
- **Acts 26:18**
"To open their eyes, *and* to **turn *them* from darkness to light**, and *from* the power of Satan unto God, that they may receive forgiveness of sins, and inheritance among them which are sanctified by faith that is in me."
When the Lord Jesus Christ appeared unto Paul on the Damascus road, He gave him a commission and a purpose. It was to turn people "*from darkness to light.*"
- **Romans 13:12**
"The night is far spent, the day is at hand: let us therefore cast off **the works of darkness**, and let us put on the armour of light."
"*Works of darkness*" should be cast off by true Christians. The armour of light must be put on as a garment.
- **2 Corinthians 4:6**
"For God, who commanded the light to shine out of **darkness**, hath shined in our hearts, to *give* the light of the knowledge of the glory of God in the face of Jesus Christ."

CHRIST THE LIGHT OF THE WORLD

The Lord Jesus Christ, as the Light of the world, has shined in the hearts of genuine Christians to give them the knowledge of God's glory.

- **2 Corinthians 6:14b**
". . . and what communion hath light with **darkness**?"
"*Darkness*" **and light have nothing in common**.
- **Ephesians 5:8**
"For **ye were sometimes darkness**, but now *are ye* light in the Lord: walk as children of light:"
For the salvation of these Ephesian Christians, they were in the darkness of unbelief and sin. Once saved, they came into the light in the Lord.
- **Ephesians 5:11**
"And have no fellowship with the unfruitful works of **darkness**, but rather reprove *them*."

> **DARKNESS SHOULD BE REPROVED AND EXPOSED**
> Not only should true Christians not fellowship with works of *"darkness,"* but this *"darkness"* should be reproved and exposed.

- **Ephesians 6:12**
"*For we wrestle not against flesh and blood, but against principalities, against powers, against the rulers of* **the darkness of this world**, *against spiritual wickedness in high places.*"

The enemies of all genuine Christians are Satanic rulers of the *"darkness"* of this world. People must know who their enemies are in order to win the battles with them.

- **Colossians 1:13**
"*Who hath delivered us from the* **power of darkness**, *and hath translated us into the kingdom of his dear Son:*"

> **CHRIST DELIVERS CHRISTIANS FROM DARKNESS**
> The Lord Jesus Christ has delivered every true Christian from the power of Satanic *"darkness."* They can now walk in the light.

- **1 Peter 2:9**
"*But ye are a chosen generation, a royal priesthood, an holy nation, a peculiar people; that ye should shew forth the praises of him who hath* **called you out of darkness** *into his marvellous light:*"

> **GENUINE CHRISTIANS CALLED OUT OF DARKNESS**
> Genuine Christians have been called out of the Devil's darkness and have been brought into God's marvelous light so they can show forth His praises.

- **Jude 1:13**
"*Raging waves of the sea, foaming out their own shame; wandering stars, to whom is reserved the blackness of* **darkness** *for ever.*"

> **NON-CHRISTIANS CALLED WANDERING STARS**
> Unsaved non-Christians are called here *"raging waves"* and *"wandering stars."* Their eternal destiny is the darkness of Hell *"for ever."* The false Gnostic religion denies that there is a Hell. And certainly they did not believe it would be *"for ever"* for those who reject the Lord Jesus Christ. This false and corrupt Gnostic Critical Greek

> Text leaves out the words, *"for ever."* Likewise, every Bible version in every language in the world that follows this corrupt Gnostic Critical Greek Text leaves out *"for ever"* as well.

1 John 1:6

"If we say that we have fellowship with him, and walk in darkness, we lie, and do not the truth:"

So-called "Christians" who say that they have fellowship with the Lord Jesus Christ and yet walk in darkness and do not the truth, are liars! They are lost, Hell-bound sinners! That's what this verse teaches us.

Verses On Fellowship

There are many verses on the subject of fellowship, but notice a few of some of the important ones:

- **Psalms 94:20**

"Shall the throne of iniquity have **fellowship** with thee, which frameth mischief by a law?"

Iniquity and sin should not have *"fellowship"* with true Christians.

- **Acts 2:42**

"And they continued stedfastly in the apostles' doctrine and **fellowship**, and in breaking of bread, and in prayers."

Genuine Christians in our days also can have *"fellowship"* one with the other in Bible-believing churches where God's Words are preached.

- **1 Corinthians 1:9**

"God *is* faithful, by whom ye were called unto the **fellowship** of his Son Jesus Christ our Lord."

If you are a true Christian, you have been called unto the *"fellowship"* with God's Son, the Lord Jesus Christ.

- **1 Corinthians 10:20**

"But I *say*, that the things which the Gentiles sacrifice, they sacrifice to devils, and not to God: and I would not that ye should have **fellowship with devils.**"

> **NO FELLOWSHIP WITH THE DEVIL OR HIS PEOPLE**
> God does not want any genuine Christian to have any *"fellowship"* with devils or those whose father is the Devil.

- **2 Corinthians 6:14b**

". . . for what **fellowship** hath righteousness with unrighteousness?"

The answer to this question is that there is no possible *"fellowship"* or common ground between righteousness and unrighteousness.

- **Galatians 2:9**
"And when James, Cephas, and John, who seemed to be pillars, perceived the grace that was given unto me, they gave to me and Barnabas the **right hands of fellowship**; that we *should go* unto the heathen, and they unto the circumcision."

RIGHT HANDS OF FELLOWSHIP GIVEN IN THE BIBLE

The *"right hand of fellowship"* is a phrase that there is an agreement and concord between two or more true Christians in a local church or in another Christian organization.

- **Ephesians 5:11**
"And have **no fellowship** with the unfruitful works of darkness, but rather reprove *them*."

There must be no *"fellowship"* with the unfruitful works of darkness. Not only must genuine Christians stay away from these works of darkness, but they must reprove and expose them.

Verses On Walk

THE MEANING OF THE GREEK WORD, "PERIPATEO"

The Greek Word for "walk" is PERIPATEO. Some of the meanings of this Greek Word are:

> *"1) to walk; 1a) to make one's way, progress; to make due use of opportunities; 1b) Hebrew for, to live; 1b1) to regulate one's life; 1b2) to conduct one's self; 1b3) to pass one's life"*

- **Romans 13:13**
"Let us **walk honestly**, as in the day; not in rioting and drunkenness, not in chambering and wantonness, not in strife and envying."

Genuine Christians should never walk in the darkness of sin and evil, but in an honest manner.

- **2 Corinthians 5:7**
"(For we **walk by faith**, not by sight:)"

The true Christian walk is based on faith in the Bible, God's Words, not by human sight.

- **Galatians 5:16**
"*This* I say then, **Walk in the Spirit**, and ye shall not fulfil the lust of the flesh."

ONLY TRUE CHRISTIANS CAN WALK IN THE SPIRIT

The only people who can "*walk in the Spirit*" are genuine Christians. They are the only ones who have God the Holy Spirit indwelling them. This "*walk*" is a step-by-step event in the power and by the control of the Holy Spirit. A "*walk in the Spirit*" must be a very cautious "*walk*" because each step might lead to a fall. Without such a "*walk*" in the Spirit's power, the lust of the flesh might be fulfilled.

- Ephesians 2:10

"For we are his workmanship, created in Christ Jesus unto good works, which God hath before ordained that we should **walk** in them."

Though they are not saved by their works, after people are born-again, God wants all these genuine Christians to walk in good works, not bad works.

- Ephesians 4:1

"I therefore, the prisoner of the Lord, beseech you that ye **walk worthy** of the vocation wherewith ye are called,"

True Christians should walk in a worthy manner, to please the Lord Jesus Christ.

- Ephesians 4:17

"This I say therefore, and testify in the Lord, that ye henceforth **walk not** as other Gentiles **walk**, in the vanity of their mind,"

Genuine Christians should no longer walk as they did before they were saved. That previous walk should cease.

- Ephesians 5:2

"And **walk in love**, as Christ also hath loved us, and hath given himself for us an offering and a sacrifice to God for a sweetsmelling savour."

True Christians should walk in a love similar to that of the Lord Jesus Christ Who died in their place on the cross.

- Ephesians 5:8

"For ye were sometimes darkness, but now *are ye* light in the Lord: **walk as children of light**:"

THE DARK WALK OF THE DEVIL'S CHILDREN

The walk of genuine Christians must not resemble the dark walk of the Devil's children. A real Christian must walk in the light of God's Words.

- Ephesians 5:15
"See then that ye **walk circumspectly**, not as fools, but as wise,"

LOOKING ALL AROUND IN OUR WALK
This means that the walk must involve making sure that no dangers or stumbling blocks be found throughout all 360 degrees around that walk. The Devil is able to confront people from the left, the right, the front, or the rear. A saved person must have a careful and a circumspect walk.

- Colossians 1:10
"That ye might **walk worthy** of the Lord unto all pleasing, being fruitful in every good work, and increasing in the knowledge of God;"

A worthy walk results in being fruitful in every good work and ever-increasing in the knowledge of God.

- Colossians 2:6
"As ye have therefore received Christ Jesus the Lord, *so* **walk** ye in him:"

The walk should be in the same way the Lord Jesus Christ was received–by faith.

- Colossians 4:5
"**Walk in wisdom** toward them that are without, redeeming the time."

The walk must be in wisdom toward the unsaved. There should be no wasted time, but every minute should be lived for the Lord's glory.

- 1 Thessalonians 2:12
"That ye would **walk worthy** of God, who hath called you unto his kingdom and glory."

This is yet another verse calling for the necessity of a worthy walk with God who saved and called these genuine Christians.

- 2 Thessalonians 3:11
"For we hear that there are some which **walk among you disorderly**, working not at all, but are busybodies."

There should be no walk that is disorderly and out of conformity with the Words of God. Work should be undertaken, without being busybodies.

- 3 John 1:4
"I have no greater joy than to hear that my children **walk in truth**."

WALKING IN TRUTH BY GOD'S WORDS
A walk in truth would be one in strict conformity to the Words of God.

Verses On Lying

There are a number of verses in both the Old and the New Testaments about lying. Here are a few of them:
- **John 8:44**

"Ye are of *your* father the devil, and the lusts of your father ye will do. He was a murderer from the beginning, and abode not in the truth, because there is no truth in him. When he speaketh a lie, he speaketh of his own: for he is a **liar**, and the father of it."

The Devil is the father of all lies and untruth. There is no truth in him at all.
- **Acts 5:3**

"But Peter said, Ananias, why hath Satan filled thine heart to **lie** to the Holy Ghost, and to keep back *part* of the price of the land?"

Ananias and Sapphira lied about how much they sold their land for. They pretended that they gave the apostles all of the price when it was only a portion of the price of the land. They were both slain because they lied to the Holy Spirit.
- **Colossians 3:9**

"**Lie not one to another**, seeing that ye have put off the old man with his deeds;"

Some of the true Christians in the church at Colosse were apparently lying. Paul told them to stop it since it was part of the deeds of their old nature.
- **2 Thessalonians 2:11**

"And for this cause God shall send them strong delusion, that they should **believe a lie**:"

STRONG DELUSION IN THE TRIBULATION PERIOD
In the seven-year period of the Tribulation, God will send people a strong delusion so that they will believe a lie. Believing lies will be more common than in our world today because God the Holy Spirit will withdraw His restraining influence during the Tribulation.

- **Titus 1:2**

"In hope of eternal life, which **God, that cannot lie**, promised before the world began;"

Though many today do not believe God and His Words, God can never lie or deceive. He deals only in the truth.
- **Hebrews 6:18**
"That by two immutable things, in which *it was* **impossible for God to lie**, we might have a strong consolation, who have fled for refuge to lay hold upon the hope set before us:"

Again, this verse teaches clearly that it is totally impossible for God to lie. Lying is against His very Nature.

1 John 1:7

"But if we walk in the light, as he is in the light, we have fellowship one with another, and the blood of Jesus Christ his Son cleanseth us from all sin."

I want you to zero in on the teachings of the Bible on the blood of the Lord Jesus Christ. Some time ago, I wrote a book entitled *John MacArthur's Heresy On The Blood Of Christ* **(BFT #2185 @ $10.00 + $4.00 S&H)**. It was written in 1995 and has 66 pages. Later, I wrote a 6-page summary of this subject entitled *"The Blood Of Christ–Fourteen Biblical Effects Of The Literal Blood Of Christ"* **(BFT #2548-T @ 4/$1.00 + $1.00 S&H)**. I will outline each one of these 14 Biblical effects on the literal blood of the Lord Jesus Christ in this section and explain the vital importance of each one.

In my opinion, John MacArthur is the greatest heretic regarding the blood of the Lord Jesus Christ living today. There are others that lived before him that were equally heretics on the *"blood"* of the Lord Jesus Christ, but he says that the *"blood"* of Christ doesn't really mean *"blood"*—it just means *"death."*

John MacArthur is a heretic on every one of these 14 Biblical effects of the precious blood of the Lord Jesus Christ. Let me sum up and clarify MacArthur's position: He repeatedly claims *"blood"* does not mean literal *"blood"* (though the Greek Word, HAIMA, means only *"blood"* and never *"death"*); He claims that *"blood"* means *"death"* (though the Greek Word, THANATOS, means only *"death"* and never *"blood"*).

I'll be quoting from *John MacArthur's Heresy On The Blood Of Christ* **(BFT #2185 @ $10.00 + $4.00 S&H)** giving the pages so you can check it out for yourself if you get this book. The material is found in the book on pages 44 through 48.

Fourteen Biblical Effects Of The Literal Blood Of Christ

1. There is REDEMPTION (Atonement, Substitution, Remission, Salvation, or Purchase) through the literal Blood of Christ:

• (Leviticus 17:11) *"For the life of the flesh {is} in the blood: and I have given IT to you upon the altar to make an atonement for your souls: for it {is} the blood {that} maketh an atonement for the soul."*
   [Literal Blood is referred to here.]

• (Matthew 26:28) *"For this is My Blood of the new testament, which is shed for many for the remission of sins."*
   [Literal Blood is referred to here for the future "shedding" at Calvary, though the cup is figurative for the Blood.]

• (Mark 14:24) *"And he said unto them, This is My Blood of the new testament, which is shed for many."*
   [Literal Blood is referred to here for the future "shedding" at Calvary, though the cup is figurative for the Blood.]

• (Luke 22:20) *"Likewise also the cup after supper, saying, This cup {is} the new testament in My Blood, which is shed for you."*
   [Literal Blood is referred to here for the future "shedding" at Calvary, though the cup is figurative for the Blood.]

• (Acts 20:28) *"Take heed therefore unto yourselves, and to all the flock, over the which the Holy Ghost hath made you overseers, to feed the church of God, which he hath purchased with his own Blood."*
   [Literal Blood is meant here as the purchased price.]

• (Romans 5:9) *"Much more then, being now justified by His Blood, we shall be saved from wrath through him."*
   [Literal Blood is referred to here.]

• (Ephesians 1:7) *"In whom we have redemption through His Blood, the forgiveness of sins, according to the riches of his grace;"*
   [Literal Blood is referred to here.]

• (Colossians 1:14) *"In whom we have redemption through His Blood, {even} the forgiveness of sins:"*
   [Literal Blood is referred to here.]

• (1 Peter 1:18) *"Forasmuch as ye know that ye were not redeemed with corruptible things, {as} silver and gold, from your vain conversation {received} by tradition from your fathers;"* (1 Peter 1:19) *"but with the precious Blood of Christ, as of a lamb without blemish and without spot:"*

[Literal Blood is referred to here.]
- (Revelation 5:9) *"And they sung a new song, saying, Thou art worthy to take the book, and to open the seals thereof: for Thou wast slain, and hast redeemed us to God by His Blood out of every kindred, and tongue, and people, and nation;"*
[Literal Blood is referred to here.]

2. There is **PROPITIATION** through the **literal Blood** of Christ:
- (Romans 3:25) *"Whom God hath set forth {to be} a propitiation through faith in His Blood, to declare his righteousness for the remission of sins that are past, through the forbearance of God;"*
[Literal Blood is referred to here.]

3. There is **JUSTIFICATION** through the **literal Blood** of Christ:
- (Romans 5:9) *"Much more then, being now justified by His Blood, we shall be saved from wrath through Him."*
[Literal Blood is referred to here.]

4. There is **FELLOWSHIP** through the **literal Blood** of Christ:
- (Ephesians 2:13) *"But now in Christ Jesus ye who sometimes were far off are made nigh by the Blood of Christ."*
[Literal Blood is referred to here.]

5. There is **PEACE** through the **literal Blood** of Christ:
- (Ephesians 1:20) *"And, having made peace through the Blood of his cross, by him to reconcile all things unto himself; by him, {I say}, whether {they be} things in earth, or things in heaven."*
[Literal Blood is referred to here.]

6. There is **FORGIVENESS** through the **literal Blood** of Christ:
- (Ephesians 1:7) *"In whom we have redemption through His Blood, the forgiveness of sins, according to the riches of his grace;"*
[Literal Blood is referred to here.]
- (Colossians 1:14) *"In whom we have redemption through His Blood, {even} the forgiveness of sins:"*
[Literal Blood is referred to here.]

7. There is **SANCTIFICATION** through the **literal Blood** of Christ:
- (Hebrews 13:12) *"Wherefore Jesus also, that He might sanctify the people with His own Blood, suffered without the gate."*

[Literal Blood is referred to here.]

8. There is RECONCILIATION through the literal Blood of Christ:

- (Colossians 1:20) *"And, having made peace through the Blood of his cross, by him to reconcile all things unto himself; by him, {I say}, whether {they be} things in earth, or things in heaven."*

[Literal Blood is referred to here.]

9. There is CLEANSING (Purging, Washing, Purifying) through the literal Blood of Christ:

- (Hebrews 9:14) *"How much more shall the Blood of Christ, who through the eternal Spirit offered himself without spot to God, purge your conscience from dead works to serve the living God?"*

[Literal Blood is referred to here.]

- (Hebrews 9:23) *"{It was} therefore necessary that the patterns of things in the heavens should be purified with these; but the heavenly things themselves with better sacrifices than these."*

[Literal Blood is implied here.]

- (1 John 1:7) *"But if we walk in the light, as he is in the light, we have fellowship one with another, and the Blood of Jesus Christ His Son cleanseth us from all sin."*

[Literal Blood is referred to here based on Calvary's events, though the cleansing is figurative yet real.]

- (Revelation 1:5) *"And from Jesus Christ, {who is} the faithful witness, {and} the first begotten of the dead, and the prince of the kings of the earth. Unto him that loved us, and washed us from our sins in His own Blood,"*

[Literal Blood is referred to here based on Calvary's events though the cleansing is figurative yet real.]

- (Revelation 7:14) *"And I said unto him, Sir, thou knowest. And he said to me, These are they which came out of great tribulation, and have washed their robes, and made them white in the Blood of the Lamb."*

[Literal Blood is referred to here based on Calvary's events, though the cleansing is figurative yet real.]

10. There is REMEMBRANCE through the literal Blood of Christ:

- (1 Corinthians 11:25) *"After the same manner also {he took} the cup, when he had supped, saying, This cup is the New Testament in My Blood: this do ye, as oft as ye drink {it}, in remembrance of Me."*

[Literal Blood is the basis here for the future "shedding" at Calvary, though the cup is figurative for the Blood.]

11. There is <u>BOLDNESS</u> (and <u>Access</u> to God's Throne) through the <u>literal Blood</u> of Christ:
- (Hebrews 10:19) *"Having therefore, brethren, <u>boldness</u> to enter into the holiest by the <u>Blood</u> of Jesus,"*
   [<u>Literal Blood</u> is referred to here.]

12. There is <u>MATURITY</u> (In <u>Doing God's Will</u>) through the <u>literal Blood</u> of Christ:
- (Hebrews 13:20) *"Now the God of peace, that brought again from the dead our Lord Jesus, that great shepherd of the sheep, through the <u>Blood</u> of the everlasting covenant," (2) Hebrews 13:21) "<u>make you perfect</u> in every good work <u>to do His will</u>, working in you that which is well pleasing in his sight, through Jesus Christ; to whom {be} glory for ever and ever. Amen."*
   [Literal Blood is referred to here.]

13. There is <u>PUNISHMENT</u> (Or <u>Weakness, Sickness, or Death</u> if we mistreat it) through the <u>literal Blood</u> of Christ:"
- (Hebrews 10:29) *"Of how much sorer <u>punishment</u>, suppose ye, shall he be thought worthy, who hath trodden under foot the Son of God, and hath counted the <u>Blood</u> of the covenant, wherewith he was sanctified, <u>an unholy</u> [or "common"] <u>thing</u>, and hath done despite unto the Spirit of grace?"*
   [Literal Blood is referred to here.]

This verse can be directly applied to John MacArthur. He treats the blood of Christ as an *"unholy"* thing. The Greek Word for *"unholy"* in this verse is KOINOS. Some of the meanings of this Greek Word are:

> "κοινός *(koinos), ἡ (ē), όν (on): adj.; 1. mutual,* **common, shared** *(Tit 1:4); 2. defiled, unclean, impure, unholy (Ac 10:14); 3. worthless, of little value (Heb 10:29); 4.* **in common, what is mutual between two or more persons** *(Jude 3); 5.* ἔχω κοινός *(echō koinos),* **share mutually**, *formally,* **have in common** *(Ac 2:44+)"*

Referring to the Lord Jesus Christ's blood, MacArthur wrote: *"Nothing in His* **human blood** *saves."* [*Grace To You*, 5/76, p. 10] To say that the blood of the Lord Jesus Christ is merely "HUMAN BLOOD" and that His blood does not *"save"* is a definite mark of apostasy! It is calling Christ's blood "human" or the same and common (KOINOS) to the blood of every human being who ever lived (*"unholy"* as in this verse). Thus John MacArthur qualifies in

Hebrews 10:29 for a *"much sorer punishment"* than those *"that despised Moses' law died without mercy under two or three witnesses:"* (Hebrews 10:28)

For many more quotations from John MacArthur regarding his blasphemous view of the blood of the Lord Jesus Christ, I refer you to my book, *John MacArthur's Heresy On The Blood Of Christ* **(BFT #2185 @ $10.00 + $4.00 S&H)**

- (1 Corinthians 11:27) *"Wherefore whosoever shall eat this bread, and drink {this} cup of the Lord, unworthily, shall be guilty of the body and Blood of the Lord."*

[Literal Blood is referred to here.]

- (1 Corinthians 11:29) *"For he that eateth and drinketh unworthily, eateth and drinketh damnation to himself, not discerning the Lord's body. (1 Corinthians 11:30) For this cause many {are} weak and sickly among you, and many sleep."*

[Literal Blood is the basis here, though "drinketh" is figurative for commemorating Christ's shed Blood.]

14. There is **VICTORY** (Over Satan) through the literal **Blood** of Christ:

- (Revelation 12:11) *"And they overcame him by the Blood of the Lamb, and by the word of their testimony; and they loved not their lives unto the death."*

[Literal Blood is referred to here based on the work of the Cross.]

So, as I said before, I have very, very serious differences with John MacArthur about his blatant heresy on the blood of the Lord Jesus Christ! I was in the Los Angeles, California area two different times, in two different churches speaking on John MacArthur's heresy and the blood of Christ. I used numerous quotations that John MacArthur made from his articles and from some of his tapes using quotations **in his own voice**.

He started out believing the blood of the Lord Jesus Christ was literal. But in his recordings, as he goes from year to year, he finally arrived at the false and unBiblical conclusion that the use of the word, *"blood"* for the blood of the Lord Jesus Christ was not to be taken literally, but that is only a metonym or a figure of speech for the death of Christ. The recordings of John MacArthur cover around a ten-year period of time.

When this serious opposition to MacArthur's view came out, MacArthur wrote an article entitled: *"I believe in the precious blood."* This title caused some of MacArthur lovers to refute my factual articles. He tried to show that he really believes in the proper view of Christ's *"precious blood."* When you read the article carefully, however, you will find that MacArthur continues to refer to the blood of the Lord Jesus Christ as only a metonym for His "*death.*" He's seeking to confuse people on the idea of the blood of the Lord Jesus Christ.

MacArthur wrote a whole commentary on the Bible. In his comments in the book of Hebrews, he continues to refer to the "*blood*" of the Lord Jesus Christ as merely his "*death.*" I had a call some time ago from a man who asked, "Hasn't John MacArthur changed his position on the blood of the Lord Jesus Christ?" I answered him that he clearly has **NOT** changed his position on this important doctrine. He likes to have people think he has changed his position. Yet, he still defines "*blood*" as "*death.*"

It is true that the Lord Jesus Christ shed His blood in His death on the cross of Calvary, but God says very clearly in the Bible that it's Christ's "*blood*" that accomplished these fourteen effects, not His "*death.*" When it says in this verse (1 John 1:7) that "*the blood of Jesus Christ his Son cleanseth us from all sin,*" that's exactly what it means. God couldn't possibly make it any simpler or plainer, could He? If it doesn't mean this, why did God the Holy Spirit give those Greek Words to the New Testament writers? Why did God use the word, "*blood*" if He didn't mean "*blood*"? The Lord knows exactly what He's talking about.

1 John 1:8

"**If we say that we have no sin, we deceive ourselves, and the truth is not in us.**"

Some people say that they have no sin. There are many holiness churches and groups in this country and around the world. They teach that a person can reach a point of pure holiness and have no sin of any kind. They are what are called "believers" in sinless perfection. However, this present verse teaches the opposite of this doctrinal error. It says very clearly, "*If we say that we have no sin, we deceive ourselves, and the truth is not in us.*"

EVERY PERSON HAS A SIN NATURE

Every human being who has ever lived, from the time of Adam and Eve to this present hour, has a sin nature within them that will never be eradicated until they die. This sin nature was inherited from Adam.

Verses On Sin

> **BIBLE VERSES ON THE SIN NATURE**
> There are many verses in the Bible, both in the Old and the New Testaments, that speak about a sin nature that resides within every human being and the various sins that this sin nature produces:

- **Romans 6:12-13**

"Let not **sin** therefore reign in your mortal body, that ye should obey it in the lusts thereof. Neither yield ye your members *as* instruments of unrighteousness unto **sin**: but yield yourselves unto God, as those that are alive from the dead, and your members *as* instruments of righteousness unto God."

It is assumed that "*sin*" refers to the "*sin nature*" possessed by all human beings, including genuine Christians. That nature must not reign and rule in these Christians' lives. Members of the body include the eyes, the feet, the hands, the ears, the mouth, the heart, and other members as well.

- **1 Kings 8:46**

"If they sin against thee, (for *there is* **no man that sinneth not**,) and thou be angry with them, and deliver them to the enemy, so that they carry them away captives unto the land of the enemy, far or near;"

There is not any man, woman, or child who is free from sin.

- **Proverbs 20:9**

'Who can say, I have made my heart clean, I am pure from my **sin**?'

No one but the Lord Jesus Christ can say this since He is, was, and ever will be free from sin.

- **John 1:29**

"The next day John seeth Jesus coming unto him, and saith, Behold the Lamb of God, which **taketh away the sin of the world**."

> **ONLY CHRIST HAS ATONED FOR ALL SINS**
> The Lord Jesus Christ is the only One who has taken away the sin of the world from those who genuinely trust in Him as their Saviour.

- **John 8:7**

"So when they continued asking him, he lifted up himself, and said unto them, He that is **without sin** among you, let him first cast a stone at her."

Not a single man picked up a stone to cast at this woman who was accused of adultery because none of them was without sin.
- **Romans 3:9**
  "What then? are we better *than they*? No, in no wise: for we have before proved both Jews and Gentiles, that **they are all under sin**;"

Everyone in the world, no matter what race, sex, or country is considered by the God of the Bible to be "*under sin*." All of these people need to truly trust the Lord Jesus Christ as their Saviour Who alone can forgive their sins.
- **Romans 3:23**
  "For **all have sinned**, and come short of the glory of God;"

All have sinned. There are no exceptions in the human family.
- **Romans 5:12**
  "Wherefore, as by one man **sin entered** into the world, and **death by sin**; and so death passed upon all men, for that all have sinned:"

ADAM'S SIN MADE ALL PEOPLE SINNERS
Because of Adam's sin, all were made sinners and all have had death passed upon them.

- **Romans 6:23**
  "For the **wages of sin** *is* death; but the gift of God *is* eternal life through Jesus Christ our Lord."

DEATH PASSED ON ALL PEOPLE THROUGH ADAM
Because of sin that has been passed upon all mankind, death has also been passed upon all mankind. Only through genuine faith in the Lord Jesus Christ can men and women receive the gift of eternal life.

Verses On Deception

Verse 8 in 1 John states: "*If we say that we have no sin, we deceive ourselves, and the truth is not in us.*"

THE MEANING OF THE GREEK WORD, "PLANAO"
The Greek Word for "*deceive*" is PLANAO. Some of the meanings of this Greek Word are:

> "*1) to cause to stray, to lead astray, lead aside from the right way; 1a) to go astray, wander, roam about; 2) metaph.; 2a) to lead away from the truth, to lead into error, to deceive; 2b) to be led into error; 2c) to be led aside from the path of*

> virtue, to go astray, sin; 2d) to sever or fall away from the truth; 2d1) of heretics; 2e) to be led away into error and sin"

From this Greek Word, we get the English word, *"planet"* which is a heavenly body that wanders through the heavens.

- **Matthew 24:4-5**

"And Jesus answered and said unto them, Take heed that **no man deceive** you. For many shall come in my name, saying, I am Christ; and **shall deceive many**."

There are all kinds of deceivers throughout the world. People should beware of deceivers who deceive many, pretending to be Christ.

- **Matthew 24:11**

"And many false prophets shall rise, and **shall deceive many**." Many are being deceived by the many false prophets that have existed for centuries all around the world.

- **Romans 16:18**

"For they that are such serve not our Lord Jesus Christ, but their own belly; and by good words and fair speeches **deceive the hearts** of the simple."

Deception of the heart comes by seemingly good words and fair speeches that are really false.

- **Ephesians 4:14**

"That we *henceforth* be no more children, tossed to and fro, and carried about with every wind of doctrine, by the sleight of men, *and* cunning craftiness, whereby they **lie in wait to deceive**;"

People deceive others by false doctrines, sleights (clever skills), and cunning craftiness.

- **Ephesians 5:6**

"**Let no man deceive you** with vain words: for because of these things cometh the wrath of God upon the children of disobedience."

DECEPTION COMES WITH EMPTY WORDS
Vain and empty words are the cause of much deception which brings God's wrath upon the disobedient.

- **2 Thessalonians 2:3**

"**Let no man deceive you** by any means: for *that day shall not come*, except there come a falling away first, and that man of sin be revealed, the son of perdition;"

The Tribulation will not come until great apostasy occurs and the man of sin is revealed.

1 John 1:9

"If we confess our sins, he is faithful and just to forgive us our sins, and to cleanse us from all unrighteousness."

THE MEANING OF THE GREEK WORD, "HOMOLOGEO"

This verse tells the true Christian what they must do when they have sinned. The Greek Word for "*confess*" is HOMOLOGEO. Some of the meanings of this Greek Word are:

> "*1) to say the same thing as another, i.e. to agree with, assent; 2) to concede; 2a) not to refuse, to promise; 2b) not to deny; 2b1) to confess; 2b2) declare; 2b3) to confess, i.e. to admit or declare one's self guilty of what one is accused of; 3) to profess; 3a) to declare openly, speak out freely; 3b) to profess one's self the worshipper of one; 4) to praise, celebrate*"

When the genuine Christian sins, he or she must say the same thing about that sin that God says. They must agree with God that what is thought, said, or done is sin.

Verses On Confession

- **Psalms 32:5**

    "I acknowledged my sin unto thee, and mine iniquity have I not hid. I said, I will confess my transgressions unto the LORD; and thou forgavest the iniquity of my sin. Selah."

David was willing to confess his transgressions unto the LORD Who forgave him.

- **Romans 14:11**

    "For it is written, *As* I live, saith the Lord, every knee shall bow to me, and every tongue shall **confess to God**."

ONE DAY EVERY KNEE SHALL BOW TO CHRIST

One day in the future God has promised that every knee shall bow to Him, whether lost sinners (at the Great White Throne Judgment) or genuine Christians (at the Judgment Seat of Christ). They will honor the Lord, whether unwillingly (like the first group) or willingly (like the second group).

1, 2, & 3 John–Preaching Verse-by-Verse

- **Philippians 2:11**

"And *that* **every tongue should confess** that Jesus Christ *is* Lord, to the glory of God the Father."
One day that will happen, as mentioned in the preceding verse.

- **James 5:16**

"**Confess *your* faults** one to another, and pray one for another, that ye may be healed. The effectual fervent prayer of a righteous man availeth much."

CONFESS "FAULTS," TO OTHERS, NOT "SINS."
This verse speaks of how true Christians should deal with one another. They should confess their "*faults*" one to one another (not their "*sins*") as the false Gnostic Critical Greek says and every version around the world based upon this false text!)

Verses On Faithfulness

- **1 Corinthians 1:9**

"**God *is* faithful**, by whom ye were called unto the fellowship of his Son Jesus Christ our Lord."
God is faithful in all that He has spoken and promised. He has never been nor ever will be unfaithful.

- **1 Corinthians 10:13**

"There hath no temptation taken you but such as is common to man: but **God *is* faithful**, who will not suffer you to be tempted above that ye are able; but will with the temptation also make a way to escape, that ye may be able to bear *it*."

IN TESTINGS, A WAY TO ESCAPE BY GOD
When temptations and testings come into the lives of true Christians, God is faithful to them in making a way to escape so that they may be able to bear it.

- **1 Thessalonians 5:24**

"**Faithful *is* he that calleth you**, who also will do *it*."
The Lord is faithful in everything He has promised to do for the true Christians as well as for those who are non-Christians. He will never fail in doing what He has promised.

- **2 Thessalonians 3:3**

"But **the Lord is faithful**, who shall stablish you, and keep *you* from evil."
The faithfulness of God to genuine Christians involves both their being established and kept from evil.

- **2 Timothy 2:13**
  "If we believe not, *yet* **he abideth faithful**: he cannot deny himself."

No matter what happens, the Lord continues to abide in complete faithfulness.

- **Hebrews 10:23**
  "Let us hold fast the profession of *our* faith without wavering; (for **he *is* faithful** that promised;)"

Our Lord is completely faithful.

- **Hebrews 11:11**
  "Through faith also Sara herself received strength to conceive seed, and was delivered of a child when she was past age, because she judged him faithful who had promised."

He is faithful. He keeps His promises.

- **1 Peter 4:19**
  "Wherefore let them that suffer according to the will of God commit the keeping of their souls to him in well doing, as unto a **faithful Creator**."

God is the faithful Creator of the entire universe and everything that is within it.

- **Revelation 1:5**
  "And from **Jesus Christ, *who is* the faithful witness**, *and* the first begotten of the dead, and the prince of the kings of the earth. Unto him that loved us, and washed us from our sins in his own blood,"

The Lord Jesus Christ is a faithful Witness. He came from Heaven to tell the truth. He did so very faithfully despite how he was hated for doing it.

Verses On Just

The Lord Jesus Christ does not only forgive the sins of those who truly trust Him as their Saviour, but He is "just" in doing so because His payment for sins was on the cross.

- **Acts 3:14**
  "But ye denied the Holy One and **the Just**, and desired a murderer to be granted unto you;"

CHRIST IS THE ONLY "JUST ONE" THAT EVER LIVED

The Lord Jesus Christ is called the Just One. He's the only Just One Who ever walked this earth.

- **Acts 7:52**
"Which of the prophets have not your fathers persecuted? and they have slain them which shewed before of the coming of **the Just One**; of whom ye have been now the betrayers and murderers:"

The Lord Jesus Christ was prophesied to come to this earth as the "Just One."

- **Acts 22:14**
"And he said, The God of our fathers hath chosen thee, that thou shouldest know his will, and see **that Just One**, and shouldest hear the voice of his mouth."

Once again, the Lord Jesus Christ is called the "*Just One*."

- **Romans 3:26**
"To declare, *I say*, at this time his righteousness: that **he might be just**, and the justifier of him which believeth in Jesus."

GOD WAS JUST IN FORGIVING SINNERS
God the Father was just in redeeming those who exercise saving faith in the Lord Jesus Christ because the Saviour, in His death, made atonement for all of their sins.

- **1 Peter 3:18**
"For Christ also hath once suffered for sins, **the just** for the unjust, that he might bring us to God, being put to death in the flesh, but quickened by the Spirit:"

The Lord Jesus Christ is again called "*the just*" Who suffered for the unjust sinners of all the world.

- **Revelation 15:3**
"And they sing the song of Moses the servant of God, and the song of the Lamb, saying, Great and marvellous *are* thy works, Lord God Almighty; **just** and true *are* thy ways, thou King of saints."

GOD IS ALWAYS JUST AND TRUE
God is always "*just*" and true in all His ways.

Verses On Forgiveness

- **Matthew 18:21-22**
"Then came Peter to him, and said, Lord, how oft shall my brother sin against me, and I **forgive** him? till seven times? Jesus saith unto him, I say not unto thee, Until seven times: but, Until seventy times seven."

The Lord Jesus Christ taught Peter that there should be no end to forgiveness. Though it is difficult, it should be endless.

- **Mark 2:10**

"But that ye may know that the Son of man hath power on earth **to forgive sins**, (he saith to the sick of the palsy,)"

> **ONLY CHRIST CAN FORGIVE SINS**
>
> The Lord Jesus Christ is the only One who has the power on earth to forgive sins. Today, He exercises that power when a person has genuine faith in Him as their Saviour Who died for them.

- **Luke 17:3**

"Take heed to yourselves: If thy brother trespass against thee, rebuke him; and if he repent, **forgive him**."

Notice, after the rebuke comes the repentance of the trespasser, and then comes the forgiveness. This order should be maintained.

- **Luke 23:34**

"Then said Jesus, **Father, forgive them**; for they know not what they do. And they parted his raiment, and cast lots."

> **CHRIST FORGAVE THOSE WHO CRUCIFIED HIM**
>
> Those who were crucifying the Lord Jesus Christ on the cross were the subjects of God's forgiveness because they didn't know what they were doing.

- **2 Corinthians 2:6-7**

"Sufficient to such a man *is* this punishment, which *was inflicted* of many. So that contrariwise ye *ought* rather to **forgive *him***, and comfort *him*, lest perhaps such a one should be swallowed up with overmuch sorrow."

This is speaking about a man in the Corinthian church who had committed incest with his father's wife. Even he should be forgiven by the Corinthian Christians.

Verses On Cleansing

- **Matthew 23:25-26**

"Woe unto you, scribes and Pharisees, hypocrites! for ye make **clean the outside** of the cup and of the platter, but within they are full of extortion and excess. *Thou* blind Pharisee, **cleanse** first that *which is* within the cup and platter, that the outside of them may be **clean also**."

Cleansing must originate from within in order to cleanse properly that which is without. The Lord Jesus Christ is able to cleanse genuine Christians from within and from without.

- **2 Corinthians 7:1**

"Having therefore these promises, dearly beloved, **let us cleanse ourselves** from all filthiness of the flesh and spirit, perfecting holiness in the fear of God."

CLEANSING NEEDED FOR FLESH AND SPIRIT

Cleansing must be from filthiness and sins of both the flesh and the spirit.

- **Ephesians 5:26**

"That he might sanctify and **cleanse** it with the washing of water by the word,"

CHRISTIANS CAN BE CLEANSED BY THE BIBLE

God cleanses true Christians as they study and are cleansed by the washing with the water of the Words of God.

- **James 4:8**

"Draw nigh to God, and he will draw nigh to you. **Cleanse *your* hands**, *ye* sinners; and purify *your* hearts, *ye* double minded."

Both hands and hearts must be cleansed and purified before the Lord will draw near to people.

- **1 John 1:9**

"If we confess our sins, he is faithful and just to **forgive us** *our* sins, and to **cleanse us** from all unrighteousness."

This verse is speaking of genuine Christians who sincerely confess their sins unto God, as I have mentioned earlier.

THE MEANING OF THE GREEK WORD, "APHIEMI"

The Greek Word for *"forgive"* is APHIEMI. Some of the many meanings of this Greek Word are:

> *"1) to send away; 1a) to bid going away or depart; 1a1) of a husband divorcing his wife; 1b) to send forth, yield up, to expire; 1c) to let go, let alone, let be; 1c1) to disregard; 1c2) to leave, not to discuss now, (a topic); 1c21) of teachers, writers and speakers; 1c3) to omit, neglect; 1d) to let go, give up a debt, forgive, to remit; 1e) to give up, keep no longer; 2) to permit, allow, not to hinder, to give up a thing to a person; 3) to leave, go way from one; 3a) in order to go to another*

> *place; 3b) to depart from any one; 3c) to depart from one and leave him to himself so that all mutual claims are abandoned; 3d) to desert wrongfully; 3e) to go away leaving something behind; 3f) to leave one by not taking him as a companion; 3g) to leave on dying, leave behind one; 3h) to leave so that what is left may remain, leave remaining; 3i) abandon, leave destitute."*

God's forgiveness is when He sends away the sins of the true Christian by saving faith in His Son, the Lord Jesus Christ. It's like the Day of Atonement, in the Old Testament in Leviticus 16. Aaron was to take two goats. One was slain, the blood was applied to the Holy of Holies. The other was the scapegoat that was free to go out alive. But before that goat went out, Aaron laid his hands on the goat and confessed the sins of all the children of Israel that they had done that whole year. After that, the goat was let free to go out in the wilderness.

THE MEANING OF THE GREEK WORD, "APHIEMI"

That's what this Greek Word APHIEMI means. To cast off, let go, and send away. The sins are gone when true Christians honestly confess them to the Lord and agree with Him that they are sins. God is just in His forgiveness of these sins and faithful in cleansing them.

1 John 1:10

"If we say that we have not sinned, we make him a liar, and his word is not in us."

GOD IS NOT A LIAR ABOUT PEOPLE'S SINS

God is not a liar. If either the unsaved people, or even genuine Christians, say that they have not sinned, they make God a liar. There are many verses that speak of the sins of human beings. His Words are very clear in this matter. Because of the presence of the sin nature in every human being, there are two kinds of sinners: (1) lost sinners, (2) saved sinners. Even if a people truly received the Lord Jesus Christ as their Saviour, they still have the sin nature and can sin if they walk after the lust of their flesh.

In 1 John 1:8, we have listed many of the verses that tell us that God considers all people to be sinners. Look back at those verses to see how clearly God has declared this fact. <u>If people do not believe this, they make God a liar.</u>

Verses On Liars

- **Proverbs 17:4**

"A wicked doer giveth heed to false lips; *and* a **liar** giveth ear to a naughty tongue."

<u>God declares here that liars often listen to wicked tongues</u> that speak many evil things.

- **Proverbs 30:6**

"Add thou not unto his words, lest he reprove thee, and thou be found a **liar**."

<u>Adding to God's Words is what the new Bible versions do repeatedly. In so doing, they are reproved by the Lord, and they are called "liars."</u>

- **John 8:44**

"Ye are of *your* father the devil, and the lusts of your father ye will do. He was a murderer from the beginning, and abode not in the truth, because there is no truth in him. When he speaketh a **lie**, he speaketh of his own: for he is a **liar**, and the father of it."

<u>The Devil speaks many lies.</u> In fact, <u>he is called here</u> a liar and <u>the father of lies.</u>

- **Romans 3:4**

"God forbid: yea, let God be true, but **every man a liar**; as it is written, That thou mightest be justified in thy sayings, and mightest overcome when thou art judged."

THOSE WHO DISAGREE WITH THE BIBLE ARE LIARS

When God states something in His Words in the Bible and people disagree with those words, the conclusion that must be drawn is that it is God Who is true, and every person who disagrees with Him is a liar.

1 John
Chapter Two

1 John 2:1

"My little children, these things write I unto you, that ye sin not. And if any man sin, we have an advocate with the Father, Jesus Christ the righteous:"

In chapter two, the Apostle John talks about *"little children."* These are genuine Christians who are probably newly-saved. In the expression *"any man,"* it is the way the King James translators in 1611 meant *"any person,"* whether male or female. The Greek Word for this is TIS which means any person. You might think of it as *"any human being."*

Even true Christians sin because they still have their flesh and their fallen nature. No one but the Lord Jesus Christ could be sinlessly perfect. But if Christians sin, they have an *"advocate with the Father, Jesus Christ the righteous."*

MEANING OF THE GREEK WORD, "PARAKLETOS"

The Greek Word for *"advocate"* is PARAKLETOS. Some of the meanings of that Greek Word are:

> *"1) summoned, called to one's side, esp. called to one's aid; 1a) one who pleads another's cause before a judge, a pleader, counsel for defense, legal assistant, an advocate; 1b) one who pleads another's cause with one, an intercessor; 1b1) of Christ in his exaltation at God's right hand, pleading with God the Father for the pardon of our sins; 1c) in the widest sense, a helper, succourer, aider, assistant; 1c1) of the Holy Spirit destined to take the place of Christ with the apostles (after*

> *his ascension to the Father), to lead them to a deeper knowledge of the gospel truth, and give them divine strength needed to enable them to undergo trials and persecutions on behalf of the divine kingdom"*

The Lord Jesus Christ is the true Christians' defense lawyer when they fall into sin when tempted by either the world, their own flesh, or the Devil. The Lord Jesus Christ is the only Lawyer and Advocate that they have.

Verses On Christ As Intercessor And Great High Priest

- **Job 9:32-33**

"For *he is* not a man, as I *am, that* I should answer him, *and* we should come together in judgment. Neither is there **any daysman** betwixt us, *that* might lay his hand upon us both."

In Job's day, before the Lord Jesus Christ, there was no daysman or advocate who could be an umpire that could lay his hand on both man and God.

- **Romans 8:34**

"Who *is* he that condemneth? *It is* **Christ** that died, yea rather, that is risen again, who is even at the right hand of God, **who also maketh intercession for us**."

That's what the genuine Christians' Advocate does when they sin– the Lord Jesus Christ intercedes for them.

- **Hebrews 7:24-25**

"But this *man*, because he continueth ever, hath an **unchangeable priesthood**. Wherefore he is able also to save them to the uttermost that come unto God by him, seeing **he ever liveth to make intercession for them**."

When true Christians sin, the Lord Jesus Christ, their Advocate and Great High Priest, intercedes for them before God the Father.

- **Hebrews 2:17**

"Wherefore in all things it behoved him to be made like unto *his* brethren, that he might be a merciful and faithful high priest in things *pertaining* to God, to make reconciliation for the sins of the people."

The Lord Jesus Christ is both a merciful and faithful High Priest and Advocate for all of the redeemed people all around the world.

- **Hebrews 3:1**
"Wherefore, holy brethren, partakers of the heavenly calling, consider the Apostle and High Priest of our profession, Christ Jesus;"

The holy brethren should consider and think about the Lord Jesus Christ as their High Priest.

- **Hebrews 4:14-15**
"Seeing then that we have a great high priest, that is passed into the heavens, Jesus the Son of God, let us hold fast *our* profession. For we have not an high priest which cannot be touched with the feeling of our infirmities; but was in all points tempted like as *we are, yet* without sin."

CHRIST NOW INTERCEDING FOR TRUE CHRISTIANS

The sinless Lord Jesus Christ is now in Heaven interceding for genuine Christians. He is sympathetic to them, understands their infirmities, and intercedes for them. Because of this, they should hold fast their faith in Him and never swerve from it.

- **Hebrews 8:1**
"Now of the things which we have spoken *this is* the sum: We have such an high priest, who is set on the right hand of the throne of the Majesty in the heavens;"

The Intercessor, Advocate, and Daysman of the true Christians is on the right hand of God the Father in Heaven.

- **Hebrews 9:11-12**
"But Christ being come an high priest of good things to come, by a greater and more perfect tabernacle, not made with hands, that is to say, not of this building; Neither by the blood of goats and calves, but by his own blood he entered in once into the holy place, having obtained eternal redemption *for us*."

By His own blood, Christ, the believers' Great High Priest, entered the Holy Place of Heaven, having obtained eternal redemption for them.

1 John 2:2

"And he is the propitiation for our sins: and not for ours only, but also for the sins of the whole world."

The Lord Jesus Christ is the propitiation not only for the sins of the genuine Christians, but also for the sins of the whole world.

> **THE MEANING OF THE GREEK WORD, "HILASMOS"**
> The Greek Word for *"propitiation"* is HILASMOS. Some of the meanings of this Greek Word are:
> *"1) an appeasing, propitiating; 2) the means of appeasing, a propitiation."*

Though this is a good theological word, the New International Version and many other versions do not use it. I guess it is too theological for them. It means that God the Father is satisfied with the work of His Son, the Lord Jesus Christ, in His death on the cross of Calvary, when he took on Himself the sins of the entire world.

> **THE HERETICAL TEACHINGS OF HYPER-CALVINISM**
> This verse teaches clearly the unlimited atonement of the Lord Jesus Christ. It repudiates the heretical teachings of the hyper-Calvinists who teach these two things: (1) They say that Christ died only for the sins of the elect and not for the sins of the entire world. (2) They say that only the elect can believe in the Lord Jesus Christ as their Saviour and no one else can believe in and trust in Him. <u>Both of these things are unscriptural and are heresies.</u> When people don't believe these two things, they make a lot of enemies from the hyper-Calvinist people—and there are many of them around the world.

<u>Other Verses On Propitiation</u>
- Romans 3:25

"Whom God hath set forth ***to be* a propitiation** through faith in his blood, to declare his righteousness for the remission of sins that are past, through the forbearance of God;"

> **PROPITIATION FOR THE SINS OF THE WORLD**
> As it says right here in 1 John 2:2, the Lord Jesus Christ is the propitiation and satisfaction, not only for the sins of the true Christians, but also for the sins of the whole world.

- 1 John 4:10

"Herein is love, not that we loved God, but that he loved us, and sent his Son *to be* the **propitiation for our sins**."

<u>God the Father sent His Son to be the propitiation for sins.</u>

Verses On Christ's "Whosoever Will" Invitation And His Unlimited Atonement

- **Isaiah 53:5**

"**But he was wounded for our transgressions**, *he was* bruised **for our iniquities**: the chastisement **of our peace** *was* upon him; and with his stripes **we are healed**."
Isaiah was prophesying about the Lord Jesus Christ, the Messiah Who was to come. I believe "*our*," in all three instances in this verse, refers to all humanity: (1) "*our transgressions*"; (2) "*our iniquities*"; (3) "*our peace*." All humanity must genuinely accept the Lord Jesus Christ as their Saviour in order to be the recipient of all these three promises.

- **Isaiah 53:6**

"**All we like sheep have gone astray**; we have turned every one to his own way; and **the LORD hath laid on him the iniquity of us all**."
"*All we like sheep have gone astray;*" This includes the entire universe of people all around the world. It refers to "*iniquity*" of all the people, not simply the iniquity of the elect as the hyper-Calvinists heretically believe.

- **Matthew 11:28**

"Come unto me, **all *ye* that labour** and are heavy laden, and **I will give you rest**."

CHRIST'S INVITATION IS FOR ALL, NOT JUST SOME
The invitation of the Lord Jesus Christ was to "**all *ye* that labour**." The invitation was not just to a small group of the elect as the hyper-Calvinists heretically teach. He clearly said that He would give "**rest**" to **all** who would come to Him in faith, not just to the elect as the hyper-Calvinists heretically teach.

- **John 1:12**

"But **as many as received him**, to them gave he power to become the sons of God, *even* to **them that believe on his name:**"

SALVATION FOR AS MANY AS RECEIVE CHRIST
Salvation is for "as many as received" the Lord Jesus Christ. It is not simply for some little group that the hyper-Calvinists call "*the elect*." Salvation is for all who receive "Him," thereby becoming the sons and daughters of God.

- **John 1:29**

"The next day John seeth Jesus coming unto him, and saith, Behold **the Lamb of God, which taketh away the sin of the world**."

This is a very clear verse about how the Lord Jesus Christ is God's Lamb Who died for and provisionally took away "*the sin of the world*," rather than only the sins of the elect.

- **John 3:14-18**

"And as Moses lifted up the serpent in the wilderness, even so must the Son of man be lifted up: That **whosoever believeth in him should not perish**, but have eternal life. For **God so loved the world**, that he gave his only begotten Son, that **whosoever believeth in him should not perish**, but have everlasting life. For God sent not his Son into the world to condemn the world; but that **the world through him might be saved**. **He that believeth on him** is not condemned: but he that believeth not is condemned already, because he hath not believed in the name of the only begotten Son of God."

The words, "*whosoever*" and "*the world*" in these verses include the whole world. They are not limited to the elect as the hyper-Calvinists heretically teach.

- **John 3:36**

"**He that believeth on the Son** hath everlasting life: and he that believeth not the Son shall not see life; but the wrath of God abideth on him."

The invitation to believe is for everyone, not just the small group of the elect as the hyper-Calvinists heretically teach.

- **John 5:24**

"Verily, verily, I say unto you, **He that heareth my word, and believeth on him** that sent me, hath everlasting life, and shall not come into condemnation; but is passed from death unto life."

Everlasting life is available for the ones who hear and sincerely believe on the Lord Jesus Christ. It is not only available for the elect.

- **John 6:35**

"And Jesus said unto them, I am the bread of life: **he that cometh to me** shall never hunger; and **he that believeth on me** shall never thirst."

Coming to and believing on the Lord Jesus Christ is available to anyone in the world, not only for the elect.

- **John 6:47**

"Verily, verily, I say unto you, **He that believeth on me** hath everlasting life."

The invitation by the Lord Jesus Christ to receive everlasting life is to "*he that believeth*" on Him. It is not limited to the elect.
- **John 7:37**
"In the last day, that great *day* of the feast, Jesus stood and cried, saying, **If any man thirst, let him come unto me**, and drink."

THE GREEK WORD, TIS, IS FOR ANY HUMAN
Once again, the Greek Word for "*man*" is TIS. It means, in the 1611 parlance of the King James Bible, "*any person*" or any "*huMAN.*" This certainly is a universal invitation to come unto the Lord Jesus Christ for salvation.

- **John 10:9**
"I am the door: by me **if any man enter in**, he shall be saved, and shall go in and out, and find pasture."

AGAIN, THE GREEK WORD, TIS, IS FOR ANY HUMAN
The Greek Word, in this verse, for "*man*" is also TIS as in other places. It means, in the 1611 parlance of the King James Bible, "*any person*" or any "*huMAN.*" Salvation is offered to any human being. It is not limited only to the elect as the hyper-Calvinists heretically proclaim.

- **John 11:25**
"Jesus said unto her, I am the resurrection, and the life: **he that believeth in me**, though he were dead, yet shall he live:"
The Lord Jesus Christ gave no restrictions whatsoever on those who can believe on Him. Salvation is not limited to the elect.

- **Romans 5:6**
"For when we were yet without strength, in due time **Christ died for** the ungodly."
The Lord Jesus Christ died for the sins of the entire world of "*ungodly*" people, not just the "*ungodly*" elect.

- **2 Corinthians 5:19**
"To wit, that God was in Christ, **reconciling the world unto himself**, not imputing their trespasses unto them; and hath committed unto us the word of reconciliation."

RECONCILIATION FOR THE WHOLE WORLD
Not simply the world of the elect only, but **God reconciled the whole world** unto Himself so that those in the world might genuinely trust His Son and partake of this reconciliation that God made available.

- **1 Timothy 2:5-6**
"For *there is* one God, and one mediator between God and men, the man **Christ Jesus; Who gave himself a ransom for all**, to be testified in due time."

The Lord Jesus Christ, on the cross, gave Himself as a ransom for all people, not just for the elect. These people must now truly trust in Him and receive His everlasting life and His forgiveness of their many sins.

- **Hebrews 2:9**
"But we see Jesus, who was made a little lower than the angels for the suffering of death, crowned with glory and honour; that **he by the grace of God should taste death for every man**."

CHRIST DIED FOR ALL PEOPLE

"*Every man*" is the Greek Word, PANTOS ("*for all*"). The Lord Jesus Christ tasted death on the cross for all people so that all who genuinely believe on Him might have Eternal life.

- **2 Peter 2:1**
"But there were false prophets also among the people, even as there shall be **false teachers** among you, who privily shall bring in damnable heresies, even **denying the Lord that bought them**, and bring upon themselves swift destruction."

HYPER-CALVINISM IS HERESY!

The Lord Jesus Christ did not die just for the elect, but He "*bought*" [that is, paid for the sins of] everyone in the world—including false teaching heretics--so that they might truly trust Him and receive His redemption.

- **1 John 4:14**
"And we have seen and do testify that the Father sent the Son *to be* **the Saviour of the world**."

GOD MADE PROVISION FOR THE WHOLE WORLD

God the Father provided the Lord Jesus Christ to be the Saviour of the entire world. The vital thing the entire world must do is to make use of God's provision and genuinely trust God's Son as their Saviour who died for their sins.

- **Luke 2:11**
"For unto you is **born this day in the city of David a Saviour**, which is Christ the Lord."

The Lord Jesus Christ will be the Saviour (not just for the elect, but) for the entire world **IF** they would only truly trust Him and accept God's invitation.

1 John 2:3

"And hereby we do know that we know him, if we keep his commandments."

THE MEANING OF THE GREEK WORD, "TEREO"

The Greek Word for *"keep"* is TEREO. Some of the meanings of this Greek Word are:

"1) to attend to carefully, take care of; 1a) to guard; 1b) metaph. to keep, one in the state in which he is; 1c) to observe; 1d) to reserve: to undergo something."

Some professing Christians often say that they know the Lord Jesus Christ as their Saviour, but they seem to live in line with the world, the flesh, or the Devil. I wonder if those people really know the Lord Jesus Christ as their Saviour.

Verses On Keeping Christ's Commandments

- John 14:15

"If ye love me, **keep my commandments**."

The evidence of the love of the Lord Jesus Christ by true Christians is that they keep His commandments.

- John 14:23

"Jesus answered and said unto him, **If a man love me, he will keep my words**: and my Father will love him, and we will come unto him, and make our abode with him."

Sincere love for the Saviour will enable genuine Christians to keep His Words.

- John 15:10

"**If ye keep my commandments, ye shall abide in my love**; even as I have kept my Father's commandments, and abide in his love."

By keeping the Saviour's commandments, faithful Christians will abide in His love.

1 John 2:4

"He that saith, I know him, and keepeth not his commandments, is a liar, and the truth is not in him."

Those who claim to be true Christians without keeping His commandments are liars. The truth is not in them.

Verses On Lying
- **John 8:44**
  "Ye are of *your* father **the devil**, and the lusts of your father ye will do. He was a murderer from the beginning, and **abode not in the truth**, because there is no truth in him. When he speaketh a lie, he speaketh of his own: for he **is a liar**, and the father of it."

Not keeping the commandments of the Lord Jesus Christ makes these people liars who don't have the truth in them.

- **Acts 5:3**
  "But Peter said, Ananias, why hath Satan filled thine heart **to lie to the Holy Ghost**, and to keep back *part* of the price of the land?"

Ananias and Sapphira lied about the price they sold their land for. God slew them because of it. God hates lying and liars.

- **Colossians 3:9**
  "**Lie not one to another**, seeing that ye have put off the old man with his deeds;"

Paul told the Christians in Colosse to stop their lying to each other. God opposes all lying.

- **2 Thessalonians 2:11**
  "And for this cause God shall send them **strong delusion, that they should believe a lie**:"

In the Tribulation period, God is going to send people "*strong delusion, that they should believe a lie*." I believe that there is much of that "*strong delusion*" with us even today. Many people are believing lies. For example, according to a close observer, President Obama, in one of his speeches, spoke eight different lies in only eight minutes. These lies were no doubt believed by his vast audience.

- **Titus 1:2**
  "In hope of eternal life, which **God, that cannot lie**, promised before the world began;"

The God of the Bible is unable to lie. People can trust everything that He says in the Bible.

- **Hebrews 6:18**
  "That by two immutable things, in which *it was* **impossible for God to lie**, we might have a strong consolation, who have fled for refuge to lay hold upon the hop e set before us:"

It is totally impossible for God to lie. People must believe Him and the truth that He declares in His Word, the Bible.

1 John 2:5

"But whoso keepeth his word, in him verily is the love of God perfected: hereby know we that we are in him."

THE MEANING OF THE GREEK WORD, "TEREO"

The Greek Word for "*keep*" is TEREO. It is the same Greek Word that was used above in verse 3. As you remember, some meanings of this Greek Word are:

> "*1) to attend to carefully, take care of; 1a) to guard; 1b) metaph. to keep, one in the state in which he is; 1c) to observe; 1d) to reserve: to undergo something.*"

Whoever observes and guards God's Words has His love perfected.

THE MEANING OF THE GREEK WORD, "TELEIOO"

The Greek Word for "*perfected*" is TELEIOO. Some of the meanings of this Greek Word are:

> "*1) to make perfect, complete; 1a) to carry through completely, to accomplish, finish, bring to an end; 2) to complete (perfect); 2a) add what is yet wanting in order to render a thing full; 2b) to be found perfect; 3) to bring to the end (goal) proposed; 4) to accomplish; 4a) bring to a close or fulfilment by event; 4a1) of the prophecies of the scriptures.*"

If genuine Christians keep God's Words, this is a proof they are "*in Him*" and really saved.

1 John 2:6

"He that saith he abideth in him ought himself also so to walk, even as he walked."

THE MEANING OF THE GREEK WORD, "MENO"

The Greek Word for "*abide*" is "MENO." Some of the meanings of this Greek Word are:

> "*1) to remain, abide; 1a) in reference to place; 1a1) to sojourn, tarry; 1a2) not to*

> *depart; 1a2a) to continue to be present; 1a2b) to be held, kept, continually; 1b) in reference to time; 1b1) to continue to be, not to perish, to last, endure; 1b1a) of persons, to survive, live; 1c) in reference to state or condition; 1c1) to remain as one, not to become another or different; 2) to wait for, await one."*

Verses On Abiding

Though the word "*abide*" is used in many of our traditional hymns and in 103 verses in our King James Bible, many of the new Bible versions do not use it. Here are some verses that use this word:

- **Psalms 91:1**

"He that dwelleth in the secret place of the most High **shall abide under the shadow of the Almighty**."

The psalmist showed that there was security when dwelling in God's secret place of fellowship.

- **John 3:36**

"He that believeth on the Son hath everlasting life: and he that believeth not the Son shall not see life; but **the wrath of God abideth on him**."

This is God's warning that those who reject genuine faith in the Lord Jesus Christ as their Saviour have God's wrath abiding on them. This is a serious warning that should be heeded by everyone.

- **John 5:38**

"And **ye have not his word abiding in you**: for whom he hath sent, him ye believe not."

The Lord Jesus Christ was speaking here to the Pharisees and other unbelievers. They did not have God's Words in them because of their unbelief.

- **John 12:46**

"I am come a light into the world, that **whosoever believeth on me should not abide in darkness**."

CHRIST THE LIGHT OF THE WORLD

The Saviour came from Heaven by His virgin birth as a light. He does not want anyone who truly believes in Him to abide in darkness. He wants them to walk in the light of God's Words. You may have lived in darkness before, but once you are in Christ, you abide and keep in Him; you stay away from that old darkness, sin, wickedness, and corruption.

- **John 14:16**
"And I will pray the Father, and he shall give you another **Comforter, that he may abide with you for ever;**"

> **THE HOLY SPIRIT INDWELLS TRUE CHRISTIANS**
> The Lord Jesus Christ promised to His genuine Christian followers that God the Father would send to them the Holy Spirit of God Who would abide with them forever. The Holy Spirit came on the day of Pentecost, (Acts 2), and fulfilled Christ's promise.

- **John 15:4-5**
"**Abide in me**, and I in you. As the branch cannot bear fruit of itself, **except it abide in the vine**; no more can ye, **except ye abide in me**. I am the vine, ye *are* the branches: **He that abideth in me**, and I in him, the same bringeth forth much fruit: for without me ye can do nothing."

The Saviour told His disciples to keep close to Him Who is the Vine that they might bear much fruit.

- **John 15:10**
"If ye keep my commandments, **ye shall abide in my love**; even as I have kept my Father's commandments, and **abide in his love**."

If people observe the Lord Jesus Christ's commandments, they will abide in His love.

Verses On Walking

If people say they are really abiding in the Lord Jesus Christ, it is evidenced by whether or not they walk as the Saviour Himself walked.

> **THE MEANING OF THE GREEK WORD, "PERIPATEO"**
> The Greek Word for "*walk*" is PERIPATEO. Some of the meanings of this Greek Word are:
> "*1) to walk; 1a) to make one's way, progress; to make due use of opportunities; 1b) Hebrew for, to live; 1b1) to regulate one's life; 1b2) to conduct one's self; 1b3) to pass one's life;*"

This is not an easy task, yet is one of the proofs that people are genuine Christians rather than "*Christians*" in name only. Here are numerous verses that speak of walking:

- **Romans 13:13**
"**Let us walk honestly**, as in the day; not in rioting and drunkenness, not in chambering and wantonness, not in strife and envying."

If people are true Christians, they should have an honest walk with the Lord in conformity to the Bible.

- **2 Corinthians 5:7**
"(For **we walk by faith, not by sight**:)"

Genuine Christians are really not able to walk by sight because they cannot see the Lord Who is their Guide. They must walk by faith in God's Words step-by-step.

- **Galatians 5:16**
"*This* I say then, **Walk in the Spirit**, and ye shall not fulfil the lust of the flesh."

True Christians are commanded here to walk step-by-step in the power of God the Holy Spirit to prevent them from getting sidetracked by the lust of their flesh.

- **Ephesians 4:1**
"I therefore, the prisoner of the Lord, beseech you that ye **walk worthy** of the vocation wherewith ye are called,"

Born-again, redeemed Christians are urged to live their lives in a worthy manner as a testimony to the Lord Who saved them.

- **Ephesians 5:2**
"And **walk in love**, as **Christ also hath loved us**, and hath given himself for us an offering and a sacrifice to God for a sweetsmelling savour."

It is very difficult for sinful human beings to carry on their lives in a loving spirit. Genuine Christians are to walk–even in the midst of hatred--in a loving manner even as the Lord Jesus Christ loved them.

- **Ephesians 5:8**
"For ye were sometimes darkness, but now *are ye* light in the Lord: **walk as children of light**:"

Before being saved, everyone was living in darkness; after salvation, they are commanded to walk in the light of God's Word as children of light.

- **Ephesians 5:15**
"See then that ye **walk circumspectly**, not as fools, but as wise,"

WALKING CIRCUMSPECTLY

"*Circumspectly*" means looking all around, 360 degrees–before, behind, to the left, and to the right–so as to avoid evil, serious harm, or foolishness.

- Colossians 4:5

"**Walk in wisdom toward them that are without**, redeeming the time."
Genuine Christians are to walk wisely, especially toward those who are without Christ, being non-Christians. Many of these people look, act, dress, and talk strangely. Much wisdom is needed in being around such people. Redeeming the time means making good use of the time without wasting any of it.

- 1 Thessalonians 2:12

"That ye would **walk worthy of God**, who hath called you unto his kingdom and glory."
God wants His sons and daughters to walk worthy of Him Who called them by grace through true faith in His Son.

- 3 John 1:4

"I have no greater joy than to hear that **my children walk in truth**."

THE KJB IS THE PROPER ENGLISH BIBLE

The Apostle John had great joy when those he led to the Lord Jesus Christ as Saviour were walking in line with the truths now found in our King James Bible. This is why the proper Bible (such as the King James Bible in English) is very necessary. Those Bibles whose New Testaments are based upon the Gnostic Critical Greek Text (which is a huge percentage of them) should be avoided. One reason for this is that they contain more than 356 doctrinal passages that are heretical and untrue.

1 John 2:7

"**Brethren, I write no new commandment unto you, but an old commandment which ye had from the beginning. The old commandment is the word which ye have heard from the beginning.**"

The Apostle John doesn't say in this verse what the commandment is, but is the commandment to "*love*."

Two Verses On Love

- John 13:34

"A new commandment I give unto you, That ye **love one another**; as I have loved you, that ye also **love one another**."

CHRISTIANS SHOULD LOVE ONE ANOTHER
The Lord Jesus Christ told His apostles to love one another. It is a commandment from Him while He was on earth.

- John 15:12

"This is my commandment, **That ye love one another**, as I have loved you."

LOVE AS CHRIST LOVED IS THE STANDARD
The standard of love for true Christians is as the Saviour loved them. Though it is very difficult to love other Christians who differ with us on many issues, love should be present despite strong differences. Paul loved Peter even though he rebuked him when Peter was wrong. We must love, in the Lord, genuine Christians who exalt the erroneous Gnostic Critical Greek New Testament Text. This is not easy, but it is the command of the Lord.

1 John 2:8

"Again, a new commandment I write unto you, which thing is true in him and in you: because the darkness is past, and the true light now shineth."

CHRIST AS LIGHT SHINES OUT OF DARKNESS
This is not the old commandment of *"love."* It is a new commandment about *"Light."* The Lord Jesus Christ is the Light of the world Who has come and Who even today shines out of the darkness of sin.

Verses On Light

- John 1:5

"And **the light shineth in darkness**; and the darkness comprehended it not."

The Lord Jesus Christ is called the "Light" that shines in the darkness of this wicked world.

- John 3:19

"And this is the condemnation, that **light is come into the world**, and men loved darkness rather than light, because their deeds were evil."

The Lord Jesus Christ has come into this evil world, but men and women as well as boys and girls love darkness rather than light

because their deeds are evil. They don't want the Light to shine upon them because it would reveal their hidden and evil deeds.
- **John 8:12**
"Then spake Jesus again unto them, saying, **I am the light of the world**: he that followeth me shall not walk in darkness, but shall have the **light of life**."

> **CHRIST THE LIGHT OF LIFE**
> What a wonderful title for our Saviour, *"the Light of the world."* He wants to light up dark sinful people and share with them His Light. By following Him, people will not walk in darkness, but will have the *"Light of life."*

- **John 12:35**
"Then Jesus said unto them, Yet a little **while is the light with you**. Walk **while ye have the light**, lest darkness come upon you: for he that walketh in darkness knoweth not whither he goeth."

> **WALKING IN THE LIGHT**
> The Lord Jesus Christ told His disciples that He was going back to Heaven soon. He urged them to walk while they had the Light with them so they would not walk in darkness, not knowing where they were going.

- **John 12:46**
"**I am come a light into the world**, that whosoever believeth on me should not abide in darkness."
The Saviour was that Light Who came into the world so that whoever genuinely believed on Him might be saved and not continue their walk in sin's darkness.

> **THE RIGHT BIBLE GIVES US LIGHT**
> God has given us His Bible so that genuine Christians can walk in God's light and truth. They have the King James Bible which is an accurate translation of the original Hebrew, Aramaic, and Greek Words. God expects all of those who are saved to walk in that light that He has shown us in our Bible.

1 John 2:9

"He that saith he is in the light, and hateth his brother, is in darkness even until now."

Those who profess to be in the light and are true Christians, yet hate their fellow Christians are in darkness.

> **THE MEANING OF THE GREEK WORD, "MISEO"**
> The Greek Word for "*hate*" is MISEO. Some of the meanings of that Greek Word are:
>> "*1) to hate, pursue with hatred, detest; 2) to be hated, detested;*"
>
> Genuine Christians might hate some of the doctrines or beliefs of fellow-Christians or what they say or do, but they should love these brethren themselves. Not to love them shows that they are in darkness rather than in the light. <u>This is a serious test which many genuine Christians fail miserably.</u>

1 John 2:10

"He that loveth his brother abideth in the light, and there is none occasion of stumbling in him."

> **THE MEANING OF THE GREEK WORD, "SKANDALON"**
> The Greek Word for "*stumbling,*" is SKANDALON. Some of the meanings of that Greek Word are:
>> "*1) the movable stick or trigger of a trap, a trap stick; 1a) a trap, snare; 1b) any impediment placed in the way and causing one to stumble or fall, (a stumbling block, occasion of stumbling) i.e. a rock which is a cause of stumbling; 1c) fig. applied to Jesus Christ, whose person and career were so contrary to the expectations of the Jews concerning the Messiah, that they rejected him and by their obstinacy made shipwreck of their salvation; 2) any person or thing by which one is (entrapped) drawn into error or sin.*"

Anything placed in the way may produce a stumbling. If a stick is holding up something, and you knock the stick away, that object falls down or stumbles. That's what this stumbling is. This verse is teaching that if genuine Christians love their fellow Christians, they're living in the light. They can see and therefore do not stumble as those who are walking in the darkness.

- **John 11:9-10**

"Jesus answered, Are there not twelve hours in the day? If any man walk in the day, he stumbleth not, because he seeth the light of this world. But if a man walk in the night, he stumbleth, because there is no light in him."

<u>Walking in the darkness, you stumble. That's why we need the light of the Scriptures so that we don't stumble over anyone or anything.</u>

1 John 2:11

"But he that hateth his brother is in darkness, and walketh in darkness, and knoweth not whither he goeth, because that darkness hath blinded his eyes."

DARKNESS BLINDS THE EYES OF CHRISTIANS

<u>This verse repeats what John said in previous verses.</u> For true Christians to hate their fellow Christians shows that such people are in darkness. They walk in darkness and don't know where they are going because darkness has blinded their eyes. Once again, I repeat that this does <u>not</u> mean that genuine Christians should go along with and agree with some of the unBiblical doctrines, teachings, or practices of their fellow Christians. They should love each other as fellow Christians who are in the family of God. Though this is difficult to do, they should allow God's love to overcome hate.

1 John 2:12

"I write unto you, little children, because your sins are forgiven you for his name's sake."

THE MEANING OF THE GREEK WORD, "APHIEMI"

The Greek Word for *"forgiveness"* is APHIEMI. Some of the many meanings of this Greek Word are:

"1) to send away; 1a) to bid going away or depart; 1a1) of a husband divorcing his wife; 1b) to send forth, yield up, to expire; 1c) to let go, let alone, let be; 1c1) to disregard; 1c2) to leave, not to discuss now, (a topic); 1c21) of teachers, writers and speakers; 1c3) to omit, neglect; 1d) to let go, give up a debt, forgive, to remit; 1e) to give up, keep no longer; 2) to

> *permit, allow, not to hinder, to give up a thing to a person; 3) to leave, go way from one; 3a) in order to go to another place; 3b) to depart from any one; 3c) to depart from one and leave him to himself so that all mutual claims are abandoned; 3d) to desert wrongfully; 3e) to go away leaving something behind; 3f) to leave one by not taking him as a companion; 3g) to leave on dying, leave behind one; 3h) to leave so that what is left may remain, leave remaining; 3i) abandon, leave destitute."*

In verses 12-14, there are three classes of people mentioned by the Apostle John:
  (1) little children
  (2) fathers
  (3) young men

In verse 12, John says he is writing to "little children."

GOD'S FORGIVENESS OF SINS THROUGH CHRIST

These were those who had been recently saved. Their sins had been forgiven because they genuinely trusted in the Lord Jesus Christ as their Saviour. It's a wonderful thing for people to have their sins forgiven. Look at all the various meanings of that Greek Word, APHIEMI, mentioned above. Here are several verses that mention God's forgiveness for those who truly trust His Son and His promises.

Verses On Forgiveness
- **Psalms 32:1**

"Blessed *is he **whose transgression is forgiven**, whose* sin *is* covered."

Even in the Old Testament, David declared how blessed and happy those people were whose transgressions were forgiven.

- **Matthew 9:2**

"And, behold, they brought to him a man sick of the palsy, lying on a bed: and Jesus seeing their faith said unto the sick of the palsy; Son, be of good cheer; **thy sins be forgiven thee**."

The Lord Jesus Christ, the only One Who could forgive sins, forgave this crippled man who was sick of the palsy.

- **Luke 7:36-50**
"And one of the Pharisees desired him that he would eat with him. And he went into the Pharisee's house, and sat down to meat. And, behold, a woman in the city, which was a sinner, when she knew that *Jesus* sat at meat in the Pharisee's house, brought an alabaster box of ointment, And stood at his feet behind *him* weeping, and began to wash his feet with tears, and did wipe *them* with the hairs of her head, and kissed his feet, and anointed *them* with the ointment.

Now when the Pharisee which had bidden him saw *it*, he spake within himself, saying, This man, if he were a prophet, would have known who and what manner of woman *this is* that toucheth him: for she is a sinner. And Jesus answering said unto him, Simon, I have somewhat to say unto thee. And he saith, Master, say on.

There was a certain creditor which had two debtors: the one owed five hundred pence, and the other fifty. And when they had nothing to pay, **he frankly forgave them both**. Tell me therefore, which of them will love him most?

Simon answered and said, I suppose that *he*, to whom he forgave most. And he said unto him, Thou hast rightly judged. And he turned to the woman, and said unto Simon, Seest thou this woman? I entered into thine house, thou gavest me no water for my feet: but she hath washed my feet with tears, and wiped *them* with the hairs of her head. Thou gavest me no kiss: but this woman since the time I came in hath not ceased to kiss my feet. My head with oil thou didst not anoint: but this woman hath anointed my feet with ointment.

Wherefore I say unto thee, **Her sins, which are many, are forgiven**; for she loved much: but to whom little is forgiven, *the same* loveth little. And they that sat at meat with him began to say within themselves, **Who is this that forgiveth sins** also?" And he said to the woman, Thy faith hath saved thee; go in peace."

The Lord Jesus Christ forgave the many sins of this woman. The Pharisees questioned whether or not He was able to forgive sins. As both Perfect God and Perfect Man, He was able then and is able today to forgive those who genuinely trust in Him as their Saviour.

- **Romans 4:7**
"*Saying*, Blessed *are* they whose iniquities are forgiven, and whose sins are covered."

Paul quotes Psalm 32:1, agreeing with David about the blessedness of those whose iniquities are forgiven.

- **Ephesians 4:32**
"And be ye kind one to another, tenderhearted, **forgiving one another**, even **as God for Christ's sake hath forgiven you**."

Genuine Christians are commanded to forgive their fellow Christians to the same extent that God, for Christ's sake, forgave them. That's quite a high standard.

- **Colossians 2:13**
"And you, being dead in your sins and the uncircumcision of your flesh, hath he quickened together with him, **having forgiven you all trespasses**;"

Those who are the recipients of God's salvation, through genuine faith in His Son, have all of their trespasses forgiven--past, present, and future.

1 John 2:13

"I write unto you, fathers, because ye have known him that is from the beginning. I write unto you, young men, because ye have overcome the wicked one. I write unto you, little children, because ye have known the Father."

John now mentions all three groups in this one verse:
(1) fathers
(2) young men
(3) little children

He writes to them and encourages them. Notice the fathers "ye have known him *that is* from the beginning." In other words, they are the early ones, who trusted the Saviour early in life. They have known the Lord Jesus Christ for years.

Then John mentions the young men. These young men are mature Christians, not old timers, but younger men. They have overcome the wicked one.

THE MEANING OF THE GREEK WORD, "NIKAO"

The Greek Word for "*overcome*" is NIKAO. Some of the meanings for this Greek Word are:

"*1) to conquer; 1a) to carry off the victory, come off victorious; 1a1) of Christ, victorious over all His foes; 1a2) of Christians, that hold fast their faith even unto death against the power of their foes, and temptations and*

> *persecutions; 1a3) when one is arraigned or goes to law, to win the case, maintain one's cause.*"

The little children are commended because they have known God the Father by coming to the Lord Jesus Christ as their Saviour.

Verses On Overcoming

- **John 16:33**

"These things I have spoken unto you, that in me ye might have peace. In the world ye shall have tribulation: but be of good cheer; **I have overcome the world**."

The Lord Jesus Christ has conquered and overcome this wicked world.

- **Romans 12:21**

"**Be not overcome of evil**, but **overcome evil with good**."

Evil should not conquer the true Christians, but they should conquer the evil with the good found in God's Words.

- **2 Peter 2:19**

"While they promise them liberty, they themselves are the servants of corruption: for **of whom a man is overcome**, of the same is he brought in bondage."

If people are overcome with some sin (such as drugs, or any other sin), they become slaves to that sin, a terrible condition.

- **1 John 4:4**

"Ye are of God, little children, and **have overcome them**: because greater is he that is in you, than he that is in the world."

The preceding verses speak of false spirits. Genuine Christians have overcome false spirits because of the power of the Holy Spirit within them.

- **1 John 5:4-5**

"**For whatsoever is born of God overcometh the world**: and this is the victory that **overcometh the world**, *even* our faith. Who is he that **overcometh the world**, but he that believeth that Jesus is the Son of God?"

Those who are born of God and believe that "Jesus is the Son of God" can overcome this wicked world around them by that faith.

- **Revelation 12:11**

"And **they overcame him by the blood of the Lamb**, and by the word of their testimony; and they loved not their lives unto the death."

During the Tribulation, those genuine Christians will overcome Satan by the blood of the Lamb and by their testimony for their Saviour.

Verses On Satan, The Wicked One
- **Matthew 13:19**
"When any one heareth the word of the kingdom, and understandeth *it* not, **then cometh the wicked *one***, and catcheth away that which was sown in his heart. This is he which received seed by the way side."

Those people who receive the seed of God's Words by the way side rather than on good ground will have that seed removed by Satan, the wicked one.
- **Matthew 13:38**
"The field is the world; the good seed are the children of the kingdom; but **the tares are the children of the wicked *one*;**"

Outwardly, the good seed appears to be the same as the tares, but there is a difference inwardly. Genuine Christians may appear to be the children of the wicked one if they allow their flesh to prevail.
- **1 John 3:12**
"Not as **Cain, *who* was of that wicked one**, and slew his brother. And wherefore slew he him? Because his own works were evil, and his brother's righteous."

Cain, a very evil man, murdered Abel, his brother. He was motivated by Satan, the wicked one.
- **1 John 5:18**
"We know that whosoever is born of God sinneth not; but he that is begotten of God keepeth himself, and **that wicked one toucheth him not**."

Being born-again and begotten by God puts up a guard against Satan.
- **Luke 22:31-32**
"And the Lord said, Simon, Simon, behold, **Satan hath desired *to have* you**, that he may sift *you* as wheat: But I have prayed for thee, that thy faith fail not: and when thou art converted, strengthen thy brethren."

The Lord Jesus Christ told Peter that Satan wanted to have him, but that Jesus would pray for him. Luke 22:1-3 indicates that Satan had a serious influence on Peter.

1 John 2:14

"I have written unto you, fathers, because ye have known him that is from the beginning. I have written unto you, young men, because ye are strong, and the word of God abideth in you, and ye have overcome the wicked one."

John speaks again about the fathers and the young men, but leaves out the little children. Three things were said about the young men:
- (1) they were strong
- (2) the Word of God abode in them
- (3) they had overcome the wicked one

Verses On Being Strong

- **Romans 4:20**

"He staggered not at the promise of God through unbelief; but was **strong in faith**, giving glory to God;"

Abraham was spiritually strong in faith.

- **1 Corinthians 16:13**

"Watch ye, stand fast in the faith, quit you like men, **be strong**."

Paul told the very carnal church at Corinth to be strong rather than weak as they currently were.

- **Ephesians 6:10**

"Finally, my brethren, **be strong in the Lord**, and in the power of his might."

The strength spoken of here is in the Lord rather than in people's personal efforts.

- **2 Timothy 2:1**

"Thou therefore, my son, **be strong in the grace** that is in Christ Jesus."

Paul told Pastor Timothy to be strong in the grace that is found in the Lord Jesus Christ.

1 John 2:15

"Love not the world, neither the things that are in the world. If any man love the world, the love of the Father is not in him."

The expression, "love not" is in the Greek present tense. Since it is a negative prohibition in that tense, it means to stop an action already in progress. Those to whom John was writing were loving the world. He told them to stop it! (If it were in the Greek aorist tense, it would mean not to begin an action.) This is the action that Genuine Christians should take in our day. They are to stop loving this wicked world with all of its wayward ways.

CHRISTIANS SHOULD LOVE NOT THE WORLD

If true Christians do not stop their love for the world, the love for God the Father will not be in them. They must choose the object of their love–the world, or God. They cannot serve two masters. They must choose between the world and God.

Verses On The World

- John 12:31

"Now is **the judgment of this world**: now shall the prince of this world be cast out."

CHRIST JUDGED SATAN AT THE CROSS

At the cross, the Lord Jesus Christ judged this world and sentenced Satan to judgment to be carried out at a later time.

- John 14:30

"Hereafter I will not talk much with you: for **the prince of this world cometh**, and hath nothing in me."

The Lord Jesus Christ predicted that Satan would manifest himself soon. He did this through the betrayal of Judas Iscariot.

- John 16:11

"Of judgment, because **the prince of this world is judged**."

THE DEVIL WILL BE SENT TO THE LAKE OF FIRE

The Devil has been sentenced. His judgment in the Lake of Fire will one day be carried out.

> *"And the devil that deceived them was cast into the lake of fire and brimstone, where the beast and the false prophet are, and shall be tormented day and night for ever and ever. "* (Revelation 20:10)

- Romans 12:2

"And **be not conformed to this world**: but be ye transformed by the renewing of your mind, that ye may prove what *is* that good, and acceptable, and perfect, will of God."

Those who are regenerated are commanded not to be conformed to this world, but be transformed instead.

- **1 Corinthians 7:31**
  "And they that use this world, as not abusing *it*: for **the fashion of this world passeth away**."

This world's fashions and customs will all pass away one day; they are only temporary and transitory.

- **2 Corinthians 4:4**
  "In whom **the god of this world hath blinded the minds** of them which believe not, lest the light of the glorious gospel of Christ, who is the image of God, should shine unto them."

The god of this world is Satan. He blinds the minds of those who do not believe on His Son for salvation and redemption.

- **Galatians 1:4**
  "Who gave himself for our sins, that he might **deliver us from this present evil world**, according to the will of God and our Father:"

CHRIST WANTS TO DELIVER FROM THE EVIL WORLD
The desire of the Lord Jesus Christ by dying for the sins of the world was to deliver those, who truly trust in Him, from this present evil world. They should not be a part of its evil.

- **Ephesians 2:2**
  "Wherein in time past ye walked **according to the course of this world**, according to the prince of the power of the air, the spirit that now worketh in the children of disobedience:"

Before genuine Christians are saved, they all walked according to the course of this world as the evil prince, Satan, directed them.

- **Ephesians 6:12**
  "For we wrestle not against flesh and blood, but against principalities, against powers, against the rulers of **the darkness of this world**, against spiritual wickedness in high *places*."

The world around us is in darkness apart from the Lord Jesus Christ, the Light of the world.

- **Colossians 2:8**
  "Beware lest any man spoil you through philosophy and vain deceit, after the tradition of men, **after the rudiments of the world**, and not after Christ."

FOLLOWING THE WORLD SPOILS CHRISTIANS
If saved people follow the rudiments of this world, they will be spoiled for the Lord's work.

- **2 Timothy 4:10**
"For Demas hath forsaken me, having **loved this present world**, and is departed unto Thessalonica; Crescens to Galatia, Titus unto Dalmatia."

When <u>Demas</u> loved this present world, he <u>forsook the ministry of the Apostle Paul</u>.

- **Titus 2:12**
"Teaching us that, denying ungodliness and worldly lusts, we should live soberly, righteously, and godly, **in this present world**;"

God wants His own to live godly, not in worldly lusts.

- **James 1:27**
"Pure religion and undefiled before God and the Father is this, To visit the fatherless and widows in their affliction, *and* to keep himself unspotted from the world."

To be undefiled before God, genuine Christians should keep themselves unspotted from the wickedness of this world.

- **James 4:4**
"Ye adulterers and adulteresses, know ye not that the **friendship of the world is enmity with God**? whosoever therefore will be **a friend of the world is the enemy of God**."

THESE CHRISTIANS WERE WORLD COMPROMISERS
James was addressing true Christians who were compromising with the world, thus becoming an enemy of God.

- **2 Peter 2:20**
"For if after they have escaped the pollutions of the world through the knowledge of the Lord and Saviour Jesus Christ, they are again entangled therein, and overcome, the latter end is worse with them than the beginning."

WORLD ENTANGLEMENT IS DEPLORABLE
If genuine Christians, who have been saved out of the world's pollutions, become entangled again in them, they are out of fellowship with the Lord. This is a deplorable condition to be in.

- **1 John 5:19**

"*And* we know that we are of God, and **the whole world lieth in wickedness**."

God's assessment of this world is that it is completely enveloped in wickedness.

1 John 2:16

"For all that is in the world, the lust of the flesh, and the lust of the eyes, and the pride of life, is not of the Father, but is of the world."

John lists three different things that are in this wicked world:
- (1) the lust of the flesh
- (2) the lust of the eyes
- (3) the pride of life

Let's look at a few verses that speak about these things that are not of the Father, but are of this world:

Verses On The Flesh

The flesh is not the same as the human body, but the flesh is an evil nature that dwells within the human body of human beings.

- **John 3:6**

"**That which is born of the flesh is flesh**; and that which is born of the Spirit is spirit."

The flesh is the sinful part of a person's nature that is received by birth and does not change, but can be controlled by the Holy Spirit.

- **John 6:63**

"It is the spirit that quickeneth; **the flesh profiteth nothing**: the words that I speak unto you, *they* are spirit, and *they* are life."

CHRISTIANS' TWO NATURES–FLESH & HOLY SPIRIT

Genuine Christians have both the indwelling Holy Spirit (obtained by their new birth) and their flesh (obtained by their natural birth). The flesh is of no profit in the sight of God.

- **Romans 7:18**

"For I know that in me (that is, **in my flesh,) dwelleth no good thing**: for to will is present with me; but *how* to perform that which is good I find not."

In people's flesh, including Paul's, there is no good thing. On the contrary, it is evil and sinful.

- **Romans 8:1**
 "*There is* therefore now no condemnation to them which are in Christ Jesus, **who walk not after the flesh**, but after the Spirit."

> ### WALKING AFTER THE SPIRIT
> Those who are "*in Christ Jesus*" have been redeemed. They should walk after the Holy Spirit, not after their flesh.

- **Romans 13:14**
 "But put ye on the Lord Jesus Christ, and **make not provision for the flesh**, to *fulfil* the lusts *thereof.*"
True Christians should make no provision for their evil flesh nature whatever.

- **1 Corinthians 1:29**
 "That **no flesh should glory in his presence**."
In God's presence there is no glory in anyone's flesh.

- **2 Corinthians 7:1**
 "Having therefore these promises, dearly beloved, let us cleanse ourselves from all **filthiness of the flesh** and spirit, perfecting holiness in the fear of God."
God calls the flesh filthy. There is no good in it at all.

- **Galatians 5:16-21**
 "*This* I say then, Walk in the Spirit, and **ye shall not fulfil the lust of the flesh. For the flesh lusteth against the Spirit**, and the Spirit against the flesh: and these are contrary the one to the other: so that ye cannot do the things that ye would. But if ye be led of the Spirit, ye are not under the law. Now **the works of the flesh are manifest**, which are *these*; Adultery, fornication, uncleanness, lasciviousness, Idolatry, witchcraft, hatred, variance, emulations, wrath, strife, seditions, heresies, Envyings, murders, drunkenness, revellings, and such like: of the which I tell you before, as I have also told *you* in time past, that they which do such things shall not inherit the kingdom of God."

> ### TRUE CHRISTIANS HAVE TWO NATURES
> In every true Christian, there are two natures--the old flesh and the indwelling Holy Spirit. The non-Christians have only one nature–their flesh. For the Christian, there is a battle between these two natures. If their flesh wins out, one or more of these seventeen works of the flesh, (mentioned in Galatians 5:19-21) will be manifested in their lives.

- **Ephesians 2:3**
"Among whom also we all had our conversation in times past in the **lusts of our flesh**, fulfilling the **desires of the flesh** and of the mind; and were by nature the children of wrath, even as others."

The former walking after the flesh should be history for the genuine Christians. They should not continue that wicked walk.

- **Philippians 3:3**
"For we are the circumcision, which worship God in the spirit, and rejoice in Christ Jesus, and **have no confidence in the flesh**."

Paul says he has no confidence in the flesh. That should be the attitude of all true Christians.

- **1 Peter 3:21**
"The like figure whereunto *even* baptism doth also now save us (**not the putting away of the filth of the flesh**, but the answer of a good conscience toward God,) by the resurrection of Jesus Christ:"

God speaks truly about "*the filth of the flesh.*"

- **2 Peter 2:18**
"For when they speak great swelling *words* of vanity, they allure through **the lusts of the flesh**, *through much* wantonness, those that were clean escaped from them who live in error."

False teachers allure their followers through "*the lusts of the flesh.*"

A Verse On The Lust Of The Eyes

The second thing that is in this wicked world is the lust of the eyes.

- **Matthew 5:28**
"But I say unto you, That **whosoever looketh on a woman to lust after her hath committed adultery with her already in his heart.**"

ADULTERY OF THE HEART

A man, using the eyes to look on a woman with "*lust after her*" is a commission of adultery in the heart.

Verses On Pride

The third thing in the world that should be shunned is "pride."

- **Proverbs 16:18**
"**Pride *goeth* before destruction**, and an haughty spirit before a fall."

- Mark 7:21-22

"For from within, out of the heart of men, proceed evil thoughts, adulteries, fornications, murders, thefts, covetousness, wickedness, deceit, lasciviousness, an evil eye, blasphemy, **pride**, foolishness:"

Pride comes right out of a person's heart.

- 1 Timothy 3:6

"Not a novice, lest being lifted up with pride he fall into the condemnation of the devil."

CHURCH OFFICERS SHOULD NOT BE PRIDEFUL

Paul is speaking about the qualifications of prospective deacons. They must not be novices. Otherwise, they might be *"lifted up with pride lest he fall into the condemnation of the devil."* None of these officers (or any of its officers) in a local church should be prideful.

1 John 2:17

"And the world passeth away, and the lust thereof: but he that doeth the will of God abideth for ever.

THEY WHO DO GOD'S WILL ABIDE FOREVER

This world, with all of its ungodly people, will one day pass away. All of its lust will pass away with it as well, *"but he that doeth the will of God abideth for ever."* John is speaking about the people who have truly received the Lord Jesus Christ as their Saviour. They are the ones who have received God's gift of eternal life. They will abide forever with their Saviour in Heaven.

1 John 2:18

"Little children, it is the last time: and as ye have heard that antichrist shall come, even now are there many antichrists; whereby we know that it is the last time."

John is writing to the *"little children"* who were probably just recently saved. As it was the *"last time"* in his day, just think how closer the Lord's coming is today.

CURRENT ANTICHRISTS DENY CHRIST'S DEITY

He tells them that the Antichrist will come one day. But even in John's day, there were many antichrists, proving that it was the *"last time."* An antichrist is one who opposes the Lord Jesus Christ in all His Perfect Deity and His Perfect Humanity as well as all of His miraculous works He did while on this earth.

ANTICHRISTS ARE IN ALL RELIGIOUS GROUPS

Those who fit this description of being antichrists are many these days. They would include all the apostate Protestants in all of their denominations. It would include the Roman Catholic Church. It would also include all of the world religions such as the Muslims, Buddhists, Shintoists, Taoists, Animists, and all of the others.

The lead Antichrist will not be revealed until the Tribulation when he will arise and deceive most of the people living on the earth.

CHRISTIANS WILL BE TAKEN IN THE RAPTURE

This Tribulation is Daniel's seventieth week (Daniel 9:24, etc.). It is called *"the time of Jacob's trouble"* (Jeremiah 30:7). It will begin right after the Rapture of genuine Christians who will meet the Lord Jesus Christ in the clouds of the air. Since we don't know when the Rapture will occur, we don't know when the Antichrist will appear; he might be living on earth today. Many, many names have been guessed through the years as to who the Antichrist is, but none so far have been correct.

Verses On The Last Time Or Last Days

- 2 Timothy 3:1

"This know also, that in the last days perilous times shall come." We are living today in very *"perilous times."*

- Hebrews 1:2

"Hath in these last days spoken unto us by *his* Son, whom he hath appointed heir of all things, by whom also he made the worlds;"

Prophets were used of the Lord to speak God's Words in the Old Testament. In the last days, God sent His only begotten Son from Heaven to die on the cross for sinners who might receive everlasting life by genuinely trusting in Him.

- **1 Peter 1:5**
"Who are kept by the power of God through faith unto salvation ready to be revealed in the last time."

> **ANIMALS WILL BE DELIVERED IN THE MILLENNIUM**
>
> Genuine Christians are kept by God's power. Their salvation will never be removed. In the last time also, salvation, in the sense of deliverance, will occur as in Romans 8:21.
>
> > *"Because the creature itself also shall be delivered from the bondage of corruption into the glorious liberty of the children of God."* (Romans 8:21)
>
> During the Millennium, wild beasts will live next to tame beasts without killing them. There will be many other deliverances as well in that *"last time."*

- **2 Peter 3:3**
"Knowing this first, that there shall come in the last days scoffers, walking after their own lusts,"

We have many scoffers, in these last days, who belittle the Lord Jesus Christ and the Bible and walk after the lusts which are clearly condemned in the Bible.

- **Jude 1:18**
"How that they told you there should be mockers in the last time, who should walk after their own ungodly lusts."

Mockers are added to the scoffers who can't stand God's truths. They continue to walk after ungodly lusts.

Verses On The Antichrist And Antichrists

- **1 John 2:22**
"Who is a liar but he that denieth that Jesus is the Christ? He is antichrist, that denieth the Father and the Son."

We have many today who deny that the Lord Jesus Christ is the Messiah sent from God and who deny God the Father and God the Son. God labels them *"antichrist."*

- **1 John 4:3**
"And every spirit that confesseth not that Jesus Christ is come in the flesh is not of God: and this is that *spirit* of antichrist, whereof ye have heard that it should come; and even now already is it in the world."

ANTICHRISTS DENY CHRIST'S INCARNATION

Another definition of being "antichrist" is to deny the Incarnation of the Lord Jesus Christ, that *"God was manifest in the flesh."*

- 2 John 1:7

"For many deceivers are entered into the world, who confess not that Jesus Christ is come in the flesh. This is a deceiver and an antichrist."

MANY PROTESTANT AND CATHOLIC ANTICHRISTS!

A deceiver and an antichrist denies the Lord Jesus Christ as God's own Son, sent from Heaven, Who came in the flesh. A deceiver and an antichrist are fitting names for all the religious apostates of the Protestants, the Catholics, and all other world religions.

1 John 2:19

"They went out from us, but they were not of us; for if they had been of us, they would no doubt have continued with us: but they went out, that they might be made manifest that they were not all of us."

ANTICHRISTS SHOULD LEAVE SOUND CHURCHES

John is speaking of these antichrist people who left fellowship with him because they did not believe in the Bible's teachings about the Lord Jesus Christ and other major doctrines of the Christian faith. Their leaving showed that they were not with John and the Bible's doctrines. Unbelievers should leave Bible-believing churches today as well. The problem, many times, is that these antichrist people stay in the churches and eventually cause these churches to depart from the truth!

- 1 Corinthians 11:19

"For there must be also heresies among you, that they which are approved may be made manifest among you."

Heresies in this sense mean the holding of certain beliefs, which in this case would be false beliefs. When people see the false teachings, those who love the truth are made manifest and speak against such heresies. They stand out clearly from the false teachers.

1 John 2:20

"**But ye have an unction from the Holy One, and ye know all things.**"

This unction is a reference to God the Holy Spirit who indwells all those who are true Christians as soon as they are saved. He gives them spiritual understanding and knowledge of God's Words and can lead them if they yield to His control and leading.

Verses On Knowing

- **1 Corinthians 2:11**

"For what man knoweth the things of a man, save the spirit of man which is in him? even so the things of God knoweth no man, but the Spirit of God."

The spirit is the part of human beings that can know and understand spiritual things. Likewise the things of God can be known only by the Spirit of God as He leads genuine Christians in their walk with the Lord.

- **1 Corinthians 2:14**

"But the natural man receiveth not the things of the Spirit of God: for they are foolishness unto him: neither can he know *them*, because they are spiritually discerned."

LOST PEOPLE CAN'T UNDERSTAND GOD'S WORDS

The natural or unsaved person doesn't receive God's things. They appear foolish unto them. These things can only be "*spiritually discerned*" or understood and known by true Christians who are indwelt by God the Holy Spirit.

1 John 2:21

"**I have not written unto you because ye know not the truth, but because ye know it, and that no lie is of the truth.**"

THE MEANING OF THE GREEK WORD, "ALETHEIA"

The Greek Word for "*truth*" is ALETHEIA. Some of the meanings of that Greek Word are:

> "*1) objectively; 1a) what is true in any matter under consideration; 1a1) truly, in truth, according to truth; 1a2) of a truth, in reality, in fact, certainly; 1b) what is true in things appertaining to God and the duties of man, moral and*

> *religious truth; 1b1) in the greatest latitude; 1b2) the true notions of God which are open to human reason without his supernatural intervention; 1c) the truth as taught in the Christian religion, respecting God and the execution of his purposes through Christ, and respecting the duties of man, opposing alike to the superstitions of the Gentiles and the inventions of the Jews, and the corrupt opinions and precepts of false teachers even among Christians; 2) subjectively; 2a) truth as a personal excellence; 2a1) that candour of mind which is free from affection, pretence, simulation, falsehood, deceit."*

John is writing to those true Christians who know the truth. They know that lies are not truth, even though many people believe the lies as truth. Lies are anything that is contrary to truth. In this sense, a so-called "*half truth*" is a "*whole lie*."

1 John 2:22

"Who is a liar but he that denieth that Jesus is the Christ? He is antichrist, that denieth the Father and the Son."

The greatest of all lies are the antichrists who deny that the Lord Jesus Christ is Christ, the anointed Messiah sent from God the Father. The antichrists deny both God the Father and God the Son. Ministers today (and there are hundreds and hundreds of them) who deny the Deity of the Lord Jesus Christ are liars and antichrists.

John 4:25-26
"The woman saith unto him, I know that Messias cometh, which is called Christ: when he is come, he will tell us all things. Jesus saith unto her, I that speak unto thee am *he*."
The woman at the well was told by the Lord Jesus Christ that He was the Messiah, sent from God.

1 John 2:23

"Whosoever denieth the Son, the same hath not the Father: (but) he that acknowledgeth the Son hath the Father also."

DENIAL OF THE SON IS A DENIAL OF THE FATHER

If anyone denies that the Lord Jesus Christ is the Son of God, equal in all attributes to God the Father, they also deny God the Father. <u>The last part of this verse is in italics, but it is in the manuscripts of our Textus Receptus and it's in the Scrivener text. I believe it is true, even though it is in italics in the King James Bible.</u>

Verses On God The Father

- John 1:14

"And the Word was made flesh, and dwelt among us, (and we beheld his glory, the glory as of the only begotten of the Father,) full of grace and truth."

<u>The Lord Jesus Christ partakes of all the glory of God the Father.</u>

- John 3:35

"The Father loveth the Son, and hath given all things into his hand."

GOD THE FATHER AND GOD THE SON ARE DISTINCT

<u>God the Father loves God the Son. They are two distinct Persons of the Godhead. There is a heretical teaching believed by some called the "Oneness Doctrine."</u> It wrongly teaches that the Lord Jesus Christ is the Father, the Son, and the Holy Spirit. <u>This is a blatant denial of the Trinity.</u> The Bible clearly teaches that there is one God in three Persons: God the Father, God the Son, and God the Holy Spirit.

- John 5:20-23

"For the Father loveth the Son, and sheweth him all things that himself doeth: and he will shew him greater works than these, that ye may marvel. For as the Father raiseth up the dead, and quickeneth *them*; even so the Son quickeneth whom he will. For the Father judgeth no man, but hath committed all judgment unto the Son: That all *men* should honour the Son, even as they honour the Father. He that honoureth not the Son honoureth not the Father which hath sent him."

> **CHRIST WAS GIVEN ALL JUDGMENT BY THE FATHER**
>
> As these verses indicate, God the Father loves God the Son. As God the Father can raise up the dead, so God the Son can do likewise to whomever He wishes. The Father has given all judgment unto His Son. He wants all people to honor God the Son as they honor God the Father. Any who do not honor God the Son do not honor God the Father Who sent Him into the world as John 3:16 clearly indicates.

- John 14:6

"Jesus saith unto him, I am the way, the truth, and the life: no man cometh unto the Father, but by me."

The only way to come to God the Father is by genuinely receiving God the Son as Saviour. The Lord Jesus Christ is the only Way to the Father.

- John 5:26

"For as the Father hath life in himself; so hath he given to the Son to have life in himself;"

God the Father has life in Himself and He has given to God the Son to have life in Himself also.

- John 8:16

"And yet if I judge, my judgment is true: for I am not alone, but I and the Father that sent me."

The judgment of God the Son is true. God the Father is always with Him in such judgments.

- John 10:30

"I and *my* Father are one."

> **THE TRINITY IS A TRI-UNITY—ONE IN THREE**
>
> There is a unity in the Trinity. It is a tri-unity. God the Son is unified (though not the same Person as) with God the Father. God the Holy Spirit is also united with God the Father and God the Son in the Godhead.

- John 10:38

"But if I do, though ye believe not me, believe the works: that ye may know, and believe, that the Father *is* in me, and I in him."

> **DISTINCT PERSONS IN THE TRIUNE GODHEAD**
>
> God the Father is in God the Son, and God the Son is in God the Father. There is a unity, yet a separation of the Persons of the Godhead.

- John 14:6

"Jesus saith unto him, I am the way, the truth, and the life: no man cometh unto the Father, but by me."

The only way any man, woman, or child can come to God the Father is through true faith in His Son, the Lord Jesus Christ.

- John 15:23

"He that hateth me hateth my Father also."

If a person hates God the Son, he also hates God the Father.

- John 16:15

"All things that the Father hath are mine: therefore said I, that he shall take of mine, and shall shew *it* unto you."

All that God the Father has is also possessed by God the Son.

- John 16:28

"I came forth from the Father, and am come into the world: again, I leave the world, and go to the Father."

THE SON CAME FROM THE FATHER AND RETURNED

The Lord Jesus Christ came from God the Father and returned to God the Father after His sacrificial death at Calvary and bodily resurrection.

1 John 2:24

"Let that therefore abide in you, which ye have heard from the beginning. If that which ye have heard from the beginning shall remain in you, ye also shall continue in the Son, and in the Father."

GOD'S TRUTH IS UNCHANGEABLE

John is talking to those genuine Christians who heard the teachings of the Lord Jesus Christ right from the beginning. If these teachings remain and abide in them, they will continue in both God the Son and God the Father. Many today are drifting from the truth. Truth doesn't change. What was true thousands of years ago is still true today. Truth continues, no matter what people might do to soften, change, or negate it.

1 John 2:25

"And this is the promise that he hath promised us, even eternal life."

God keeps His promise regarding eternal life. He keeps all of His promises. The word, "*promise*," is found one hundred and eleven times in our King James Bible. Though politicians and others do not always keep their promises, God always keeps those promises which He has made.

Verses On Promises

- **Joshua 23:5**

"And the LORD your God, he shall expel them from before you, and drive them from out of your sight; and ye shall possess their land, as the LORD your God hath promised unto you."

Joshua believed the promises of God about His driving out the Canaanites and possessing the land of Canaan. True Christians should believe His promises found in His Words, the Bible. He never fails.

- **Joshua 23:10**

"One man of you shall chase a thousand: for the LORD your God, he *it is* that fighteth for you, as he hath promised you."

God kept that miracle promise to Joshua as well.

- **1 Kings 5:12**

"And the LORD gave Solomon wisdom, as he promised him: and there was peace between Hiram and Solomon; and they two made a league together."

God promised Solomon wisdom, and He gave it to him.

- **Luke 24:49**

"And, behold, I send the promise of my Father upon you: but tarry ye in the city of Jerusalem, until ye be endued with power from on high."

THE ELECTION OF MATTHIAS WAS DISOBEDIENCE

This was God's promise of the Holy Spirit that the Lord Jesus Christ told to His apostles. They were to tarry in Jerusalem until the power of the Holy Spirit came unto them. Instead of waiting for God the Holy Spirit, Peter and the others had an election to replace Judas that was not authorized by God. At the proper time, the Lord Jesus Christ Himself selected Paul to replace Judas rather than Matthias.

- **Acts 1:4**

"And, being assembled together with *them*, commanded them that they should not depart from Jerusalem, but wait for the promise of the Father, which, *saith he*, ye have heard of me."

> **THE APOSTLES WERE TO WAIT FOR THE SPIRIT**
> This is the second time the Lord Jesus Christ told His apostles to *"wait"* rather than to hold an election. Again, they did not wait for the promise of the Father, but had an election led by the flesh rather than by God the Holy Spirit.

- Acts 2:33
"Therefore being by the right hand of God exalted, and having received of the Father the promise of the Holy Ghost, he hath shed forth this, which ye now see and hear."

> **THE HOLY SPIRIT'S COMING WAS PROMISED**
> God the Holy Spirit's coming to this earth was promised by God the Father and by God the Son. This was fulfilled on the Day of Pentecost as recorded in Acts 2.

- Acts 13:23
"Of this man's seed hath God according to *his* promise raised unto Israel a Saviour, Jesus:"

God promised David that a Saviour would one day come from his lineage. It was fulfilled in the birth of the Lord Jesus Christ.

- Romans 4:20
"He staggered not at the promise of God through unbelief; but was strong in faith, giving glory to God;"

> **ABRAHAM BELIEVED IN A SON THROUGH SARAH**
> Abraham was strong in believing God's promise that the Saviour would come from his heritage through Sarah. As Abraham, genuine Christians should never stagger at the promises of God in the Bible. They should be strong in faith.

- Titus 1:2
"In hope of eternal life, which God, that cannot lie, promised before the world began;"

Before the world was created, the Lord Jesus Christ existed; God the Father, Who can never lie, promised eternal life for those who genuinely receive the Lord Jesus Christ as Saviour.

- Hebrews 6:13
"For when God made promise to Abraham, because he could swear by no greater, he sware by himself,"

God made a promise to Abraham and fulfilled that promise faithfully.

- Hebrews 10:23
"Let us hold fast the profession of *our* faith without wavering; (for he *is* faithful that promised;)"

God is faithful in keeping all of his promises.
- **Hebrews 10:36**
"For ye have need of patience, that, after ye have done the will of God, ye might receive the promise."

CHRISTIANS SHOULD WAIT FOR GOD'S PROMISES
True Christians should do God's will and patiently wait for His promises connected with doing it.

- **Hebrews 11:11**
"Through faith also Sara herself received strength to conceive seed, and was delivered of a child when she was past age, because she judged him faithful who had promised."

SARAH BELIEVED GOD'S PROMISE OF A SON
Though the birth of Isaac seemed to be impossible because of Abraham's and Sarah's advanced ages, Sarah believed God would perform His promise. They were both too old. They couldn't have a child, but God said you're going to have a baby. Sarah believed God is Faithful Who promised.

- **James 1:12**
"Blessed *is* the man that endureth temptation: for when he is tried, he shall receive the crown of life, which the Lord hath promised to them that love him."

This crown of life has been promised to those who love the Lord Jesus Christ sincerely and endure temptation successfully.

- **2 Peter 3:9**
"The Lord is not slack concerning his promise, as some men count slackness; but is longsuffering to us-ward, not willing that any should perish, but that all should come to repentance."

The Lord is not slack or holding back in fulfilling any of His promises.

Verses On Eternal Life

- **John 3:15**
"That whosoever believeth in him should not perish, but have eternal life."

Genuine faith in the Lord Jesus Christ as Saviour is the only way a person can receive eternal life and not perish in Hell. All the new English and other language Bibles that are based on the false Gnostic Critical Greek Text omit "*should not perish*" from this verse. Gnosticism believes that everyone goes to Heaven; they don't believe there is a Hell. English versions that follow the false Greek text include the NIV, NASV, ESV, RSV and many, many others.

- **John 10:27-28**
  "My sheep hear my voice, and I know them, and they follow me: And I give unto them eternal life; and they shall never perish, neither shall any *man* pluck them out of my hand."

It is the Lord Jesus Christ, the Shepherd Who alone can give true believers eternal life which will never pass away or be taken from them.

- **Romans 6:23**
  "For the wages of sin *is* death; but the gift of God *is* eternal life through Jesus Christ our Lord."

Eternal life is God's gift to those genuine Christians. Being a gift, eternal life cannot be worked for or man-made.

- **1 John 5:11**
  "And this is the record, that God hath given to us eternal life, and this life is in his Son."

THE SOURCE OF ETERNAL LIFE IS THE SON OF GOD

Eternal life has its Source only in the Son of God. If people don't have Him as their Saviour, they don't have eternal life.

- **1 John 5:13**
  "These things have I written unto you that believe on the name of the Son of God; that ye may know that ye have eternal life, and that ye may believe on the name of the Son of God."

Those who genuinely trust in the Lord Jesus Christ have assurance that they possess eternal life.

- **1 John 5:20**
  "And we know that the Son of God is come, and hath given us an understanding, that we may know him that is true, and we are in him that is true, *even* in his Son Jesus Christ. This is the true God, and eternal life."

CHRIST IS CALLED "THE TRUE GOD"

In this verse, the Lord Jesus Christ is called "*the true God*" and is also given the title of "Eternal Life." This is a clear verse on the Deity of the Saviour.

1 John 2:26

"These things have I written unto you concerning them that seduce you."

THE MEANING OF THE GREEK WORD, "PLANAO"

This seduction is a terrible thing. The Greek Word for "seduce" is PLANAO. Some of the meanings of this Greek Word are:

> "1) to cause to stray, to lead astray, lead aside from the right way; 1a) to go astray, wander, roam about; 2) metaph.; 2a) to lead away from the truth, to lead into error, to deceive; 2b) to be led into error; 2c) to be led aside from the path of virtue, to go astray, sin; 2d) to sever or fall away from the truth; 2d1) of heretics; 2e) to be led away into error and sin."

John is warning people. We have people that are seducing multitudes today, including some genuine Christians. They are leading them astray into false beliefs and practices, whether great or small.

SOME OF THE FALSE DOCTRINAL SEDUCERS

Here are a few such seducers: Mary Baker Eddy, Harry Emerson Fosdick, E. Stanley Jones, Bill Hybels, Robert Schuler, Rick Warren, Joel Osteen, Benny Hinn, Jim Bakker, Jimmy Swaggart, Billy Graham, John MacArthur, Peter Ruckman, Gail Riplinger, and many, many others have led or are leading many people astray from sound Bible doctrine and teaching them false doctrines–either big or small. In fact, all of the leaders of the world religions teach false doctrines–either big or small.

- Ezekiel 13:10

"Because, even because they have seduced my people, saying, Peace; and *there was* no peace; and one built up a wall, and, lo, others daubed it with untempered *morter*:"

Seducing by false prophets was practiced in the Old Testament as well as the New Testament, thus leading many people astray into errors and sins.

- 2 Timothy 3:13

"But evil men and seducers shall wax worse and worse, deceiving, and being deceived."

EVIL MEN WILL BECOME WORSE AND WORSE
Paul told Pastor Timothy that seducers would become worse and worse in the coming days. This prophecy has been greatly fulfilled in our day. In Timothy's day, evil men and seducers existed. It's getting worse day after day and year after year. Many, many politicians through the years and today as well have been and are big time and serious seducers that have led people astray with false ideas. The radio, TV, and the Internet are filled with seducers and deceivers.

- Revelation 2:20

"Notwithstanding I have a few things against thee, because thou sufferest that woman Jezebel, which calleth herself a prophetess, to teach and to seduce my servants to commit fornication, and to eat things sacrificed unto idols."

Here's a woman preacher, Jezebel, who seduced God's servants to commit fornication and sacrifice to idols.

1 John 2:27

"But the anointing which ye have received of him abideth in you, and ye need not that any man teach you: but as the same anointing teacheth you of all things, and is truth, and is no lie, and even as it hath taught you, ye shall abide in him."

THE HOLY SPIRIT CAN GUIDE CHRISTIANS
John is speaking again about God the Holy Spirit Who indwells every genuine Christian. One of His duties is to teach and make clear the Words of the Bible. Born-again Christians should know and follow their Bibles, asking for guidance from the Holy Spirit to understand and apply the Words.

1 John 2:28

"And now, little children, abide in him; that, when he shall appear, we may have confidence, and not be ashamed before him at his coming."

John is addressing the newly-saved Christians. They should stick closely to and abide with the Lord Jesus Christ so that when He would appear at His return, they would have confidence and not be ashamed before Him when He returns.

The next event prophetically in Scripture, is the coming of the Lord Jesus Christ in the Rapture to take up to Heaven all those who are genuine Christians. No one knows the day or hour when this will take place.

There are various verses about the coming again of the Lord Jesus Christ. There are two phases of that coming. The first phase of His coming again is the Rapture.

ABIDING IN CHRIST, NOT BE ASHAMED OF HIM

The Lord Jesus Christ will appear in the clouds to take away all genuine Christians who have died and who are alive at the time. Those in the grave will receive incorruptible bodies. Those who are alive will receive immortal bodies.

THE THOUSAND-YEAR REIGN OF CHRIST

The second phase of the return of the Lord Jesus Christ will be after the seven years of Tribulation. In that phase, He will come to earth and begin His reign for one thousand years in the Millennium.

Verses On The Second Coming Of Christ

- **Colossians 3:4**

"When Christ, *who is* our life, shall appear, then shall ye also appear with him in glory."

This refers to His coming in the Rapture. All true Christians will appear with Him in glory.

- **1 Timothy 6:14**

"That thou keep *this* commandment without spot, unrebukeable, until the appearing of our Lord Jesus Christ:"

This also refers to the Rapture. True Christians are to keep and follow the Words of God faithfully until the Rapture occurs.

- **2 Timothy 4:1**

"I charge *thee* therefore before God, and the Lord Jesus Christ, who shall judge the quick and the dead at his appearing and his kingdom;"

The "appearing" is the Rapture; His "kingdom" is His Millennial reign. The Lord Jesus Christ will be the judge of both the living and the dead.

- **2 Timothy 4:8**

"Henceforth there is laid up for me a crown of righteousness, which the Lord, the righteous judge, shall give me at that day:

and not to me only, but unto all them also that love his appearing."

> **CHRISTIANS SHOULD LOVE CHRIST'S APPEARING**
>
> True Christians should love the appearing of the Lord Jesus Christ. A crown of righteousness will be granted to those who love that appearing.

- **Titus 2:13**
"Looking for that blessed hope, and the glorious appearing of the great God and our Saviour Jesus Christ;"

> **TWO PHASES OF CHRIST'S SECOND COMING**
>
> Here are both phases of Christ's second coming in one verse. The *"blessed hope"* is the Rapture. The *"glorious appearing"* is His Millennial reign. Both phrases should be looked for. <u>Notice the Deity of the Lord Jesus Christ. He is called *"the great God"* as well as the *"Saviour."*</u>

- **1 Peter 1:7**
"That the trial of your faith, being much more precious than of gold that perisheth, though it be tried with fire, might be found unto praise and honour and glory at the appearing of Jesus Christ:"

<u>This refers to the Rapture of the Saviour to transform the bodies of all the genuine Christians and take them to Heaven.</u>

- **1 Peter 5:2-4**
"Feed the flock of God which is among you, taking the oversight *thereof*, not by constraint, but willingly; not for filthy lucre, but of a ready mind; Neither as being lords over *God's* heritage, but being ensamples to the flock. And when the chief Shepherd shall appear, ye shall receive a crown of glory that fadeth not away."

<u>Faithful pastors who perform as mentioned in this verse will receive a crown of glory at the appearing of the Lord Jesus Christ.</u>

- **1 John 3:2**
"Beloved, now are we the sons of God, and it doth not yet appear what we shall be: but we know that, when he shall appear, we shall be like him; for we shall see him as he is."

> **AT THE RAPTURE, CHRISTIANS GET NEW BODIES**
>
> <u>At the Rapture, every genuine Christian will receive a glorified body like the glorified body of the Lord Jesus Christ. Those Christians who are still living and are mortal shall become immortal. Those Christians who have died</u>

and are corruptible shall become incorruptible. This is the teaching of both 1 Thessalonians 4:13-18 and 1 Corinthians 15:51-54.

Verses On Confidence

- **Proverbs 14:26**

"In the fear of the LORD is strong confidence: and his children shall have a place of refuge."

In the LORD, true Christians can place their total confidence. He will never let them down. They should be bold and courageous as they, with confidence, take their stand for their Saviour.

THE MEANING OF THE GREEK WORD, "PARRESIA"

The Greek Word for "*confidence*" is PARRESIA. Some of the meanings of this Greek Word are:

"*1) freedom in speaking, unreservedness in speech; 1a) openly, frankly, i.e without concealment; 1b) without ambiguity or circumlocution; 1c) without the use of figures and comparisons; 2) free and fearless confidence, cheerful courage, boldness, assurance; 3) the deportment by which one becomes conspicuous or secures publicity.*"

- **Philippians 3:3**

"For we are the circumcision, which worship God in the spirit, and rejoice in Christ Jesus, and have no confidence in the flesh."

The flesh of both the saved and the lost will let them down. There should be no confidence in it.

- **Hebrews 10:35**

"Cast not away therefore your confidence, which hath great recompence of reward."

Genuine Christians should never cast away their confidence that they have in the Lord Jesus Christ. He is trustworthy and dependable at all times and in every circumstance.

- **1 John 3:21**

"Beloved, if our heart condemn us not, *then* have we confidence toward God."

Confidence comes when the heart does not condemn us.

Verses On Ashamed

True Christians should not be ashamed before the Lord Jesus Christ at His coming.

- **Mark 8:38**
"Whosoever therefore shall be ashamed of me and of my words in this adulterous and sinful generation; of him also shall the Son of man be ashamed, when he cometh in the glory of his Father with the holy angels."

NO ONE SHOULD BE ASHAMED OF GOD'S WORDS
Genuine Christians should never be ashamed of His Words. This is why we stand so strongly for the preserved Hebrew, Aramaic, and Greek Words on which our King James Bible is based and against the false Words on which the modern Bibles are based. If we are ashamed of His Words, He will be ashamed of us.

- **Romans 1:16**
"For I am not ashamed of the gospel of Christ: for it is the power of God unto salvation to every one that believeth; to the Jew first, and also to the Greek."

Paul wasn't ashamed of the gospel of the Lord Jesus Christ, nor should any true Christian be ashamed. Even though he was in prison, Paul kept preaching the gospel. It's God's power unto salvation for all those who truly believe it.

- **Romans 9:33b**
". . . and whosoever believeth on him shall not be ashamed."

Genuine Christians should never be ashamed of the Lord Jesus Christ their Saviour, no matter what.

- **Philippians 1:20**
"According to my earnest expectation and *my* hope, that in nothing I shall be ashamed, but *that* with all boldness, as always, *so* now also Christ shall be magnified in my body, whether *it be* by life, or by death."

PAUL WANTED CHRIST TO BE MAGNIFIED
Even though in the Roman prison, Paul was not ashamed of His Saviour. He wanted Christ to be magnified in his body whether by life or by death.

- **2 Timothy 1:8**
"Be not thou therefore ashamed of the testimony of our Lord, nor of me his prisoner: but be thou partaker of the afflictions of the gospel according to the power of God;"

TIMOTHY WAS NOT TO BE ASHAMED OF CHRIST
Paul told Pastor Timothy, in this last letter he would write, that he was never to be ashamed of the testimony of

the Lord Jesus Christ or of Paul His prisoner. He warned Timothy that, in time, he, too, as Paul, would be a partaker of the afflictions of the gospel.

- 2 Timothy 1:12

"For the which cause I also suffer these things: nevertheless I am not ashamed: for I know whom I have believed, and am persuaded that he is able to keep that which I have committed unto him against that day."

PAUL WAS NOT ASHAMED OF CHRIST

Though Paul suffered many things because of his faith, he was not ashamed of the Lord Jesus Christ in Whom he had believed. He was sure that the Lord Jesus Christ would keep him, Paul, for all eternity. 2 Corinthians 11:23-28 lists 26 kinds of suffering that Paul endured.

- 2 Timothy 1:16

"The Lord give mercy unto the house of Onesiphorus; for he oft refreshed me, and was not ashamed of my chain:"
Onesiphorus was a godly Christian man who was not ashamed of Paul being in the Roman prison, but visited him and refreshed him many times. May many more Christians be as Onesiphorus.

- 2 Timothy 2:15

"Study to shew thyself approved unto God, a workman that needeth not to be ashamed, rightly dividing the word of truth."

CHRISTIANS MUST STUDY GOD'S WORDS

Every genuine Christian should study the Words of God to be **approved by God** and not be ashamed because they are rightly dividing those Words.

- Hebrews 2:11b

". . . for which cause he is not ashamed to call them brethren,"
The Lord Jesus Christ is not ashamed to call true Christians "brethren." They are all part of His Heavenly family.

- 1 Peter 4:16

"Yet if *any man suffer* as a Christian, let him not be ashamed; but let him glorify God on this behalf."

NOT ASHAMED EVEN IN SUFFERING FOR CHRIST

When true Christians suffer for their testimony, they should not be ashamed, but should glorify God.

1 John 2:29

"If ye know that he is righteous, ye know that every one that doeth righteousness is born of him."

There are some people that don't do righteousness. One of two things might be true of them.

(1) They may be lost, Hell-bound sinners, not doing righteousness but doing iniquity.

(2) They be genuine Christians who are walking according to the flesh rather than according to the Spirit. Doing righteousness is an indication that people are born-again and saved.

1 John
Chapter Three

1 John 3:1

"Behold, what manner of love the Father hath bestowed upon us, that we should be called the sons of God: therefore the world knoweth us not, because it knew him not."

Just think of the manner of love that God the Father had for wicked people like we are, that He would send His Son to die for their sins and give eternal life to those who truly trust in Him.

- **John 3:16**

"For God so loved the world, that he gave his only begotten Son, that whosoever believeth in him should not perish, but have everlasting life."

GOD'S LOVE SENT HIS SON TO DIE FOR US

It was God's great love that caused Him to send His Son so that those who genuinely believe in Him wouldn't perish, but have everlasting life and become the children of God.

Verses On Children Of God

- **John 1:12**

"But as many as received him, to them gave he power to become the **sons of God**, *even* to them that believe on his name:"

"Sons of God" are made only by receiving and truly believing in the Lord Jesus Christ.

- **Galatians 3:26**

"For ye are all the **children of God** by faith in Christ Jesus."

The only way to become *"children of God"* is when people have genuine faith in the Lord Jesus Christ as their Saviour.

1 John 3:2

"Beloved, now are we the sons of God, and it doth not yet appear what we shall be: but we know that, when he shall appear, we shall be like him; for we shall see him as he is."

Right now, those who are genuine Christians are called the "sons of God." When the Lord Jesus Christ will appear in the Rapture, the "sons of God" shall receive glorified bodies like His glorified body.

The Greek Word used here for "*like*" is HOMOIOS. Some of the meanings of this Greek Word are:

"1) like, similar, resembling; 1a) like: i.e. resembling; 1b) like: i.e. corresponding to a thing."

TRUE CHRISTIANS WILL BE LIKE CHRIST

These Christians will be "*like*" Him, but not the same as He is. That Greek Word would be HOMOS which is different from HOMOIOS. This limits the title of "*sons*" or "*children*" of God. At the Rapture, these "children" shall see the Lord Jesus Christ as He is.

Verses On Christ's Appearing Again

- Colossians 3:4

"**When Christ, *who is* our life, shall appear**, then shall ye also appear with him in glory."

TWO PHASES OF CHRIST'S SECOND COMING

The Lord Jesus Christ will appear again at his return both in the air and to the earth in the two phases of His coming.

- John 14:3

"And if I go and prepare a place for you, **I will come again**, and receive you unto myself; that where I am, *there* ye may be also."

This is a promise that the Lord Jesus Christ will fulfill.

- Hebrews 9:28

"So Christ was once offered to bear the sins of many; and unto them that look for him **shall he appear the second time** without sin unto salvation."

In His future appearing, it will not have anything to do with the sin

question. He paid for sins at his first coming.
- **1 Peter 5:4**
"And when the chief Shepherd shall appear, ye shall receive a crown of glory that fadeth not away."

One day the Lord Jesus Christ, the "*Chief Shepherd*," will appear in, what is called, His second coming.
- **1 John 2:28**
"And now, little children, abide in him; that, **when he shall appear**, we may have confidence, and not be ashamed before him at his coming."

> **NOT ASHAMED BEFORE HIM AT HIS COMING**
> True Christians should live for their Saviour so that when He shall appear, they will not be ashamed before Him when He comes.

Verses On What Happens At Christ's Coming
- **1 Corinthians 15:51-52**
"Behold, I shew you a mystery; We shall not all sleep, but **we shall all be changed**, In a moment, in the twinkling of an eye, at the last trump: for the trumpet shall sound, and **the dead shall be raised incorruptible, and we shall be changed**."

> **CORRUPTIBLE TO INCORRUPTIBLE BODIES**
> If the Lord Jesus Christ would come today, the genuine Christians who have died would have their corruptible bodies instantly changed to incorruptible bodies.

- **Philippians 3:20-21**
"For our conversation is in heaven; from whence also we look for the Saviour, the Lord Jesus Christ: Who shall change our vile body, that it may be fashioned like unto his glorious body, according to the working whereby he is able even to subdue all things unto himself."

True Christians who are living when the Lord Jesus Christ returns will have their bodies of humiliation made like unto His glorious body.
- **1 Thessalonians 4:16-17**
"For the Lord himself shall descend from heaven with a shout, with the voice of the archangel, and with the trump of God: and **the dead in Christ shall rise first: Then we which are alive *and* remain shall be caught up together with them in the clouds**, to meet the Lord in the air: and so shall we ever be with the Lord."

> **THE DEAD IN CHRIST RISE FIRST**
> At His second coming, those genuine Christian believers who have died, will be raised first to meet the Lord Jesus Christ in the air. Then, those Christians who are alive and remain shall be caught up together with them to meet the Lord in the clouds. They will all be with the Lord forever.

1 John 3:3

"And every man that hath this hope in him purifieth himself, even as he is pure."

As I have said before, our King James Bible often uses the expression, "*every man*," to refer to every person or every "huMAN." This is the reference here.

> **"PAS" REFERS TO EVERY TRUE CHRISTIAN**
> The Greek Word used is PAS (meaning "*all.*") Every true Christian has this hope of being made like the Lord Jesus Christ's glorious body. Because of that, they want to make themselves pure as He is pure.

Verses On Hope
- 1 Corinthians 15:19
"If in this life only we have **hope in Christ**, we are of all men most miserable."

Paul looked for hope in his Saviour in Heaven. Hope did not stop with this life which, for Paul, was miserable.
- 1 Timothy 1:1
"Paul, an apostle of Jesus Christ by the commandment of God our Saviour, and **Lord Jesus Christ, *which is* our hope**;"

He is the Hope of genuine Christians.

> **HOPE IS FUTURE YET ASSURED**
> The Greek Word for "*hope*" is ELPIS. This is something in the future, yet is certain to come to pass.

- Titus 2:13
"**Looking for that blessed hope**, and the glorious appearing of the great God and our Saviour Jesus Christ;"

That blessed hope is the Rapture, when the Lord Jesus Christ will transform the bodies of all true Christians, whether living or dead. The glorious appearing refers to the second phase of the coming of the Lord and Saviour, Jesus Christ, to begin his thousand-year reign on this earth in the Millennium.

Verses On Purity

- **Matthew 5:8**

"**Blessed *are* the pure in heart**: for they shall see God."

God wants His genuine Christians to be pure, not only in their bodies, but also in their hearts.

- **2 Corinthians 6:4-6**

"But in all *things* approving ourselves as the ministers of God, in much patience, in afflictions, in necessities, in distresses, In stripes, in imprisonments, in tumults, in labours, in watchings, in fastings; **By pureness**, by knowledge, by longsuffering, by kindness, by the Holy Ghost, by love unfeigned,"

One of the ways that Paul, the apostle, kept himself approved by God was by "pureness." That included purity of heart and purity of life.

- **1 Timothy 3:9**

"Holding the mystery of the faith **in a pure conscience**."

The conscience should also be pure, not defiled in any way.

- **1 Timothy 5:2**

"The elder women as mothers; the younger **as sisters, with all purity**."

When men are dealing with younger women, they should treat them as sisters, with all purity.

- **1 Timothy 5:22**

"Lay hands suddenly on no man, neither be partaker of other men's sins: **keep thyself pure**."

Paul told Pastor Timothy to keep himself pure. So should all pastors and fellow Christians today.

- **2 Timothy 1:3**

"I thank God, whom **I serve** from *my* forefathers **with pure conscience**, that without ceasing I have remembrance of thee in my prayers night and day;"

When the Lord Jesus Christ saved his soul, Paul served the Lord with a pure conscience.

- **2 Timothy 2:22**

"Flee also youthful lusts: but follow righteousness, faith, charity, peace, with **them that call on the Lord out of a pure heart**."

Paul told Pastor Timothy that he was to pray from a pure heart to the Lord. All genuine Christians should do this as well.

- **Titus 1:15**
"**Unto the pure all things *are* pure**: but unto them that are defiled and unbelieving *is* **nothing pure**; but even their mind and conscience is defiled."
There's no purity in defiled and unbelieving minds and consciences.
- **Titus 2:14**
"Who gave himself for us, that he might redeem us from all iniquity, and **purify unto himself a peculiar people**, zealous of good works."

CHRIST DIED FOR THE SINS OF THE WORLD
The Lord Jesus Christ died for the sins of the world to redeem those who truly trust in Him and to purify to Himself a special people.

- **James 3:17**
"But the **wisdom that is from above is first pure**, then peaceable, gentle, *and* easy to be intreated, full of mercy and good fruits, without partiality, and without hypocrisy."
God's wisdom, found in the Words of the Bible, is pure and without any hypocrisy.
- **1 Peter 1:22**
"Seeing **ye have purified your souls** in obeying the truth through the Spirit unto unfeigned love of the brethren, *see that ye* love one another **with a pure heart** fervently:"
True Christians have purified souls. They should love their fellow Christians with pure hearts.
- **2 Peter 3:1**
"This second epistle, beloved, I now write unto you; in *both* which **I stir up your pure minds** by way of remembrance:"
Peter wanted to stir up the pure minds of the genuine Christians he was addressing.

1 John 3:4

"Whosoever committeth sin transgresseth also the law: for sin is the transgression of the law."

Continuous committing of sin is a transgression of the Law of Moses, or any other law that man might establish. Only by being controlled by the indwelling Holy Spirit can the true Christian stay away from transgressing God's laws or man's laws.

1 John 3:5

"**And ye know that he was manifested to take away our sins; and in him is no sin.**"

The Lord Jesus Christ came into this world for the purpose of taking away the sins of the world so that those who truly trust Him might receive everlasting life. I believe "*our*" refers to the sins of the whole world. The Lord Jesus Christ is sinlessly perfect. He is Perfect God and Perfect Man.

Verses On Christ's Dying For Sins

- John 1:29b

"... Behold **the Lamb of God**, which **taketh away the sin of the world**."

THE MEANING OF THE GREEK WORD, "AIRO"

The Greek Word for "*take away*" is AIRO. Some of the meanings of this Greek Word are:

1) to raise up, elevate, lift up; 1a) to raise from the ground, take up: stones; 1b) to raise upwards, elevate, lift up: the hand; 1c) to draw up: a fish; 2) to take upon one's self and carry what has been raised up, to bear; 3) to bear away what has been raised, carry off; 3a) to move from its place; 3b) to take off or away what is attached to anything; 3c) to remove; 3d) to carry off, carry away with one; 3e) to appropriate what is taken; 3f) to take away from another what is his or what is committed to him, to take by force; 3g) to take and apply to any use; 3h) to take from among the living, either by a natural death, or by violence; 3i) cause to cease."

On the cross, the Lord Jesus Christ took upon Himself the sins of the world so that those who genuinely trust Him might have forgiveness and eternal life.

- **Romans 5:6**

"For when we were yet without strength, in due time **Christ died for the ungodly**."

> **CHRIST DIED FOR ALL UNGODLY, NOT JUST ELECT**
> He died for all the "ungodly," not just for some small "elect" group as the hyper-Calvinists heretically teach.

- **Romans 5:8**

"But God commendeth his love toward us, in that, <u>**while we were yet sinners, Christ died for us**</u>."

The Lord Jesus Christ died for ALL of the "*sinners*" and for all the "*us*" of the world, not just for a tiny "elect" group.

- **1 Corinthians 15:3**

"For I delivered unto you first of all that which I also received, how that **Christ died for our sins** according to the scriptures;"

> **CHRIST DIED FOR THE SINS OF THE WHOLE WORLD**
> The Lord Jesus Christ died for "*our*" sins. Again, the "*our*" includes the sins of the entire world.

- **2 Corinthians 5:14**

"For the love of Christ constraineth us; because we thus judge, that if <u>**one died for all**</u>, then were all dead:"

The Saviour died for ALL the people in the world.

- **Galatians 1:4**

"<u>**Who gave himself for our sins**</u>, that he might deliver us from this present evil world, according to the will of God and our Father:"

> **"OUR SINS" MEANS THE WHOLE WORLD'S SINS**
> The Lord Jesus Christ gave Himself on the cross for "*our*" sins--the sins of the whole world.

- **Galatians 2:20**

"I am crucified with Christ: nevertheless I live; yet not I, but Christ liveth in me: and the life which I now live in the flesh I live by the faith of **the Son of God**, who loved me, and <u>**gave himself for me**</u>."

> **CHRIST, THE SUBSTITUTE FOR EVERYONE**
> Christ gave Himself not only for Paul, but as a substitute for every person in the world. He came to die for our sins. That was the purpose of His coming.

- **1 Timothy 2:6**

"<u>**Who gave himself a ransom for all**</u>, to be testified in due time."

This refers to the Lord Jesus Christ. The ransom that He paid on the cross was for "*all*" the world.
- **1 Peter 2:24**
"**Who his own self bare our sins** in his own body on the tree, that we, being dead to sins, should live unto righteousness: **by whose stripes ye were healed**."

In His own self, the Lord Jesus Christ bare "*our*" sins–including those of the entire world.

Verses On The Sinlessness Of Christ

The last part of 1 John 3:5 states that "*in him, is no sin.*"
- **John 8:46**
"**Which of you convinceth me of sin**? And if I say the truth, why do ye not believe me?"

No one, when the Lord Jesus Christ was on earth, and no one today, after His ascension to Heaven, can point to any sin in the Lord Jesus Christ. God the Son and the Son of God was and is impeccable and sinless.
- **2 Corinthians 5:21**
"For he hath made him *to be* sin for us, **who knew no sin**; that we might be made the righteousness of God in him."

The Lord Jesus Christ knew no sin at all, but was perfectly righteous. He was made a sin offering for the sins of the entire world.
- **1 Peter 2:22**
"**Who did no sin**, neither was guile found in his mouth:"

THE SAVIOUR WAS AND IS PERFECT AND SINLESS

The Saviour was absolutely perfect, without sin of any kind until He took upon Himself the sins of the whole World.

1 John 3:6

"**Whosoever abideth in him sinneth not: whosoever sinneth hath not seen him, neither known him.**"

GREEK PRESENT TENSE IS CONTINUOUS ACTION

Both the words, "*abideth*" and "*sinneth*" (both places in this verse) are in the Greek present tense. That tense indicates a continuous action.

ABIDING IN CHRIST FORSAKES SINS

What John is saying is that if genuine Christians are continuously abiding in the Lord Jesus Christ, they will not continue to sin. If His people carry on in continual sinfulness, it is a sign that they have never been born-again by God the Holy Spirit.

The verse does not deny the presence of the sinful flesh in every true Christian, nor does it teach sinless perfection on their part. This verse simply talks about the persistence of sinfulness on the part of people who make superficial professions of faith in the Saviour and yet continue in their sinful lifestyle.

SIN NEEDS TO BE CONFESSED AND FORSAKEN

It is true that even genuine Christians sin when they walk in the flesh rather than in dependence upon the Holy Spirit. This is where John 1:9 must be used as soon as sin appears in their lives to bring the needed cleansing and restoration of fellowship with the Lord.

1 John 3:7

"Little children, let no man deceive you: he that doeth righteousness is righteous, even as he is righteous."

STOP BEING DECEIVED

In the clause, "*let no man deceive you,*" the word, "*deceive*" is in the Greek present tense. This is a negative prohibition. If it were the Greek aorist tense, it would mean not even begin an action. The Greek present tense means stop an action already in progress. Apparently, these newly-saved Christians were being deceived. John told them to "*stop letting anyone deceive you.*" People who continue to do (Greek present tense) righteousness are righteous just as the Lord Jesus Christ is righteous.

THE MEANING OF THE GREEK WORD, "PLANO"

The Greek Word for "*deceive*" is PLANAO. Some of the meanings of this Greek Word (which we have seen before in 1 John 1:8 and 2:26) are:

> "*1) to cause to stray, to lead astray, lead aside from the right way; 1a) to go astray, wander, roam about; 2) metaph.; 2a) to lead away from the truth, to lead into error, to deceive; 2b) to be led into error; 2c) to be led aside from the path of*

> *virtue, to go astray, sin; 2d) to sever or fall away from the truth; 2d1) of heretics; 2e) to be led away into error and sin"*

God does not want His genuine Christians to be deceived by anyone or anybody. God does not want us to be deceived at all! Often, deception is difficult to detect until deception has affected a person's behavior.

Verses On Deception

- **Matthew 24:4-5**

"And Jesus answered and said unto them, Take heed that no man deceive you. For many shall come in my name, **saying, I am Christ; and shall deceive many**."

The Lord Jesus Christ was well aware of deceivers. He warned that many would come in His Name pretending to be Christ, the Anointed Messiah, and would deceive many people.

- **Ephesians 4:14**

"That we *henceforth* be no more children, tossed to and fro, and carried about with every wind of doctrine, **by the sleight of men**, *and* cunning craftiness, **whereby they lie in wait to deceive**;"

Paul warned the true Christians at Ephesus not to be like easily-swayed children being deceived by the false doctrines of men.

- **Ephesians 5:6**

"**Let no man deceive you with vain words**: for because of these things cometh the wrath of God upon the children of disobedience."

Another method that deceives even genuine Christians is the use of vain or empty words. Paul cautioned against being taken in by such words.

- **Revelation 20:3**

"And cast him into the bottomless pit, and shut him up, and set a seal upon him, **that he should deceive the nations no more**, till the thousand years should be fulfilled: and after that he must be loosed a little season."

> **SATAN THE MASTER DECEIVER**
>
> Satan is the master deceiver. God will shut him up during the Millennium when the Lord Jesus Christ is reigning upon this earth to prevent any further deception during those thousand years.

- Revelation 20:8

"And shall go out to **deceive the nations** which are in the four quarters of the earth, Gog and Magog, to gather them together to battle: the number of whom *is* as the sand of the sea."

SATAN LOOSED FOR WAR AFTER THE MILLENNIUM

After the Millennium is over, Satan will be loosed from his captivity and will go out to deceive all the nations on the earth.

1 John 3:8

"He that committeth sin is of the devil; for the devil sinneth from the beginning. For this purpose the Son of God was manifested, that he might destroy the works of the devil."

CONTINUING IN SIN IS THE DEVIL'S DESIRE

Once again, the word for "*committeth*" is in Greek present tense. As mentioned before, this sets forth an action that is continuous. What John is saying is that persons who continue in unending sin are of the Devil. They are children of the Devil and have never been born-again into God's family by genuine faith in the Lord Jesus Christ. The Lord Jesus Christ came to destroy the works of the Devil. The Saviour gives true Christians the indwelling Holy Spirit to restrain them from a continuous life of sinfulness. When they occasionally sin, they are to apply 1 John 1:9.

- 1 John 1:9

"If we confess our sins, he is faithful and just to forgive us *our* sins, and to cleanse us from all unrighteousness."

THE MEANING OF "CONFESS" IS TO "AGREE"

When genuine Christians "*confess*" (HOMOLOGEO) (agree with God about) their sins, God is faithful in forgiving them. He is just in forgiving them because His Son paid for every sin that they might commit. He will cleanse them from all unrighteousness. Only by means of the sacrifice of the Lord Jesus Christ at Calvary was this righteousness made available at all times.

1 John 3:9

"**Whosoever is born of God doth not commit sin; for his seed remaineth in him: and he cannot sin, because he is born of God.**"

We must understand the tenses here. If we don't, we're going to be in serious trouble. "*Whosoever is born of God*"—referring to people who are born-again and saved by genuine faith in the Lord Jesus Christ, "*Doth not commit sin.*"

MEANING OF THE PRESENT TENSE OF "COMMIT'

The word for "*commit*" is in the Greek present tense. It doesn't mean that these people are sinlessly perfect. But it does mean that they do not continue always, always, always, sinning and sinning and sinning.

GOD'S SEED IS THE HOLY SPIRIT

"*For His seed,*" that is, God's seed, the Holy Spirit of God "*remaineth in him.*" He cannot (Greek present tense again) continue, and continue and continue in sin "*because he is born of God.*" God says, from this verse, that someone who continues and continues in sin, that's all they do, is lost and bound for Hell.

Verses On Being Born-Again

- John 1:13

"**Which were born**, not of blood, nor of the will of the flesh, nor of the will of man, but **of God**."

People are born of God by genuine trust in the Lord Jesus Christ.

- John 3:3

"Jesus answered and said unto him, Verily, verily, I say unto thee, **Except a man be born again**, he cannot see the kingdom of God."

New birth is necessary for the kingdom of God.

- John 3:7-8

"**Marvel not that I said unto thee, Ye must be born again**. The wind bloweth where it listeth, and thou hearest the sound thereof, but canst not tell whence it cometh, and whither it goeth: so is every one that is **born of the Spirit**."

Nicodemus was a ruler of the Jews and a Pharisee, but he needed to be born-again. He needed to be "*born of the Spirit.*"

- 1 Peter 1:23

"**Being born again**, not of corruptible seed, but of incorruptible, by the word of God, which liveth and abideth for ever."

The new birth by God the Holy Spirit gives people a new nature and a new spiritual life.

- 1 John 4:7

"Beloved, let us love one another: for love is of God; and every one that loveth is **born of God**, and knoweth God."

The new birth enables a person to know God.

- 1 John 5:1

"Whosoever believeth that Jesus is the Christ is **born of God**: and every one that loveth him that begat loveth him also that is begotten of him."

Genuinely trusting the Lord Jesus Christ as their Saviour makes people who are born of God.

- 1 John 5:4

"For whatsoever is **born of God** overcometh the world: and this is the victory that overcometh the world, *even* our faith."

INDWELLING OF THE HOLY SPIRIT IN THE SAVED

The Scriptures teach us clearly that once people are genuinely saved, they have God the Holy Spirit living within their hearts and lives. Their whole body is the temple of the Spirit of God. God the Holy Spirit indwells all those who are genuinely born-again.

1 John 3:10

"**In this the children of God are manifest, and the children of the devil: whosoever doeth not righteousness is not of God, neither he that loveth not his brother."**

GOD'S CHILDREN MANIFESTED

God's born-again children are manifested and the children of the Devil are also manifested. When people who do not (Greek present tense) want to do continuously that which is righteous but that which is unrighteous, they are not of God. A second standard of genuine Christians is that they continuously (Greek present tense) love their fellow Christians. If this be the case, they are manifested to be true Christians.

Verses On The Devil

- **Matthew 25:41**

"Then shall he say also unto them on the left hand, Depart from me, ye cursed, into **everlasting fire, prepared for the devil and his angels**:"

HELL WAS PREPARED FOR THE DEVIL

The everlasting fire of Hell was prepared for the devil and his angels. Hell was not prepared for people. However, if they reject the Lord Jesus Christ as their Saviour Who is the only One Who can deliver them from Hell, they will go there where the Devil and his angels are.

- **John 8:44**

"Ye are of *your* father **the devil**, and the lusts of your father ye will do. **He was a murderer** from the beginning, and abode not in the truth, because **there is no truth in him**. When he speaketh a lie, he speaketh of his own: for **he is a liar, and the father of it**."

SATAN IS A LIAR AND A MURDERER

Satan is a murderer, a liar, and the father of all lies. All people are born into his family, and don't leave his family until and unless they become genuine Christians and enter God's Family by true faith in the Lord Jesus Christ.

- **John 13:2**

"And supper being ended, **the devil having now put into the heart of Judas Iscariot**, Simon's *son*, **to betray him**;"

The Devil put into Judas Iscariot's heart to betray the Lord Jesus Christ.

- **Acts 13:10**

"And said, O full of all subtilty and all mischief, *thou* child of the devil, *thou* enemy of all righteousness, wilt thou not cease to pervert the right ways of the Lord?"

Paul talked to Elymas, the unsaved sorcerer, calling him a child of the Devil.

- **Acts 26:18**

"To open their eyes, *and* **to turn *them*** from darkness to light, and ***from* the power of Satan unto God**, that they may receive forgiveness of sins, and inheritance among them which are sanctified by faith that is in me."

> **TURNING FROM SATAN'S POWER**
>
> One of the things Paul was told to do, when the Lord Jesus Christ saved him, was to turn people from the power of Satan unto God. Satan has power and control over all of his children. He should not exercise his power over true Christians in any way.

- Revelation 2:9

"I know thy works, and tribulation, and poverty, (but thou art rich) and *I know* the blasphemy of them which say they are Jews, and are not, but **are the synagogue of Satan**."

John speaks plainly to one of the early churches of Asia Minor. He says they are the synagogue of Satan. They were trying to fool others, but they couldn't fool God.

1 John 3:11

"For this is the message that ye heard from the beginning, that we should love one another."

This message that genuine Christians should love one another was given clearly by the Lord Jesus Christ Himself.

- John 13:34-35

"A new commandment I give unto you, **That ye love one another**; as I have loved you, that **ye also love one another**. By this shall all *men* know that ye are my disciples, **if ye have love one to another**."

> **LOVE REGARDLESS OF DISAGREEMENTS**
>
> There are many examples of this command of the Lord Jesus Christ not being carried out in our days. You don't have to agree with your brothers and sisters in Christ in all of their doctrines and practices; certainly we don't agree with some doctrines and teachings, but if they're saved, we are to love them even if they don't love us back!
>
> For example, I've said many times, on the doctrine of the Bible, we differ completely with our fundamentalist brethren at Bob Jones University, but we still have love for the brethren. I wish they'd love us back, but sometimes I get the feeling that they won't.
>
> There are some Christian believers who say they are born-again believers, being Pentecostal. We don't agree with the Pentecostal situation. They speak in tongues. But if they are genuinely born-again Christians, God commands

us, to continue to love the brethren.
We've got some hyper-Calvinists that teach that Christ only died for the sins of the elect. I don't agree with it at all but, if they are genuinely saved, I must love those brethren. We can differ in doctrine, and we do, and we should. We should have the freedom to disagree on various doctrines.
Paul differed from Peter. Remember, in the book of Galatians, Paul withstood Peter to his face. But Paul and Peter loved one another since they were brothers in Christ. John is teaching the importance of love among the brethren.

1 John 3:12

"Not as Cain, who was of that wicked one, and slew his brother. And wherefore slew he him? Because his own works were evil, and his brother's righteous."

CAIN HATED HIS BROTHER, ABEL

Cain didn't love his brother. John said, love the brethren, not as Cain who hated his brother. Cain killed Abel because Cain's works were evil.

Verses On Cain

- **Genesis 4:1-5**

"And Adam knew Eve his wife; and she conceived, and bare Cain, and said, I have gotten a man from the LORD. And she again bare his brother Abel. And Abel was a keeper of sheep, but **Cain was a tiller of the ground**. And in process of time it came to pass, that Cain brought of the fruit of the ground an offering unto the LORD. And Abel, he also brought of the firstlings of his flock and of the fat thereof. And the LORD had respect unto Abel and to his offering: But **unto Cain and to his offering he had not respect**. And Cain was very wroth, and his countenance fell."

God didn't want the fruit offering; He wanted the blood offering of the lamb to propitiate for sin. Cain rose up and slew his brother.

- **Genesis 4:8-9**

"And Cain talked with Abel his brother: and it came to pass, when they were in the field, that **Cain rose up against Abel his brother, and slew him**. And the LORD said unto Cain, Where *is* Abel thy brother? And he said, I know not: *Am* I my brother's keeper?"

> **CAIN MURDERED ABEL AND LIED ABOUT IT**
> Cain murdered his brother Abel, then lied about it to the Lord. We are to love the brethren, even though we may differ with them in many areas.

- **Genesis 4:11-13**

"And now *art* thou cursed from the earth, which hath opened her mouth to receive thy brother's blood from thy hand; When thou tillest the ground, it shall not henceforth yield unto thee her strength; **a fugitive and a vagabond shalt thou be in the earth**. And Cain said unto the LORD, My punishment *is* greater than I can bear."

God judged Cain very severely.

- **Genesis 4:15**

"And the LORD said unto him, Therefore whosoever slayeth Cain, vengeance shall be taken on him sevenfold. And **the LORD set a mark upon Cain, lest any finding him should kill him**."

> **GOD PROTECTED CAIN, THE MURDERER**
> God protected Cain, the murderer, and let him go free. Cain went out from the presence of the Lord.

- **Hebrews 11:4**

"**By faith Abel offered unto God a more excellent sacrifice than Cain**, by which he obtained witness that he was righteous, God testifying of his gifts: and by it he being dead yet speaketh."

Cain's vegetable offering was not accepted by God

- **Jude 1:11**

"Woe unto them! for **they have gone in the way of Cain**, and ran greedily after the error of Balaam for reward, and perished in the gainsaying of Core."

> **FALSE TEACHERS TODAY GO IN CAIN'S WAYS**
> False teachers in our day have gone the way of Cain in total disobedience to the will of God.

1 John 3:13

"Marvel not, my brethren, if the world hate you."

This is a section involving both love and hate. The first thing genuine Christians must get through their heads is that the world is not going to love them, who are saved, born-again, and redeemed by grace through true faith in the Lord Jesus Christ.

STOP MARVELING AT THE WORLD'S HATRED

The negative prohibition, *"marvel not,"* is in the Greek present tense. As such, <u>it means stop an action already in progress</u>. Those to whom the Apostle John was writing were to stop marveling when the world is hating you.

THE MEANING OF THE GREEK WORD, "THAUMAZO"

The Greek Word for *"marvel"* is THAUMAZO. Some of the meanings of that Greek Word are:

"1) to wonder, wonder at, marvel; 2) to be wondered at, to be had in admiration."

Verses On Hate

- John 7:7

"**The world cannot hate you; but me it hateth**, because I testify of it, that the works thereof are evil."

The wicked world hates the true Christians because they know that Christ indwells them and that the true Christians belong to Him.

- John 15:18-19

"**If the world hate you, ye know that it hated me before it hated you**. If ye were of the world, the world would love his own: but because ye are not of the world, but I have chosen you out of the world, therefore **the world hateth you**."

THE WORLD'S HATRED OF CHRISTIANS

The world's hatred goes with the territory of being genuine Christians.

- John 17:14

"I have given them thy word; and **the world hath hated them**, because they are not of the world, even as I am not of the world."

<u>Christ our Great High Priest mentioned the world's hatred in His prayer to God the Father.</u>

1 John 3:14

"We know that we have passed from death unto life, because we love the brethren. He that loveth not his brother abideth in death."

One of the indications that true Christians have passed from death unto life is that they love fellow Christians.

> **THE MEANING OF THE GREEK WORD, "METABAINO"**
> The Greek Word for *"passed"* is , METABAINO. Some of the meanings of this Greek Word are:
> > *"1) to pass over from one place to another, to remove, depart"*
>
> This verb is in the Greek perfect tense. This speaks of an action that occurred in the past, but whose results continue on into the present and future. Genuine Christians have passed from death to eternal life, and nothing can remove that from them.

If a professing Christian, or any other person, doesn't have love for true Christians, this is an indication that they are abiding in death and do not possess everlasting life. This is a very serious statement that God makes here. All Christians should ponder why they love or hate someone. It is one to be pondered by everyone.

> **THE MEANING OF THE GREEK WORD, "AGAPAO"**
> The Greek Word for *"love"* is AGAPAO. Some of the meanings of this Greek Word are:
> > *"1) of persons; 1a) to welcome, to entertain, to be fond of, to love dearly; 2) of things; 2a) to be well pleased, to be contented at or with a thing."*

That verb is in the Greek present tense which would emphasize a continuous and lasting love. The Holy Spirit of God gives the saved people the ability to love the brethren that are saved. If genuine Christians do not love fellow Christians (regardless of how much they might differ in some doctrines), according to this verse, they are not in the family of God, but are lost and are bound for Hell. This is a sober statement, but goes along with this verse.

- John 13:35

"By this shall all *men* know that ye are my disciples, **if ye have love one to another.**"

> **MAINTAINING LOVE DESPITE DIFFERENCES**
> There are many kinds of differences that people have with one another. For example, a husband or a wife might have some differences with their mate over some matters, but that shouldn't stop them from loving one another. On the part of true Christians, there should always be a love for their fellow Christians no matter what differences they

might have on doctrines or practices. This is one of the signs that they are disciples of the Lord Jesus Christ.

1 John 3:15

"Whosoever hateth his brother is a murderer: and ye know that no murderer hath eternal life abiding in him."

Here is another verse that tests someone's being born-again or being lost. The Greek Word for "hate" is in the Greek present tense. It means if people have a continuous hatred for genuine Christians, they are murderers and do not possess eternal life. That's quite a test!

Verses On Murder

- John 8:44

"Ye are of *your* father **the devil**, and the lusts of your father ye will do. **He was a murderer from the beginning**, and abode not in the truth, because there is no truth in him. When he speaketh a lie, he speaketh of his own: for he is a liar, and the father of it."

THE DEVIL IS THE LEADING MURDERER OF ALL TIME

The Devil is the leading murderer of all time. He effectively kills for all eternity in the Lake of Fire those who reject the Lord Jesus Christ. He gives them the second, eternal death.

- Acts 3:14

"But ye denied the Holy One and the Just, and **desired a murderer** to be granted unto you;"

The Jews demanded that Barabbas, the murderer, be released; they had the Lord Jesus Christ crucified.

- 1 Peter 4:15

"But **let none of you suffer as a murderer**, or *as* a thief, or *as* an evildoer, or as a busybody in other men's matters."

If people hate their fellow true Christians, they are like murderers. That should never be the case.

1 John 3:16

"Hereby perceive we the love of God, because he laid down his life for us: and we ought to lay down our lives for the brethren."

LAYING DOWN YOUR LIFE FOR FELLOW CHRISTIANS
The Lord Jesus Christ died on our behalf, in our place, for us, as a substitute, and true Christians ought to be willing, if need be, to lay down their lives for the brethren. Genuine love for the brethren would cause true Christians, when required, to lay down their lives for the brethren. That is not human love; it is superhuman. Fellow Christians should be prepared to help other genuine Christians which might mean laying down their lives.

Verses On Christ's Laying Down His Life
- John 10:15

"As the Father knoweth me, even so know I the Father: and **I lay down my life for the sheep**."

CHRIST DIED FOR ALL LOST SHEEP OF THE WORLD
At Calvary's Cross, the Lord Jesus Christ voluntarily laid down His life for the whole world of lost sheep.

- John 10:17

"Therefore doth my Father love me, because **I lay down my life**, that I might take it again."

The Lord Jesus Christ, God the Son, had the power to lay down His life and to be resurrected again.

- John 13:37-38

"**Peter said** unto him, Lord, why cannot I follow thee now? **I will lay down my life for thy sake**. Jesus answered him, Wilt thou **lay down thy life for my sake**? Verily, verily, I say unto thee, The cock shall not crow, till thou hast denied me thrice."

Peter lied, and the Lord Jesus Christ caught him in that lie.

- John 15:13

"Greater love hath no man than this, **that a man lay down his life for his friends**."

CHRIST'S GREATER LOVE–DYING FOR EVERYONE
The Lord Jesus Christ exercised this *"greater love"* by laying down His life for all the lost sinners of the world.

1 John 3:17

"But whoso hath this world's good, and seeth his brother have need, and shutteth up his bowels of compassion from him, how dwelleth the love of God in him?"

Genuine Christians who have material blessings should want to help, if they are able, other fellow Christians in the Christian family who have needs. Not to respond to such needs puts a question on their love for God. This is another very strict test for true Christians.

MEANING OF THE GREEK WORD, "SPLANCHNON"

The Greek Word for *"bowels"* is SPLANCHNON. Some of the meanings of this Greek Word are:

"1) bowels, intestines, (the heart, lungs, liver, etc.); 1a) bowels; 1b) the bowels were regarded as the seat of the more violent passions, such as anger and love; but by the Hebrews as the seat of the tenderer affections, esp. kindness, benevolence, compassion; hence our heart (tender mercies, affections, etc.); 1c) a heart in which mercy resides."

Genuine Christians should "put their money where their mouth is," as the saying goes. If they say they love their fellow Christians in need, if they are able, they should seek to help them, even if it is a little bit of help.

1 John 3:18

"My little children, let us not love in word, neither in tongue; but in deed and in truth."

John is addressing "little children." He's probably meaning those who were just recently saved.

LOVE IN DEED AND TRUTH, NOT IN WORD ONLY

This verb for *"love"* is in the Greek present tense. It's a prohibition. John is telling his readers to stop loving only in word and tongue, but to love in deed and in truth. This is the proof of sound true Christian love. This genuine love should prevail among real Christians despite differences in doctrines or practices. This is very difficult.

1 John 3:19

"And hereby we know that we are of the truth, and shall assure our hearts before him."

The word, "*hereby*" refers back to the previous verses. People who love fellow Christians and want to help them by deeds gives assurance that they are of the truth and are genuinely saved.

Verses On Assurance

- **Deuteronomy 28:66**

"And thy life shall hang in doubt before thee; and thou shalt fear day and night, and **shalt have none assurance of thy life**:"

This is an Old Testament instance of having no assurance of life.

- **Isaiah 32:17**

"And the work of righteousness shall be peace; and **the effect of righteousness** quietness and **assurance for ever**."

God gives true Christians assurance that they're saved forever.

- **Acts 2:36**

"Therefore **let all the house of Israel know assuredly**, that God hath made that same Jesus, whom ye have crucified, both Lord and Christ."

Israel should have assurance that God made the Lord Jesus Christ Whom they crucified both Lord and Christ.

- **Acts 17:31**

"Because he hath appointed a day, in the which he will judge the world in righteousness by *that* man whom he hath ordained; *whereof* **he hath given assurance unto all *men***, in that he hath raised him from the dead."

Paul preached to those on Mars Hill. He said that God would assuredly judge the world in righteousness by the Lord Jesus Christ Whom He raised from the dead.

- **1 Thessalonians 1:5**

"For **our gospel came** not unto you in word only, but also in power, and in the Holy Ghost, and **in much assurance**; as ye know what manner of men we were among you for your sake."

The gospel of the Lord Jesus Christ is an assured gospel. Christ died for the sins of the world that people might truly trust in Him and assuredly receive everlasting life.

- **2 Timothy 3:14**

"But **continue thou in the things which thou** hast learned and **hast been assured of**, knowing of whom thou hast learned *them*;"

Paul told Pastor Timothy in the church of Ephesus to <u>continue in the things he had learned and been assured of</u>.
- **Hebrews 10:22**
"Let us **draw near with a true heart in full assurance of faith**, having our hearts sprinkled from an evil conscience, and our bodies washed with pure water."

Paul urges the Hebrew Christians to draw near, with a true heart in full assurance, to the Lord, that Great High Priest Who has gone into the heavens.

1 John 3:20

" **For if our heart condemn us, God is greater than our heart, and knoweth all things.**"

KEEPING IN FELLOWSHIP WITH THE LORD

It is hoped that genuine Christians will have their hearts clean and without condemnation. This can only be done if they diligently read and heed God's Words day by day, month by month, and year by year, making good use of 1 John 1:9 when sin enters in:

"If we confess our sins, he is faithful and just to forgive us our sins, and to cleanse us from all unrighteousness."

They can be assured that their omnipotent and omniscient God knows all the things that go on in their hearts, minds, and lives. He is greater than their hearts and knows how to help His own people.

1 John 3:21

"**Beloved, if our heart condemn us not, then have we confidence toward God.**"

CONFIDENCE TOWARD GOD

When true Christians have hearts that are not condemned, they have great confidence toward God.

Verses On Confidence
- **Psalms 118:8-9**
"It is better to trust in the LORD than to put **confidence in man**. *It is* better to trust in the LORD than to put **confidence in princes**."

Genuine Christians should not put confidence in man or in princes.

- **Proverbs 3:26**
"For **the LORD shall be thy confidence**, and shall keep thy foot from being taken."

> **CONFIDENCE IN GOD AND HIS WORDS**
> The LORD will never let true Christians down. They can have absolute and total confidence in Him and in His Words.

- **Proverbs 14:26**
"**In the fear of the LORD *is* strong confidence**: and his children shall have a place of refuge."

There can be strong confidence when people trust in the Lord and in His Words.

- **Proverbs 25:19**
"**Confidence in an unfaithful man in time of trouble** *is like* a broken tooth, and a foot out of joint."

No one should put any confidence in an unfaithful man, especially in time of trouble.

- **Acts 28:31**
"**Preaching** the kingdom of God, **and teaching** those things which concern the Lord Jesus Christ, **with all confidence**, no man forbidding him."

Paul preached and taught about the things of the Lord Jesus Christ with all confidence.

- **2 Corinthians 7:16**
"I rejoice therefore that **I have confidence in you in all *things*.**"

Paul had confidence in the genuine Christians at Corinth.

- **Ephesians 3:12**
"**In whom we have boldness and access with confidence** by the faith of him."

The Lord Jesus Christ gives true Christians boldness and access to Him with confidence.

- **Philippians 3:3**
"For we are the circumcision, which worship God in the spirit, and rejoice in Christ Jesus, and **have no confidence in the flesh**."

Genuine Christians should have no confidence in their flesh, but in God the Holy Spirit Who indwells them.

- **1 John 2:28**
"And now, little children, abide in him; that, when he shall appear, **we may have confidence**, and not be ashamed before him at his coming."

True Christians should not be ashamed before the Lord Jesus Christ when He returns in the Rapture. They should have confidence in Him.

1 John 3:22

"And whatsoever we ask, we receive of him, because we keep his commandments, and do those things that are pleasing in his sight."

For the real Christians, their prayer life is important. God answers their prayers if they keep His Words and do pleasing things in His sight.

Verses On Pleasing

- **Colossians 1:10**

"That ye might **walk worthy of the Lord unto all pleasing**, being fruitful in every good work, and increasing in the knowledge of God;"

Genuine Christians should walk worthy of the Lord to please Him.

- **Colossians 3:20**

"**Children, obey *your* parents** in all things: for **this is well pleasing unto the Lord**."

Children who obey their parents are well pleasing to the Lord.

- **1 Thessalonians 2:4**

"But as we were allowed of God to be put in trust with the gospel, even so we speak; **not as pleasing men, but God, which trieth our hearts**."

True Christians should not seek to please men, but should please God.

1 John 3:23

"And this is his commandment, That we should believe on the name of his Son Jesus Christ, and love one another, as he gave us commandment."

Both of these two things should be practiced by genuine Christians:

(1) They should genuinely believe in God's Son, thus receiving everlasting life.

(2) They should love one another.

Verses On Love

- **John 13:34-35**

"A new commandment I give unto you, That ye **love one another; as I have loved you**, that ye also **love one**

another. By this shall all *men* know that ye are my disciples, if ye have **love one to another**."

True Christians are commanded to love one another as the Lord Jesus Christ has loved them. This is the goal, even if impossible to fulfill.

- **John 15:12**

"This is my commandment, **That ye love one another, as I have loved you**."

This is the real Christians' goal, even though impossible to attain.

- **John 3:16**

"For **God so loved the world**, that he gave his only begotten Son, that whosoever believeth in him should not perish, but have everlasting life."

> **GOD WANTS ALL TO TRULY TRUST IN HIS SON**
> God so loved the world that He sent His Son to come to earth and to die for all their sins so they might trust him and receive eternal life.

- **John 15:13**

"**Greater love hath no man** than this, that a man **lay down his life for his friends**."

This is exactly what the Lord Jesus Christ did at the cross.

- **John 15:17**

"These things I command you, that ye **love one another**."

Love for fellow Christians is a command by the Lord Jesus Christ.

- **John 17:26**

"And I have declared unto them thy name, and will declare *it*: that **the love wherewith thou hast loved me may be in them**, and I in them."

> **CHRIST WANTS GOD'S LOVE IN TRUE CHRISTIANS**
> The Lord Jesus Christ asked God the Father to put the love He had for His Son in all genuine Christians.

- **Romans 5:5**

"And hope maketh not ashamed; because **the love of God is shed abroad in our hearts by the Holy Ghost** which is given unto us."

The love of God is shed abroad in the hearts of true Christians by the Holy Spirit of God Who indwells them.

1 John 3:24

"**And he that keepeth his commandments dwelleth in him, and he in him. And hereby we know that he abideth in us, by the Spirit which he hath given us.**"

GOD THE HOLY SPIRIT INDWELLS TRUE CHRISTIANS

The Apostle John is writing to real Christian believers. By keeping God's Words, genuine Christians dwell in God and God dwells in them. God the Father abides in these Christians by His Holy Spirit which He has given them. God the Holy Spirit indwells these Christians the moment they are saved and never leaves them.

Verses On The Indwelling Holy Spirit
- John 14:17

"*Even* **the Spirit of truth**; whom the world cannot receive, because it seeth him not, neither knoweth him: but ye know him; for **he dwelleth with you, and shall be in you**."

THE HOLY SPIRIT WOULD BE IN THE DISCIPLES

Notice what the Lord Jesus tells His disciples here, "*for he dwelleth with you, and shall be in you.*" Before the descent of the Holy Spirit, in Acts chapter two, the Holy Spirit was with them but not in them. After that time, all genuine Christians have the Holy Spirit dwelling in them.

- Romans 8:9

"But ye are not in the flesh, but in the Spirit, **if so be that the Spirit of God dwell in you**. Now if any man have not the Spirit of Christ, he is none of his."

The indwelling Spirit of God is the distinction between true Christians and those who are lost.

- 1 Corinthians 3:16

"Know ye not that ye are the temple of God, and *that* **the Spirit of God dwelleth in you**?"

Genuine Christians have God the Holy Spirit indwelling them. This is a sound Biblical truth.

- 2 Timothy 1:14

"That good thing which was committed unto thee keep by **the Holy Ghost which dwelleth in us**."

This can be said only of true Christians.

- **James 4:5**

"Do ye think that the scripture saith in vain, **The spirit that dwelleth in us** lusteth to envy?"

> **THE INDWELLING HOLY SPIRIT OF GOD**
> The Holy Spirit dwells in every real Christian.

- **1 Corinthians 6:19**

"What? know ye not that **your body is the temple of the Holy Ghost *which is* in you**, which ye have of God, and ye are not your own? For ye are bought with a price: therefore glorify God in your body, and in your spirit, which are God's."

> **TRUE CHRISTIANS SHOULD GLORIFY GOD**
> Because true Christians have been "*bought with a price*," the Spirit of God can indwell them and teach them the things that they ought to know from the Bible.

1 John
Chapter Four

1 John 4:1

"Beloved, believe not every spirit, but try the spirits whether they are of God: because many false prophets are gone out into the world."

The Greek verb for "*believe not*" is a Greek present tense. It is a negative prohibition. As such, the force of the Greek is for someone to stop an action that they have been doing or thinking. John is telling his readers to stop believing every spirit that is around. Apparently, these people were like vacuum cleaners, sucking up and swallowing every false doctrine that came along.

SPIRITS MUST BE TESTED FOR ERRORS

The command is for them to "*try*" or "*test out*" these spirits to see if they are from God or if they're false teachings. The Greek Word for "*try*" is DOKIMAZO. Some of the meanings of this Greek Word are:

"1) to test, examine, prove, scrutinise (to see whether a thing is genuine or not), as metals; 2) to recognise as genuine after examination, to approve, deem worthy."

There are many, many false prophets and false teachings in the United States and all around the world. We have TV programs, radio programs, and Internet programs that are continually setting forth false teachings. Everything that people read, listen to, or watch on the TV or Internet should be tested out.

In the religious world, the Roman Catholic Church, the cults, New Evangelicalism, and even some fundamentalists must be tested by the yardstick of Bible truth.

Verses On Trying And Testing
- **Judges 7:4**

"And the LORD said unto Gideon, The people *are* yet *too* many; bring them down unto the water, and **I will try them for thee there**: and it shall be, *that* of whom I say unto thee, This shall go with thee, the same shall go with thee; and of whomsoever I say unto thee, This shall not go with thee, the same shall not go."

Gideon was told by the LORD to try or test out his warriors before having them in his army.

- **Psalms 26:2**

"Examine me, O LORD, and prove me; **try my reins and my heart.**"

David asked the LORD to examine, prove, and try or test his reins and heart. Only God can do this.

- **Psalms 139:23**

"Search me, O God, and know my heart: **try me, and know my thoughts**:"

David wanted to be searched out, tried, and tested by God for his heart and his thoughts.

- **Jeremiah 17:9-10**

"The heart *is* deceitful above all *things*, and desperately wicked: who can know it? **I the LORD search the heart, *I* try the reins**, even to give every man according to his ways, *and* according to the fruit of his doings."

Only the LORD can search, try, and test out persons' reins and hearts.

- **Lamentations 3:40**

"**Let us search and try our ways**, and turn again to the LORD."

RETURN TO THE LORD'S WAYS
After people try and test their ways, they can see how they need to go back to the LORD's ways.

- 1 Corinthians 3:13

"Every man's work shall be made manifest: for the day shall declare it, because it shall be revealed by fire; and **the fire shall try every man's work of what sort it is**."

THE JUDGMENT SEAT OF CHRIST'S TEST OF WORKS
At the Judgment Seat of Christ, the fire will try or test out every Christian's work, of what sort it is, whether gold, silver, and precious stones, or hay, wood, and stubble.

1, 2, & 3 John–Preaching Verse-by-Verse 135

- 1 Peter 4:12

"Beloved, think it not strange concerning **the fiery trial which is to try you**, as though some strange thing happened unto you:"

Dangerous and sometimes fiery trials try and test out Christians who are living in this wicked world. This is not strange; it is often routine.

Verses On Unclean And Evil Spirits

- Leviticus 19:31

"**Regard not them that have familiar spirits, neither seek after wizards**, to be defiled by them: I *am* the LORD your God."

False and evil spirits should not be regarded or listened to.

- Matthew 10:1

"And when he had called unto *him* his twelve disciples, he gave them **power *against* unclean spirits, to cast them out**, and to heal all manner of sickness and all manner of disease."

One of the powers the Lord Jesus Christ gave to His disciples was the casting out of unclean and evil spirits.

- 1 Timothy 4:1

"Now the Spirit speaketh expressly, that in the latter times some shall depart from the faith, giving heed to **seducing spirits**, and doctrines of devils;"

Genuine Christians should never give heed to seducing or evil spirits.

Verses On False Prophets

John also warns about false prophets that have gone into the world.

- Matthew 7:15

"**Beware of false prophets**, which come to you in sheep's clothing, but inwardly they are ravening wolves."

WOLVES LOOKING LIKE SHEEP

True Christians should beware of these false prophets. They look like sheep, but they are really wolves.

- Matthew 24:11

"And **many false prophets shall rise, and shall deceive many**."

DECEPTION IS THE DEVIL'S KEY METHOD

Deception is the Devil's key method. Be very careful not to be deceived by false prophets.

- Matthew 24:24

"For **there shall arise false Christs, and false prophets**, and shall shew great signs and wonders; insomuch that, if *it were* possible, they shall deceive the very elect."

These false prophet miracle workers are on TV and the Internet, deceiving many genuine Christians.

- 2 Peter 2:1

"But **there were false prophets also among the people**, even as there shall be false teachers among you, who privily shall bring in damnable heresies, even denying the Lord that bought them, and bring upon themselves swift destruction."

False prophets were and are many in number. This includes false teachers who teach Biblical errors.

1 John 4:2

"Hereby know ye the Spirit of God: Every spirit that confesseth that Jesus Christ is come in the flesh is of God:"

THE DOCTRINE OF THE INCARNATION OF CHRIST

"Jesus Christ is come in the flesh" refers to the Incarnation of the Lord Jesus Christ. This is a vital doctrine of the Bible.

Verses On The Incarnation– Christ Coming In The Flesh

- 1 Timothy 3:16

"And without controversy great is the mystery of godliness: **God was manifest in the flesh**, justified in the Spirit, seen of angels, preached unto the Gentiles, believed on in the world, received up into glory."

CHRIST WAS GOD MANIFEST IN THE FLESH

"God was manifest in the flesh" is a clear teaching about the Incarnation of the Lord Jesus Christ. The word, *"God,"* is omitted by the Gnostic Critical Greek Texts and left out of all the Bible versions in all the languages of the world that follow these Satanic Gnostic Critical Greek Texts. In English versions, this includes the ASV, NASV, RSV, NIV, ESV and many, many more.

- **2 John 1:7**
"For many deceivers are entered into the world, **who confess not that Jesus Christ is come in the flesh**. This is a deceiver and an antichrist."

APOSTATE ANTICHRIST PREACHERS
Think about all the modernist, liberal, apostate preachers, of whatever denomination or church group. They do not believe that the Lord Jesus Christ came in the flesh in the Incarnation. They are deceivers and antichrists.

THE MEANING OF THE GREEK WORD, "HOMOLOGEO"
The Greek Word for "*confess*" is HOMOLOGEO. Some of the meanings of this Greek Word are:

"1) to say the same thing as another, i.e. to agree with, assent; 2) to concede; 2a) not to refuse, to promise; 2b) not to deny; 2b1) to confess; 2b2) declare; 2b3) to confess, i.e. to admit or declare one's self guilty of what one is accused of; 3) to profess; 3a) to declare openly, speak out freely; 3b) to profess one's self the worshipper of one; 4) to praise, celebrate."

They deny "*Jesus*" which, in the Greek language means "Saviour." They also deny "Christ" which is the Anointed One of God the Father.

Verses On Recognizing Christ As The Messiah
- **Matthew 16:16**
"And Simon Peter answered and said, **Thou art the Christ**, the Son of the living God."

Peter confessed the Lord Jesus was "*the Christ*," the Son of God.

- **John 4:42**
"And said unto the woman, Now we believe, not because of thy saying: for we have heard *him* ourselves, and know that **this is indeed the Christ, the Saviour of the world**."

Even the woman at the well who had five husbands finally recognized that the Lord Jesus Christ was indeed "*the Christ, the Saviour of the world.*"

- **John 11:27**
"She saith unto him, Yea, Lord: **I believe that thou art the Christ, the Son of God**, which should come into the world."

Mary, Martha's sister, believed that Christ was the Messiah Who should come into the world.

- John 20:31

"But these are written, **that ye might believe that Jesus is the Christ, the Son of God**; and that believing ye might have life through his name."

> **JOHN'S PURPOSE IN WRITING HIS GOSPEL**
>
> This was John's purpose in writing his Gospel–that his readers might believe that the Lord Jesus was the Christ, that is, the Messiah, promised from the Old Testament.

- 1 John 2:22

"Who is a liar but **he that denieth that Jesus is the Christ**? He is antichrist, that denieth the Father and the Son."

> **ANTICHRISTS AND LIARS ARE DEFINED BY JOHN**
>
> That includes every Jewish rabbi, every apostate Protestant preacher, every Unitarian, every member of any of the world religions, or anyone else who denies that the Lord Jesus Christ is God's Messiah Christ. According to this verse, all the above are both liars and antichrists.

1 John 4:3

"And every spirit that confesseth not that Jesus Christ is come in the flesh is not of God: and this is that spirit of antichrist, whereof ye have heard that it should come; and even now already is it in the world."

> **GNOSTIC VERSIONS DENY CHRIST'S INCARNATION**
>
> Every spirit that confesseth not that the Lord Jesus Christ has come in the flesh by means of the Incarnation is not of God and is of the spirit of antichrist. <u>The Gnostic Critical Greek Text and all the translations that follow that false Greek text omit *"Christ is come in the flesh."*</u> They deny the Incarnation of God the Son, the Lord Jesus Christ, and again are called antichrists. This denial is a horrible heresy. <u>That clause is not in the ASV, NASV, NIV, RSV, ESV or any of the other erroneous English versions.</u>

Verses On Antichrist

- 1 John 2:18

"Little children, it is the last time: and as ye have heard that **antichrist shall come, even now are there many antichrists**; whereby we know that it is the last time."

Even in John's time, in 90 A.D., there were many antichrists. There are many more today.
- 1 John 2:22
"Who is a liar but he that denieth that Jesus is the Christ? **He is antichrist, that denieth the Father and the Son.**"
This is another definition of *"liar"* and *"antichrist."*
- 2 John 1:7
"For many deceivers are entered into the world, who **confess not that Jesus Christ is come in the flesh**. This is a deceiver and an antichrist."
The Incarnation of the Lord Jesus Christ is a pivotal doctrine of the New Testament. To deny it makes people deceivers and antichrists.

1 John 4:4

"Ye are of God, little children, and have overcome them: because greater is he that is in you, than he that is in the world."

John might mean by *"little children"* those who recently became true Christians. Though new in the Lord, they have still overcome the world around them.

THE MEANING OF THE GREEK WORD, "NIKAO"

The Greek Word for *"overcome"* is NIKAO. Some of the meanings of this Greek Word are:

"1) to conquer; 1a) to carry off the victory, come off victorious; 1a1) of Christ, victorious over all His foes; 1a2) of Christians, that hold fast their faith even unto death against the power of their foes, and temptations and persecutions; 1a3) when one is arraigned or goes to law, to win the case, maintain one's cause"

The reason for this victory is the greatness of God the Holy Spirit Who indwells them. This Power is greater than any power this world can muster.

1 John 4:5
"They are of the world: therefore speak they of the world, and the world heareth them."

ANTICHRISTS ARE OF THIS WORLD
Those who have the spirit of antichrist are of this world. Because of this, they speak about the things of the world; those who are of the world, not genuine Christians, listen to them. Their primary interest is this sinful world and those who inhabit it.

1 John 4:6
"We are of God: he that knoweth God heareth us; he that is not of God heareth not us. Hereby know we the spirit of truth, and the spirit of error."

People who are true Christians are of God. Those who also know God by genuine faith in His Son listen to one another. Those who do not know God by true faith in His Son do not listen to those who are real Christians. Those who are saved have within them the Spirit of truth. Those who are not saved have within them the spirit of error.

Verses On The Indwelling Holy Spirit
- John 14:16

"And I will pray the Father, and he shall give you **another Comforter, that he may abide with you for ever**;"
The abiding presence of God the Holy Spirit never leaves the genuine Christians.
- John 15:26

"But when **the Comforter is come, whom I will send unto you from the Father, *even* the Spirit of truth**, which proceedeth from the Father, he shall testify of me:"
The Holy Spirit Who indwells true Christians is identified as the "*Spirit of truth*" in this verse. He was sent from God the Father. His ministry is to testify about the Lord Jesus Christ. He exalts the Saviour.
- John 16:13

"Howbeit when he, **the Spirit of truth, is come, he will guide you into all truth:** for he shall not speak of himself; but whatsoever he shall hear, *that* shall he speak: and he will shew you things to come."

CHRIST'S GAVE THE WORDS OF THE BIBLE

God the Holy Spirit does not speak from Himself; but, what the Lord Jesus Christ has told Him to speak, He speaks. This is how the New Testament came about. The Lord Jesus Christ gave the Holy Spirit the Words He wanted to be recorded in the Bible, and those Words were the Words the Holy Spirit delivered unto the New Testament writers. He showed them things to come in the future.

1 John 4:7

"Beloved, let us love one another: for love is of God; and every one that loveth is born of God, and knoweth God."

John is speaking to genuine Christians. He urges them to love one another because love is from God. Real Christian love is one of the fruits of being born-again by God and knowing God as Divine Father. Real Christian love is almost an external litmus test that evidences eternal life.

Verses On Christian Love

- John 13:34

"A new commandment I give unto you, That ye **love one another; as I have loved you, that ye also love one another**."

The degree that true Christians should love one another is as the Lord Jesus Christ loved them. Though impossible to achieve, this is the goal that the Lord Jesus Christ laid down.

- John 15:12

"This is my commandment, That ye **love one another, as I have loved you**."

The Lord Jesus Christ repeated this command and its standard once again.

- John 15:17

"These things I command you, that ye **love one another**."

CHRIST COMMANDED MUTUAL CHRISTIAN LOVE

This is a strong order from the Lord Jesus Christ. It's just like when a military officer commands another person of a lower rank. There must be an attempt, at least, to obey such a command.

- **Romans 13:8**
"Owe no man any thing, but to **love one another**: for he that loveth another hath fulfilled the law."

Even though there might be things on which fellow Christians differ, there should be genuine love extended for one another.

- **1 Thessalonians 4:9**
"But as touching brotherly love ye need not that I write unto you: for **ye yourselves are taught of God to love one another**."

LOVING FELLOW-CHRISTIANS TAUGHT BY GOD

Loving fellow Christians is taught by God. It is expected of every genuine Christian.

- **1 Peter 1:22**
"Seeing ye have purified your souls in obeying the truth through the Spirit unto **unfeigned love of the brethren, see that ye love one another with a pure heart fervently**:"

UNFEIGNED NON-HYPOCRITICAL LOVE

The love involved here must be *"unfeigned,"* without any hypocrisy involved in it. It must be honest and sincere as being with a pure and fervent heart. In other words, it must not be smiling with a big grin to your fellow Christians, but behind their backs, slicing, dicing, and hating them.

- **1 John 3:11**
"For this is the message that ye heard from the beginning, that **we should love one another**."

John repeats this need for loving fellow Christians here in his letter of 1 John.

- **2 John 1:5**
"And now I beseech thee, lady, not as though I wrote a new commandment unto thee, but that which we had from the beginning, **that we love one another**."

Here again is a clear command for genuine fellow Christians to love one another no matter what else is true about their differences of doctrine.

1 John 4:8

"He that loveth not knoweth not God; for God is love."

LACK OF LOVE=NOT KNOWING GOD

This is a severe test of true Christians. This verse clearly states that such Christians who do not love their fellow Christians do not really know God because God is love. This is a Biblical and evidential test of salvation that is very shocking, yet true. God knows all persons' hearts and must be the final judge of love or lack of love in those hearts.

1 John 4:9

"In this was manifested the love of God toward us, because that God sent his only begotten Son into the world, that we might live through him."

GOD'S LOVE SHOWN BY SENDING HIS SON

God's love was manifested toward the entire world by sending His only begotten Son into the world that people who trust in Him might have everlasting life.

Verses On God's Sending His Son From Heaven
- John 3:16-17

"**For God so loved the world, that he gave his only begotten Son**, that whosoever believeth in him should not perish, but have everlasting life. For God sent not his Son into the world to condemn the world; but that the world through him might be saved."

Because He loved the entire world, God sent the Lord Jesus Christ into the world to die on a cross in order to provide salvation for whoever truly trusts in Him.

- John 3:34

"For **he whom God hath sent** speaketh the words of God: for God giveth not the Spirit by measure *unto him*."

The Lord Jesus Christ is He whom God has sent into the world in order to speak His Words to all mankind.

- John 4:34

"Jesus saith unto them, My meat is **to do the will of him that sent me**, and to finish his work."

The Lord Jesus Christ was sent by God to do God's will and finish His work for which He was sent.

- **John 5:23-24**

"That all *men* should honour the Son, even as they honour the Father. He that honoureth not the Son honoureth not **the Father which hath sent him**. Verily, verily, I say unto you, He that heareth my word, and believeth on him that sent me, hath everlasting life, and shall not come into condemnation; but is passed from death unto life."

TRUE TRUST IN CHRIST BRINGS ETERNAL LIFE

The Father sent His Son so that whoever hears God's Word and believes on the Lord Jesus Christ might have everlasting life and pass from death unto life.

- **John 5:30**

"I can of mine own self do nothing: as I hear, I judge: and my judgment is just; because I seek not mine own will, but **the will of the Father which hath sent me**."

The Lord Jesus Christ came to do the will of the Father Who sent Him into the world.

- **John 5:36**

"But I have greater witness than *that* of John: for the works which the Father hath given me to finish, the same works that I do, bear witness of me, that **the Father hath sent me**."

The works and miracles of the Lord Jesus Christ show that God the Father sent Him into the world.

- **John 6:29**

"Jesus answered and said unto them, This is the work of God, that ye **believe on him whom he hath sent**."

God wanted people to believe on Him Whom He has sent into the world. This is the work of God that people might believe on the Lord Jesus Christ.

- **Galatians 4:4**

"But when the fulness of the time was come, **God sent forth his Son**, made of a woman, made under the law,"

THE MIRACLE OF THE VIRGIN BIRTH

In God's own time, He sent His Son into the world by means of the miracle of a virgin birth.

- **John 6:51**
"**I am the living bread which came down from heaven**: if any man eat of this bread, he shall live for ever: and the bread that I will give is my flesh, which I will give for the life of the world."
The Lord Jesus Christ came down from Heaven, having been sent by His Father, so that people might have the opportunity to live forever.
- **John 6:58**
"**This is that bread which came down from heaven**: not as your fathers did eat manna, and are dead: he that eateth of this bread shall live forever."
The Lord Jesus Christ is the Living Bread.

Verses On Everlasting And Eternal Life
- **John 3:16**
"For God so loved the world, that he gave his only begotten Son, that whosoever believeth in him **should not perish, but have everlasting life**."
The Lord Jesus Christ came to provide everlasting life for those who genuinely trust Him.
- **John 3:36**
"**He that believeth on the Son hath everlasting life**: and he that believeth not the Son shall not see life; but the wrath of God abideth on him."
Genuine faith in Christ is the requisite to receiving everlasting life. If this is missing, God's wrath is the result.
- **John 6:47**
"Verily, verily, I say unto you, **He that believeth on me hath everlasting life**."

"ON ME" REMOVED FROM JOHN 6:47 BY GNOSTICS

Genuine faith in the Lord Jesus Christ is the requisite for receiving everlasting life. The Gnostic Critical Greek Text removes the two vital Words in this verse, "*on me*" because the Gnostic religion teaches that Jesus Christ was just a sinful man who couldn't save anybody. The English and other language versions around the world that are built on this perverse Greek Text are in agreement with this Gnostic heresy. The Westcott and Hort, the United Bible Society, and the Nestle Aland Greek Texts all follow slavishly this wicked and corrupt Gnostic Greek Text.

- **John 10:28**
"And **I give unto them eternal life**; and they shall never perish, neither shall any *man* pluck them out of my hand."

Only the Lord Jesus Christ can give His genuine believers eternal and everlasting life. There is no other way to receive it.
- John 20:31
"But these are written, that ye might believe that Jesus is the Christ, the Son of God; and that **believing ye might have life through his name.**"

TRUE FAITH IN CHRIST BRINGS EVERLASTING LIFE
True believing in the Lord Jesus Christ alone brings everlasting life.

1 John 4:10
" **Herein is love, not that we loved God, but that he loved us, and sent his Son to be the propitiation for our sins."**

God made the first move in loving lost, Hell-bound sinners. True Christians love God because He loved them first. The reason that God sent His Son, the Lord Jesus Christ, into this wicked world is given in this verse. It was for Him to be the propitiation for the sins of the entire world.

THE MEANING OF THE GREEK WORD, "HILASMOS"
The Greek Word for *"propitiation"* is HILASMOS. Some of the meanings of this Greek Word are:
> "*1) an appeasing, propitiating; 2) the means of appeasing, a propitiation*"

God was appeased or satisfied with the redemptive work of His Son on the cross at Calvary when He died for the sins of the world.

Why did He send his Son? *"To be the propitiation for our sins."* Many of the new Bible versions don't use "propitiation" here. They removed it, such as the English Standard Version, the New International Version, the Contemporary English Version, and others.

GOD WAS PROPITIATED BY CHRIST'S SACRIFICE
God is propitious. He was satisfied and appeased by the substitutionary death of the Lord Jesus Christ at Calvary. 1 Peter 2:24 sets this forth clearly:
> "*Who his own self bare our sins in his own body on the tree, that we, being dead to sins, should live unto righteousness: by whose stripes ye were healed.*"

Because God the Father was satisfied with the propitiation by God the Son for the sins of the world, these sins have been atoned for. Now it is up to every person in the world to accept by true faith what the Lord Jesus Christ did for them in dying for their sins.

Verses On Propitiation

- Romans 3:25

"**Whom God hath set forth *to be* a propitiation through faith in his blood**, to declare his righteousness for the remission of sins that are past, through the forbearance of God;"

WHY GOD SENT HIS SON FROM HEAVEN

That is why God sent the Lord Jesus Christ from Heaven to this earth. It was so that **He might be set forth as a propitiation, appeasement, and satisfaction for the sins of the world**. This is made possible when people genuinely trust the Lord Jesus Christ as their Saviour. It is then that their sins can be forgiven, and that they might receive everlasting life.

- 1 John 2:2

"And **he is the propitiation for our sins**: and not for ours only, **but also for *the sins of* the whole world**."

THE HYPER-CALVINISTS' ERRORS OF THE CROSS

The Lord Jesus Christ's work on the cross was for the propitiation not only for the sins of the true Christians, but also for the sins of the entire world. The hyper-Calvinists are in serious error with their teaching that the Lord Jesus Christ's death was exclusively for the little body of what they term "*the elect*." Much more, He is the satisfaction for the sins of the whole world.

1 John 4:11

"**Beloved, if God so loved us, we ought also to love one another.**"

The love of God is mentioned many times and also the love for genuine Christian brethren. We may not agree with everything that other true Christians believe, but we are to love them anyway.

THE MEANING OF THE GREEK WORD, "OPHEILO"

The Greek Word for "*ought*" is "OPHEILO." Some of the meanings of that Greek Word are:

> *"1) to owe; 1a) to owe money, be in debt for; 1a1) that which is due, the debt; 2) metaphor, the goodwill due"*

It is in the Greek present tense. As such it signifies a continuous debt that is owed and due. It never lets up or is lessened. It is a debt that can never be paid off, but is continually owed to all genuine Christians–by fellow Christians–to love and not stop loving.

At what point should a true Christian draw the line to separate from false doctrines? We should love the Christians, but should not have fellowship with their unBiblical doctrines or practices, but rather separate from them.

THE MEANING OF THE GREEK WORD, "ALLELON"

The Greek Word for *"one another"* is *"*ALLELON.*"* Some of the meanings of that Greek Word are:

"1) one another, reciprocally, mutually"

It's not a one-sided love. It is a reciprocal and mutual love on the part of both true Christian people.

Verses On Loving Genuine Christian Brethren
- **John 13:34**

"A new commandment I give unto you, That ye <u>love one another; as I have loved you, that ye also love one another</u>."

The Lord Jesus Christ told His apostles that the unreachable yet stated goal of <u>true Christian love is as the Saviour has loved them</u>. That's a very high target to shoot at.

- **Romans 13:8**

"Owe no man any thing, but to <u>love one another</u>: for he that loveth another hath fulfilled the law."

Again, that Greek Word is ALLELON as above. <u>It necessitates reciprocity and mutuality of love</u>.

- **1 Thessalonians 4:9**

"But as touching brotherly love ye need not that I write unto you: for ye yourselves are taught of God to <u>love one another</u>."

<u>God teaches genuine Christians to love one another</u>.

- **1 Peter 1:22**

"Seeing ye have purified your souls in obeying the truth through the Spirit unto <u>unfeigned love of the brethren</u>, *see that ye* <u>love one another with a pure heart fervently</u>:"

<u>The love that one true Christian should have for one another should not be unfeigned and phony</u>. Rather, it should be pure and fervent.

1 John 4:12

"No man hath seen God at any time. If we love one another, God dwelleth in us, and his love is perfected in us."

Notice three things in this verse that are true of genuine Christians:

(1) They are to *"love one another."*

(2) If they do, *"God dwelleth"* in them.

(3) If they do, God's *"love is perfected"* in them, "if we love one another."

That's the "if" clause. Genuine Christians should love one another. The second thing, if that's the case, *"God dwelleth in us."* That's almost a sign of salvation. The third thing, "his love is perfected in us." His love is made perfect and mature, if we love one another. *"God dwelleth in us,"* and people can see Christ in us. It says in Colossians "Christ in you the hope of glory." Love is perfected and made mature.

GOD'S FULNESS HAS NOT BEEN SEEN

No man has seen God in His fulness. To do so would mean death. But there are a number of verses that show some in the Bible who saw part of God's glory while on earth. Only in their resurrected bodies can genuine Christians see the Lord when they get to Heaven.

Verses On Those Who Partially Saw God

- Exodus 33:11

"And <u>the LORD spake unto Moses face to face</u>, as a man speaketh unto his friend. And he turned again into the camp: but his servant Joshua, the son of Nun, a young man, departed not out of the tabernacle."

<u>The LORD spoke to Moses face-to-face as a man speaking to his friend</u>.

- Exodus 33:13-15

"Now therefore, I pray thee, if I have found grace in thy sight, shew me now thy way, that I may know thee, that I may find grace in thy sight: and consider that this nation *is* thy people. And he said, <u>My presence shall go *with thee*</u>, and I will give thee rest. And he said unto him, If thy presence go not *with me*, carry us not up hence."

> **GOD WENT WITH MOSES IN THE WILDERNESS**
> God promised Moses that His presence would go with him through the wilderness and on into the promised land.

- **Exodus 33:18-23**

"And he said, I beseech thee, shew me thy glory. And he said, I will make all my goodness pass before thee, and I will proclaim the name of the LORD before thee; and will be gracious to whom I will be gracious, and will shew mercy on whom I will shew mercy. And he said, Thou canst not see my face: for there shall no man see me, and live. And the LORD said, Behold, *there is* a place by me, and thou shalt stand upon a rock: And it shall come to pass, while my glory passeth by, that I will put thee in a clift of the rock, and will cover thee with my hand while I pass by: And I will take away mine hand, and thou shalt see my back parts: but my face shall not be seen."

People would die if they would see the face of God. So God put Moses in a clift of the rock and covered him with His hand while He passed by. Moses saw only the back parts of the LORD, but not His face.

- **Job 19:26**

"And *though* after my skin *worms* destroy this *body*, yet in my flesh shall I see God:"

Job would see God in his newly-resurrected body. Peter writes to the Christians that are already saved; he talks about the Lord Jesus Christ.

- **1 Peter 1:8**

"Whom having not seen, ye love; in whom, though now ye see *him* not, yet believing, ye rejoice with joy unspeakable and full of glory:"

> **PETER'S READERS HAD NOT SEEN CHRIST**
> The people to whom Peter was writing had not seen the Lord Jesus Christ, but still loved Him. So with true Christians today.

- **1 John 3:2**

"Beloved, now are we the sons of God, and it doth not yet appear what we shall be: but we know that, when he shall appear, we shall be like him; for we shall see him as he is."

Genuine Christians in their resurrected bodies will be made like to the Lord Jesus Christ and shall see Him as He is.

- **Revelation 1:7**
"Behold, he cometh with clouds; and every eye shall see him, and they *also* which pierced him: and all kindreds of the earth shall wail because of him. Even so, Amen."
The second phase of the coming of the Lord Jesus Christ is to set up His millennial reign; every eye shall see Him.

1 John 4:13

"Hereby know we that we dwell in him, and he in us, because he hath given us of his Spirit."

To the true Christians, Peter said they dwell in the Lord and He in them because He has given them His Holy Spirit.

Verses On The Indwelling Of The Holy Spirit

- **John 14:17**
"*Even* the Spirit of truth; whom the world cannot receive, because it seeth him not, neither knoweth him: but ye know him; for he dwelleth with you, and shall be in you."

THE CHRISTIANS' INDWELLING HOLY SPIRIT

The Lord Jesus Christ talked with His disciples about the Holy Spirit. The Holy Spirit was dwelling with them, but one day, in the future Age of Grace, He would be dwelling in the genuine Christians.

- **Romans 8:11**
"But if the Spirit of him that raised up Jesus from the dead dwell in you, he that raised up Christ from the dead shall also quicken your mortal bodies by his Spirit that dwelleth in you."
The indwelling of the Spirit of God is mentioned by Paul as being a present reality for all true Christians.

- **1 Corinthians 3:16**
"Know ye not that ye are the temple of God, and *that* the Spirit of God dwelleth in you?"
This is another clear teaching that God the Holy Spirit dwells in every genuine Christian. They are His temple.

- **2 Timothy 1:14**
"That good thing which was committed unto thee keep by the Holy Ghost which dwelleth in us."

TRUE CHRISTIANS HAVE BOTH FLESH AND SPIRIT

The "*us*" here, refers to true Christians. Today, every genuine Christian has God the Holy Spirit indwelling them in addition to their old flesh nature.

1 John 4:14

"**And we have seen and do testify that the Father sent the Son to be the Saviour of the world.**"

The Apostle John observed the Lord Jesus Christ very carefully.

THE MEANING OF THE GREEK WORD, "THEAOMAI"

The Greek Word for "*have seen*" here is THEAOMAI. Some of the meanings of this Greek Word are:

> "*1) to behold, look upon, view attentively, contemplate (often used of public shows); 1a) of important persons that are looked on with admiration; 2) to view, take a view of; 2a) in the sense of visiting, meeting with a person; 3) to learn by looking, to see with the eyes, to perceive.*"

SALVATION OFFERED TO THE ENTIRE WORLD

God the Father sent His Son into this world to be the "*Saviour of the world.*" The Father wanted all people to trust His Son, not just a small group of "*the elect*" as the hyper-Calvinists heretically teach. He made provision for the whole world to have a Saviour. However, they must meet God's conditions before they are saved by this Saviour. They must genuinely trust and accept the Lord Jesus Christ as their Saviour before they can receive His gift of everlasting life.

Verses On Christ As The Saviour

- Luke 2:11

"For unto you is born this day in the city of David a Saviour, which is Christ the Lord."

SALVATION FOR ALL WHO ACCEPT CHRIST

The Lord Jesus Christ the Saviour provided for the entire world. It's not that all the world is saved, but all the world is able to be saved if they would accept and trust the Lord Jesus Christ as their Saviour.

- **John 4:42**
"And said unto the woman, Now we believe, not because of thy saying: for we have heard *him* ourselves, and know that this is indeed the Christ, the Saviour of the world."

Even the woman at the well recognized the Lord Jesus Christ as the Saviour of the world.

- **Acts 5:31**
"Him hath God exalted with his right hand *to be* a Prince and a Saviour, for to give repentance to Israel, and forgiveness of sins."

The mission of the Lord Jesus Christ was to be both a Prince and a Saviour.

- **Acts 13:23**
"Of this man's seed hath God according to *his* promise raised unto Israel a Saviour, Jesus:"

The Saviour was from the seed of David.

- **Philippians 3:20**
"For our conversation is in heaven; from whence also we look for the Saviour, the Lord Jesus Christ:"

Genuine Christians should look for the return of the Saviour, the Lord Jesus Christ.

- **2 Timothy 1:10**
"But is now made manifest by the appearing of our Saviour Jesus Christ, who hath abolished death, and hath brought life and immortality to light through the gospel:"

Our Saviour is one of the Lord Jesus Christ's titles.

- **Titus 1:4**
"To Titus, *mine* own son after the common faith: Grace, mercy, *and* peace, from God the Father and the Lord Jesus Christ our Saviour."

The Saviour's title is used in Paul's greeting to Pastor Titus.

- **Titus 2:13**
"Looking for that blessed hope, and the glorious appearing of the great God and our Saviour Jesus Christ;"

True Christians will meet their Saviour, the Lord Jesus Christ, at His pre-Tribulation Rapture.

- **Titus 3:6**
"Which he shed on us abundantly through Jesus Christ our Saviour;"

God's grace comes through the Lord Jesus Christ, the Saviour.

- **2 Peter 1:1**
"Simon Peter, a servant and an apostle of Jesus Christ, to them that have obtained like precious faith with us through the righteousness of God and our Saviour Jesus Christ:"
- **2 Peter 1:11**
"For so an entrance shall be ministered unto you abundantly into the everlasting kingdom of our Lord and Saviour Jesus Christ."

The Lord Jesus Christ, the Saviour, will one day set up His Millennial Kingdom on this earth.

- **2 Peter 2:20**
"For if after they have escaped the pollutions of the world through the knowledge of the Lord and Saviour Jesus Christ, they are again entangled therein, and overcome, the latter end is worse with them than the beginning."

The Lord and Saviour can keep genuine Christians from being entangled in the sins of the world.

- **2 Peter 3:2**
"That ye may be mindful of the words which were spoken before by the holy prophets, and of the commandment of us the apostles of the Lord and Saviour:"

Peter was one of the apostles of the Lord and Saviour.

- **2 Peter 3:18**
"But grow in grace, and *in* the knowledge of our Lord and Saviour Jesus Christ. To him *be* glory both now and for ever. Amen."

True Christians must grow in their knowledge of their Lord and Saviour, Jesus Christ. This is found by studying the Bible.

1 John 4:15

"Whosoever shall confess that Jesus is the Son of God, God dwelleth in him, and he in God."

"THE SON OF GOD" A TITLE FOR CHRIST

The Son of God is one of the many titles for the Lord Jesus Christ. That's why God had trouble with the Jews and the Romans. They said Christ blasphemed because He said he was the Son of God. This title clearly implies His Deity.

Verses On The Son Of God

- **Daniel 3:25**
"He answered and said, Lo, I see four men loose, walking in the midst of the fire, and they have no hurt; and the form of the fourth is like the Son of God."

The modern corrupt versions are completely wrong in their translation of this verse. When Shadrach, Meshach and Abednego, were put in the fiery furnace, the king said that he saw a fourth person "*like the Son of God*" which was the Lord Jesus Christ in His pre-incarnate state. The modern versions say: "*like unto a son of the gods.*"

- **Matthew 4:3**

"And when the tempter came to him, he said, If thou be the Son of God, command that these stones be made bread."

Satan questioned whether or not the Lord Jesus Christ was the Son of God. He didn't take up Satan's challenge at that time, though He could have performed such a miracle.

- **Matthew 4:6**

"And saith unto him, If thou be the Son of God, cast thyself down: for it is written, He shall give his angels charge concerning thee: and in *their* hands they shall bear thee up, lest at any time thou dash thy foot against a stone."

Satan again doubted whether the Lord Jesus Christ was the Son of God.

- **Matthew 8:29**

"And, behold, they cried out, saying, What have we to do with thee, Jesus, thou Son of God? art thou come hither to torment us before the time?"

The devils knew the Lord Jesus Christ was indeed the Son of God.

- **Matthew 14:33**

"Then they that were in the ship came and worshipped him, saying, Of a truth thou art the Son of God."

The disciples realized the Lord Jesus Christ was the Son of God by His miracle of quieting this storm.

- **Matthew 26:63**

"But Jesus held his peace. And the high priest answered and said unto him, I adjure thee by the living God, that thou tell us whether thou be the Christ, the Son of God."

The Jewish high priest wanted the Lord Jesus Christ to commit blasphemy to the Jews by admitting He was the Son of God.

- **Matthew 27:40**

"And saying, Thou that destroyest the temple, and buildest *it* in three days, save thyself. If thou be the Son of God, come down from the cross."

> **A CENTURION DENIED CHRIST AS THE SON OF GOD**
> One of the Roman centurions asked the Saviour to come down from the cross if He really was the Son of God. He remained on the cross, taking on Himself the sins of the world.

- **Matthew 27:43**

"He trusted in God; let him deliver him now, if he will have him: for he said, I am the Son of God."

One of the centurions mocked the Lord Jesus Christ and God His Father.

- **Matthew 27:54**

"Now when the centurion, and they that were with him, watching Jesus, saw the earthquake, and those things that were done, they feared greatly, saying, Truly this was the Son of God."

> **THIS CENTURION SAW CHRIST AS THE SON OF GOD**
> This Roman centurion believed that the Lord Jesus Christ was truly the Son of God because of the earthquake and the things that happened at His death.

- **Mark 1:1**

"The beginning of the gospel of Jesus Christ, the Son of God;" Mark used this term at the beginning of his Gospel.

- **Luke 1:35**

"And the angel answered and said unto her, The Holy Ghost shall come upon thee, and the power of the Highest shall overshadow thee: therefore also that holy thing which shall be born of thee shall be called the Son of God."

> **THE NECESSITY OF CHRIST'S VIRGIN BIRTH**
> The Lord Jesus Christ is the Son of God. Because of His virgin birth, He became a perfect Son of Man as well, combining perfect Deity with Perfect Humanity.

- **Luke 22:70**

"Then said they all, Art thou then the Son of God? And he said unto them, Ye say that I am."

The Jewish Sanhedrin asked the Lord Jesus Christ if He were the Son of God in order to condemn Him for blasphemy.

- **John 1:34**

"And I saw, and bare record that this is the Son of God."

John the Baptist bare record that the Saviour is the Son of God.

- **John 3:18**
"He that believeth on him is not condemned: but he that believeth not is condemned already, because he hath not believed in the name of the only begotten Son of God."

> **CHRIST WAS AND IS THE ETERNAL SON OF GOD**
> The Lord Jesus Christ is the only eternally begotten (an eternal relationship with God the Father) Son of God. Because of this uniqueness, people must genuinely believe on Him to receive forgiveness and everlasting life.

John 5:25
"Verily, verily, I say unto you, The hour is coming, and now is, when the dead shall hear the voice of the Son of God: and they that hear shall live."
At the time of the resurrection of the genuine Christians, they will hear the voice of the Son of God and be raised in glorified bodies.

- **John 11:27**
"She saith unto him, Yea, Lord: I believe that thou art the Christ, the Son of God, which should come into the world."
Martha was certain that the Lord Jesus Christ was the Son of God.

- **John 20:31**
"But these are written, that ye might believe that Jesus is the Christ, the Son of God; and that believing ye might have life through his name."

> **ETERNAL LIFE THROUGH FAITH IN THE SON OF GOD**
> The Apostle John gives, as the purpose of his book, that people might believe that the Lord Jesus Christ is the Son of God and that believing in Him, they might have everlasting life.

- **Acts 8:37**
"And Philip said, If thou believest with all thine heart, thou mayest. And he answered and said, I believe that Jesus Christ is the Son of God."
Phillip, one of the deacons of the early church, was taken out by the Spirit of God into the wilderness to meet a eunuch. Before Phillip baptized him, the eunuch said he believed that the Lord Jesus Christ was the Son of God. The Bible versions, in all languages of the world, that are based on the Gnostic Critical Greek text, omit this verse entirely.

- **Acts 9:20**
"And straightway he preached Christ in the synagogues, that he is the Son of God."

> **PAUL PREACHED CHRIST AS THE SON OF GOD**
> After Paul was saved by faith in the Lord Jesus Christ, he preached in the synagogues that He was the Son of God.

- **Romans 1:4**
"And declared *to be* the Son of God with power, according to the spirit of holiness, by the resurrection from the dead:"

The Lord Jesus Christ is declared in the Bible to be the Son of God.

- **Galatians 2:20**
"I am crucified with Christ: nevertheless I live; yet not I, but Christ liveth in me: and the life which I now live in the flesh I live by the faith of the Son of God, who loved me, and gave himself for me."

Paul lived by faith in the Son of God, the Lord Jesus Christ.

- **Hebrews 4:14**
"Seeing then that we have a great high priest, that is passed into the heavens, Jesus the Son of God, let us hold fast *our* profession."

Jesus, the Son of God, is the true Christians' Great High Priest Who is in Heaven.

- **1 John 3:8**
"He that committeth sin is of the devil; for the devil sinneth from the beginning. For this purpose the Son of God was manifested, that he might destroy the works of the devil."

> **DESTROYING THE WORKS OF THE DEVIL**
> One of the reasons that the Lord Jesus Christ, Son of God, came into the world, was to destroy the works of the Devil.

- **1 John 5:5**
"Who is he that overcometh the world, but he that believeth that Jesus is the Son of God?"

Believing in Jesus as the Son of God, overcomes the world.

- **1 John 5:12-13**
"He that hath the Son hath life; *and* he that hath not the Son of God hath not life. These things have I written unto you that believe on the name of the Son of God; that ye may know that ye have eternal life, and that ye may believe on the name of the Son of God."

> **ASSURANCE OF SALVATION NEEDED**
> Believing on the Lord Jesus Christ, as the Son of God, gives people assurance of their salvation.

1 John 4:16

"And we have known and believed the love that God hath to us. God is love; and he that dwelleth in love dwelleth in God, and God in him."

> **GOD LOVES RIGHTEOUSNESS AND HATES SIN**
> John's readers were genuine Christians who knew and believed in the love that God has for them. <u>One of the attributes of God is love. For these Christians to dwell in love with their fellow Christians means they are dwelling in fellowship with God.</u> The Bible's God loves righteousness and hates iniquity of any kind. He is righteous and holy in His love.

1 John 4:17

"Herein is our love made perfect, that we may have boldness in the day of judgment: because as he is, so are we in this world."

The love of the genuine Christians should be made perfect so they might have boldness.

> **THE MEANING OF THE GREEK WORD, "TELEIOO"**
> The Greek Word for *"perfect"* is TELEIOO. Some of the meanings of this Greek Word are:
>
> > *"1) to make perfect, complete; 1a) to carry through completely, to accomplish, finish, bring to an end; 2) to complete (perfect); 2a) add what is yet wanting in order to render a thing full; 2b) to be found perfect; 3) to bring to the end (goal) proposed; 4) to accomplish; 4a) bring to a close or fulfilment by event; 4a1) of the prophecies of the scriptures."*

God wants all true Christians to have boldness in their testimony for the Lord Jesus Christ.

> **THE MEANING OF THE GREEK WORD, "PARESIA"**
> The Greek Word for "*boldness*" is PARESIA. Some of the meanings of this Greek Word are:
>> "*1) freedom in speaking, unreservedness in speech; 1a) openly, frankly, i.e without concealment; 1b) without ambiguity or circumlocution; 1c) without the use of figures and comparisons; 2) free and fearless confidence, cheerful courage, boldness, assurance; 3) the deportment by which one becomes conspicuous or secures publicity.*"

<u>Genuine Christians can have and should have boldness in the day of judgment</u>. Those who are lost might be bold in a wicked way, but true Christians must be bold in a godly way.

<u>Notice the last part of this verse: "*as he is, so are we in this world.*" This is speaking about genuine Christians who are living in this world. The Lord Jesus was despised, hated, and ridiculed. So it will happen to true Christians who love the Lord Jesus Christ. The world does not love saved people. They love their worldly kind.</u>

Verses On Boldness
- Acts 4:13

"Now when <u>they saw the boldness of Peter and John</u>, and perceived that they were unlearned and ignorant men, they marvelled; and they took knowledge of them, that they had been with Jesus."

> **BOLDNESS IN CHRIST THOUGH UNLEARNED**
> <u>The boldness for their Saviour by these ignorant and unlearned fishermen was observed by those who saw them.</u> It was evident that they had been with the Lord Jesus Christ.

- Acts 4:29

"And now, Lord, behold their threatenings: and grant unto thy servants, that <u>with all boldness they may speak thy word</u>," <u>The disciples prayed for boldness</u> to speak God's Words in the midst of threats by the Roman unbelievers. <u>That must be the prayer of genuine Christians today as well.</u>

- Acts 4:31

"And when they had prayed, the place was shaken where they were assembled together; and they were all filled with the Holy Ghost, and they spake the word of God with boldness."

When they were assembled together, Peter and John were filled with the Holy Spirit and spoke God's Words with all boldness.

- Ephesians 3:12

"In whom we have boldness and access with confidence by the faith of him."

TRUE CHRISTIANS HAVE BOLDNESS AND ACCESS

Paul told the church at Ephesus that they, as well as true Christians today, have boldness and access to God the Father and His Son, the Lord Jesus Christ.

- Philippians 1:20

"According to my earnest expectation and *my* hope, that in nothing I shall be ashamed, but *that* with all boldness, as always, *so* now also Christ shall be magnified in my body, whether *it be* by life, or by death."

Paul was in jail when he wrote these words. He hoped that he would never be ashamed of his Saviour, but with all boldness He would be magnified by him, whether by his life, or by his death.

- Hebrews 10:19

"Having therefore, brethren, boldness to enter into the holiest by the blood of Jesus,"

Genuine Christians have boldness to enter into the holiest place in Heaven by the blood of the Lord Jesus Christ.

Verses On Judgment

TWO JUDGMENTS FOR PEOPLE–FOR SAVED & LOST

There are two future judgments for people. For the true Christians, there will be the judgment seat of Christ. For all the non-Christians, there will be the Great White Throne Judgment.

- Romans 14:10

"But why dost thou judge thy brother? or why dost thou set at nought thy brother? for we shall all stand before the judgment seat of Christ."

May genuine Christians have boldness as they appear before the Judgment Seat of Christ.

- **1 Corinthians 4:5**

"Therefore judge nothing before the time, until the Lord come, who both will bring to light the hidden things of darkness, and will make manifest the counsels of the hearts: and then shall every man have praise of God."

Final judgment must be postponed from the present to the future when the Lord Jesus Christ will be the Judge.

- **2 Corinthians 5:10**

"For we must all appear before the judgment seat of Christ; that every one may receive the things *done* in *his* body, according to that he hath done, whether *it be* good or bad."

This is the judgment of all true Christians. It will be based on what they have done or not done for the Lord Jesus Christ after being saved.

1 John 4:18

"There is no fear in love; but perfect love casteth out fear: because fear hath torment. He that feareth is not made perfect in love."

NO FEAR IN TRUE CHRISTIAN LOVE

This verse teaches that there is no fear in genuine Christian love, but perfect love casts out fear. Fear means that love is not perfect.

Verses On Fear

- **John 19:38**

"And after this Joseph of Arimathaea, being a disciple of Jesus, but secretly for fear of the Jews, besought Pilate that he might take away the body of Jesus: and Pilate gave *him* leave. He came therefore, and took the body of Jesus."

True Christians must not be afraid like Joseph of Arimathaea.

- **John 20:19**

"Then the same day at evening, being the first *day* of the week, when the doors were shut where the disciples were assembled for fear of the Jews, came Jesus and stood in the midst, and saith unto them, Peace *be* unto you."

MEETING ON THE FIRST DAY OF THE WEEK

The disciples of the Lord Jesus Christ met on the first day of the week (Sunday). This is why genuine Christian churches worship on Sunday rather than Saturday or some other day. The doors were shut because the disciples feared the Jews. The Lord Jesus Christ appeared in their midst and gave them His peace for their fear.

- Acts 5:5

"And Ananias hearing these words fell down, and gave up the ghost: and great fear came on all them that heard these things."

This was a case where Ananias and Sapphira had lied to the Holy Spirit and to the church. When God took their lives because of this, great fear came upon all those who heard about this.

- 2 Timothy 1:7

"For God hath not given us the spirit of fear; but of power, and of love, and of a sound mind."

THE EFFECTS OF THE SPIRIT OF GOD

The spirit of fear is not from God. That's not what the Holy Spirit is but of power, and of love, and of a sound mind. That's what the Spirit of God brings to us who are saved.

- Hebrews 2:14-15

"Forasmuch then as the children are partakers of flesh and blood, he also himself likewise took part of the same; that through death he might destroy him that had the power of death, that is, the devil; And deliver them who through fear of death were all their lifetime subject to bondage."

CHRIST'S BODILY RESURRECTION REMOVED FEAR

The Lord Jesus Christ's bodily resurrection was to remove the fear of death from His true Christian followers.

- Hebrews 13:6

"So that we may boldly say, The Lord *is* my helper, and I will not fear what man shall do unto me."

With the Lord Jesus Christ as their Helper, genuine Christians do not have to fear what man might do to them.

1 John 4:19

"We love him, because he first loved us."

GOD'S LOVE WAS FIRST
God loved sinful mankind first. True Christians are enabled to love Him because He first loved them.

Verses On God's Love

- **Romans 5:8**

"But <u>God commendeth his love toward us</u>, in that, while we were yet sinners, Christ died for us."

GOD'S LOVE EXPRESSED IN CHRIST'S DEATH
God's love was expressed to mankind by Christ's dying for them while they were yet sinners.

- **Ephesians 2:4**

"But <u>God</u>, who is rich in mercy, <u>for his great love wherewith he loved us</u>,"

God's richness of mercy was shown by His great love that He showed for sinful people.

- **Titus 3:4-5**

"But after that the kindness and <u>love of God</u> our Saviour toward man appeared, Not by works of righteousness which we have done, but according to his mercy he saved us, by the washing of regeneration, and renewing of the Holy Ghost;"

LOVE IS A GREAT MOTIVATOR
Motivated by His love, God can save those who sincerely trust in His Son, the Lord Jesus Christ.

- **1 John 3:1**

"Behold, <u>what manner of love the Father hath bestowed upon us</u>, that we should be called the sons of God: therefore the world knoweth us not, because it knew him not."

God's manner of love made it possible for genuine Christians to become His children.

- **1 John 3:16**

"Hereby perceive we <u>the love *of God*</u>, because he laid down his life for us: and we ought to lay down *our* lives for the brethren."

CHRISTIANS MUST CARE FOR ONE ANOTHER
Because the Lord Jesus Christ laid down His life for every human being, those who have trusted Him as their Saviour should lay down their lives, if need be, for their brethren.

- 1 John 4:9-10

"In this was manifested the love of God toward us, because that God sent his only begotten Son into the world, that we might live through him. Herein is love, not that we loved God, but that he loved us, and sent his Son *to be* the propitiation for our sins."

The Lord Jesus Christ laid down His life as a propitiation for all mankind so that genuine Christians might live through Him.

1 John 4:20

"If a man say, I love God, and hateth his brother, he is a liar: for he that loveth not his brother whom he hath seen, how can he love God whom he hath not seen?"

GOD'S DEFINITION OF A "LIAR"
God gives a definition of a *"liar"* here. It applies to people who say they love God but hate their fellow Christians. These kinds of people God calls *"liars."* I know personally many such *"liars"*--do you as well?

Verses On Hatred

- Matthew 5:43-44

"Ye have heard that it hath been said, Thou shalt love thy neighbour, and hate thine enemy. But I say unto you, Love your enemies, bless them that curse you, do good to them that hate you, and pray for them which despitefully use you, and persecute you;"

MUSLIMS MURDER THEIR ENEMIES
The Muslims murder their enemies, calling Jews and Christians infidels. The Lord Jesus Christ commanded His followers to love their enemies and do good to them who persecute them. This is a difficult command to obey in the natural flesh. It can be accomplished only by the power and direction of the Lord.

- **Matthew 24:9-10**
"Then shall they deliver you up to be afflicted, and shall kill you: and <u>ye shall be hated of all nations for my name's sake</u>. And then shall many be offended, and shall betray one another, and shall hate one another."

Hatred by non-Christians for true Christians was prophesied by the Lord Jesus Christ.

- **Luke 6:22**
"<u>Blessed are ye, when men shall hate you</u>, and when they shall separate you *from their company*, and shall reproach *you*, and cast out your name as evil, for the Son of man's sake."

> **HATED FOR CHRIST'S SAKE**
> The Lord Jesus Christ said that being hated for being true Christians <u>is a form of a blessing</u>. Make sure it's for His sake that the hatred comes.

- **John 15:18**
"<u>If the world hate you</u>, ye know that it hated me before *it hated* you."

> **HATRED FOR CHRIST AND HATRED FOR CHRISTIANS**
> The world's hatred of genuine Christians was preceded by their hatred of the Lord Jesus Christ.

Verses On Christian Love

- **John 13:34**
"A new commandment I give unto you, <u>That ye love one another</u>; as I have loved you, that ye also love one another."

> **TRUE CHRISTIANS ARE TO LOVE AS CHRIST LOVED**
> The measure of fellow Christians' love for each other is as the Lord Jesus Christ loved them.

- **Romans 13:8**
"Owe no man any thing, but to <u>love one another</u>: for he that loveth another hath fulfilled the law."

Fellow Christians who love one another have fulfilled the law. In the comments on 1 John 5:2, commands given in the New Testament are discussed.

- **1 Thessalonians 4:9**
"But as touching <u>brotherly love</u> ye need not that I write unto you: for ye yourselves are taught of God to <u>love one another</u>."

> **RECIPROCAL LOVE NOT PRACTICED MUCH TODAY**
> Reciprocal Christian love, though somewhat scarce today, is taught by God.

- 1 Peter 1:22

"Seeing ye have purified your souls in obeying the truth through the Spirit unto unfeigned love of the brethren, see that ye love one another with a pure heart fervently:"

> **LOVING FELLOW CHRISTIANS**
> Fellow Christians should have pure and fervent love with one another.

1 John 4:21

And this commandment have we from him, That he who loveth God love his brother also."

> **DIVINE LOVE FOR TRUE FELLOW CHRISTIANS**
> The command that true Christians have from the God of the Bible is that <u>if we love Him, we must love our fellow Christians also</u>. This Divine love for fellow Christians must be maintained regardless of how many false doctrines they might hold. We can despise and hate any false doctrine, but God expects us to love those who are genuinely born-again and saved. <u>Though this is extremely difficult, God expects it of all genuine Christians</u>.

1 John
Chapter Five

1 John 5:1

"Whosoever believeth that Jesus is the Christ is born of God: and every one that loveth him that begat loveth him also that is begotten of him."

The Apostle John insists that those who truly love the Lord Jesus Christ must love others who are also genuine Christians. It doesn't mean that there must be agreement in each other's doctrines and practices, but love should be present regardless of other differences.

BORN OF GOD DEFINED CLEARLY

He defines who are *"born of God."* It is those who believe *"that Jesus is the Christ."* *"Christ"* means the Anointed One. It is the Old Testament Word *"Messiah"* which also means the Anointed One. If people believe the Lord Jesus Christ is the One that God promised in the Old Testament and genuinely trust in Him as their Saviour, they are *"born of God."*

THE MEANING OF THE GREEK WORD, "GENNAO"

The Greek verb for *"born"* is GENNAO. It is in the Greek perfect tense which indicates an action that began in the past and whose results continue into the present and on into the future. What this means is that once people are genuinely *"born of God,"* they possess eternal life forever and will never lose it. They might be disobedient on occasion and lose their fellowship, but they do not lose their eternal life and their salvation.

- 1 John 1:9

"If we confess our sins, he is faithful and just to forgive us *our* sins, and to cleanse us from all unrighteousness."

1 John 5:2

"By this we know that we love the children of God, when we love God, and keep his commandments."

> **LOVING GOD AND LOVING FELLOW CHRISTIANS**
>
> When people are genuine Christians and love God, they also should love other true Christians. This is true if these Christians keep God's commandments.

Recently I was given a list of New Testament commandments or orders. Do you know how many commandments or orders there are in the New Testament that every Christian should obey? There are a total of 1,050 such orders and commands. There are 23 pages of these New Testament commandments divided into 68 different categories. For example, there are 7 commands to abstain, 7 commands to avoid, 3 commands to ask, 74 to be, and so on. If you want a copy of this 23-page document, just request *"COMMANDMENTS IN THE NEW TESTAMENT"* and send a gift to the Bible For Today of $6.00 + $4.00 S&H.

> **THE MEANING OF THE GREEK WORD, "TEREO"**
>
> The Greek Word for *"keep"* is TEREO. Some of the meanings of that Greek Word are:
>
> *"1) to attend to carefully, take care of;
> 1a) to guard; 1b) metaph. to keep, one in
> the state in which he is; 1c) to observe;
> 1d) to reserve: to undergo something."*
>
> God wants all genuine Christians to be obedient to His New Testament commands and orders. May God give each of them the will, grace, and power to do this.

1 John 5:3

"For this is the love of God, that we keep his commandments: and his commandments are not grievous."

The love of God is shown clearly when true Christians keep His commandments, referring to those 1,050 found in the New Testament. These commandments are not grievous.

THE MEANING OF THE GREEK WORD, "BARUS"

The Greek Word for *"grievous"* is BARUS. Some of the meanings of that Greek Word are:

> *"1) heavy in weight; 2) metaph. 2a) burdensome; 2b) severe, stern; 2c) weighty; 2c1) of great moment; 2d) violent, cruel, unsparing"*

They are meant for the good and welfare of the genuine Christians who keep them.

Many of the Old Testament commandments were very burdensome and strict. The Jews were not supposed to travel more than a Sabbath day's journey. Taking God's Name in vain or cursing your father or mother would bring the death penalty as well as performing many other violations.

1 John 5:4

"For whatsoever is born of God overcometh the world: and this is the victory that overcometh the world, even our faith."

As used before, the Greek Word for *"born"* is GENNAO. It is in the Greek perfect tense which signifies an action that happened in the past and continues to the present and future. Those who are thus born of God and thus born-again have gained a "victory" that can continue to overcome this wicked world.

THE MEANING OF THE GREEK WORD, "NIKE"

The Greek Word for *"victory"* is NIKE. It is related to the Greek Word for *"overcome"* which is NIKAO. Some of the meanings of this Greek Word are:

> *"1) to conquer; 1a) to carry off the victory, come off victorious; 1a1) of Christ, victorious over all His foes; 1a2) of Christians, that hold fast their faith even unto death against the power of their foes, and temptations and persecutions; 1a3) when one is arraigned or goes to law, to win the case, maintain one's cause"*

Those who are genuine Christians should not be defeated by the wicked world that surrounds them. They have three enemies:
(1) the world around them
(2) the flesh inside them
(3) the Devil who resists them

The genuine Christian should never be defeated and overcome by this world. And yet, even many true Christians are going right along with the sinful practices of the world, often fashioning themselves to look like the world, dress like the world, talk like the world, act like the world, and go to worldly and ungodly places like the world. God does not want them to participate in these evil things in this world, but has given them a victory to overcome all of them. God has given them a new birth, a new destiny, and a new power to overcome the sins that abound in this world. The thing that continues to overcome and defeat the sins of this world is their faith.

"THE FAITH" REFERS TO BIBLE DOCTRINES

The Greek Word for *"faith"* is PISTIS. Without the Greek article, it would refer to their personal faith in the Lord Jesus Christ. In this verse, it has the Greek article. As such, it refers to the doctrines and theology found in the Bible. It is the reading, study, and following of the Bible that can overcome this wicked world.

This is why it is very important that you have the proper and accurate Bible to read and to obey. In English, it is very important for people to read and follow the King James Bible because of its proper foundational original and preserved Words of Hebrew, Aramaic, and Greek as well as its accurate translation of those original Words.

GNOSTIC TEXTS ALTER 356 DOCTRINAL PASSAGES

The other English translations that are based on the false Gnostic Critical Greek text (such as the ASV, RSV, NIV, NASV, ESV, and many others) change the Greek New Testament in over 8,000 places including over 356 doctrinal passages. Almost all of these 356 doctrinal passages are because of their conformity to the false theology of Gnosticism that contaminated the Vatican and Sinai Greek New Testament manuscripts in Alexandria, Egypt, the headquarters of the Gnostic religion.

The doctrines of the faith, if believed, exalted, and practiced by genuine Christians, will overcome the wicked teachings and practices of the world. These Bible doctrines include the Deity of Christ, His miracles, His bodily resurrection, His blood atonement, His coming again, and all of the other Biblical doctrines.

1 John 5:5

"Who is he that overcometh the world, but he that believeth that Jesus is the Son of God?"

True Christians can overcome and have victory over the evil world because they believe that the Lord Jesus Christ is the Son of God. They believe, without any question, in the Deity of the Lord Jesus Christ as well as in His perfect and sinless Humanity. He is and was the God-Man, perfect God and perfect Man.

1 John 5:6

"This is he that came by water and blood, even Jesus Christ; not by water only, but by water and blood. And it is the Spirit that beareth witness, because the Spirit is truth."

> **CHRIST'S INCARNATION BY WATER AND BLOOD**
> He's talking about the Son of God, but not simply the One who is Deity, but the One who came *"by water and by blood."* I believe this refers to the Incarnation of the Lord Jesus Christ, and how God the Son became perfect Man through the miraculous virgin birth.

The "water" would speak of the breaking of the water before birth. The blood would mean that the Lord Jesus Christ had "blood" in His perfect Human body which was given by the Holy Spirit. Since medical information has blood coming from the father of a child, not its mother, the Lord Jesus Christ had no human blood, but blood from the power of God. The Lord Jesus Christ's blood was perfect and sinless blood, prepared by God the Father (Hebrews 10:5) without any of Adam's sinfulness in it.

> **Hebrews 10:5** *"Wherefore when he cometh into the world, he saith, Sacrifice and offering thou wouldest not, but a body hast thou prepared me:"*

From this verse, it is clear that every part of the body of the Lord Jesus Christ was prepared by God the Father. This included

His bones, His sinews, His blood, and every part of His body. This was accomplished by the miracle of His virgin birth.

"*And it is the Spirit that beareth witness, because the Spirit is truth*" (1 John 5:6c) God the Holy Spirit, by communicating the Words from the Lord Jesus Christ to the human writers, bears record of the truth found in our Bible.

> **John 16:12** "*I have yet many things to say unto you, but ye cannot bear them now.*"
>
> **John 16:13** "*Howbeit when he, the Spirit of truth, is come, he will guide you into all truth: for he shall not speak of himself; but whatsoever he shall hear, that shall he speak: and he will shew you things to come.*"
>
> **John 16:14** "*He shall glorify me: for he shall receive of mine, and shall shew it unto you.*"
>
> **John 16:15** "*All things that the Father hath are mine: therefore said I, that he shall take of mine, and shall shew it unto you.*"

THE HOLY SPIRIT WITNESSES ABOUT CHRIST

God the Holy Spirit bears truthful witness about the Lord Jesus Christ in all of His Person and work. He is perfect God and perfect Man. Jesus is a merciful and faithful High Priest for all genuine Christians. He died for the sins of the world, rose again bodily, ascended up to Heaven, and is now the Great High Priest for those whom He has redeemed and saved.

The Spirit is truth and bears witness of all the doctrines of the Bible both of the New Testament and the Old Testament. That's the reason we must use the proper Hebrew, Aramaic, and Greek Words, properly translated, as in our King James Bible, so we can know the truth. The translations not founded upon the proper original-language Words and not properly translated should not be used. Incorrectly chosen and mistranslated Words cannot reveal the full truth the Holy Spirit has given to us.

The New Testament translations founded on the false Gnostic, Critical Greek Texts such as used by the Westcott and Hort, Nestle Aland, and United Bible Society editions, change the King James Bible's Greek text in over 8,000 places, including over 356 doctrinal passages. These details can be found in Dr. Jack Moorman's book *8,000 Differences Between The Critical Text and the Received Text* (**BFT #3984 @ $29.00 + $10.00 S&H**).

Bibles in all languages of the world must come from the proper Hebrew, Aramaic, and Greek Words and must be translated accurately to preserve the Holy Spirit's truth for today.

1 John 5:7-8

"For there are three that bear record [in heaven, the Father, the Word, and the Holy Ghost: and these three are one. (v. 8) And there are three that bear witness in earth,] the Spirit, and the water, and the blood: and these three agree in one."

> **THE TRINITY IS TAUGHT IN THESE VERSES**
>
> I have put verses 7 and 8 together to show the words of the Trinity that are denied by the Gnostics and all the other modern apostates. All the [BRACKETED] words above indicate what the Gnostic Critical Greek Text, based on the false Vatican and Sinai manuscripts, have removed.
>
> This is a denial of the Trinity. *"In heaven"* [where God dwells] is gone, *"the Father"* [God the Father] is gone, and *"the Word"* [God the Son] is gone, *"the Holy Ghost"* [God the Holy Spirit] is gone, *"and these three are one"* [the Trinity of God] is gone, *"And there are three that bear witness in earth,"* [the earthly witnesses]; they're all gone except in the King James Bible.

The false Greek text merely reads these two verses as follows: *"For there are three that bear record the Spirit, and the water, and the blood: and these three agree in one."* I recommend Dr. Jack Moorman's brief summary defending 1 John 5:7-8 for all to read. It is *1 John 5:7-8 Authenticated & Summarized* **(BFT #2249 @ $5.00 + $3.00 S&H).**

(1) Dr. Moorman lists the six Greek manuscripts and the eleven Early Church Fathers who quoted from the verses in full.

(2) He gives the internal evidence and grammatical contradictions with masculine and neuter genders of these above words which are left out from these verses.

(3) He gives the reason that those in charge of the Greek Orthodox Church at the time who denied the Trinity had them removed from many Greek manuscripts.

> **WHY WORDS OMITTED FROM THE GNOSTIC GREEK**
> Someone speculated that in around the 300's A.D., the head man in the Greek Orthodox Church, was an Arian. He denied the Trinity and possibly took out all the Greek manuscripts that have the verses 1 John 5:7-8 written out in full. He might have had the Words wiped out, in order to satisfy his denial of the Trinity.

1 John 5:9

"If we receive the witness of men, the witness of God is greater: for this is the witness of God which he hath testified of his Son."

It is sad that most people in the world receive the "witness of men" whether in newspapers, magazines, television, Internet, or other sources, but totally and completely reject the greater and much more truthful and reliable witness of God in the Words of the Bible.

Much of the witness that comes from human beings are lies, deception, or only half-truths. The lies of evolution, the lies of apostate doctrines and teachings of ministers, the lies about global warming, and many other lies have been accepted and believed by many humans on the earth today.

> **THE PERSON AND WORK OF CHRIST**
> The witness of God in the Bible concerns His testimony concerning His Son. This is a true witness.
> (1) It includes the Lord Jesus Christ's Incarnation
> (2) His virgin birth
> (3) His Deity
> (4) His omniscience
> (5) His omnipresence
> (6) His omnipotence
> (7) His miracles
> (8) His substitutionary death on the cross for the sins of the world
> (9) His bodily resurrection
> (10) His bodily ascension into Heaven
> (11) His session in Heaven as the Great High Priest
> (12) His return in the Rapture to remove all genuine

> Christians to Heaven
> (13) His return to reign in the Millennium for one thousand years

The only place that you'll find the testimony of God's Son, the Lord Jesus Christ, is in the Scriptures, the Word of God. It must be in a sound Bible like the King James Bible, which is based on the proper, inspired, and preserved Hebrew, Aramaic, and Greek Words. There are at least 356 passages in the New Testament which include doctrinal matters, many of them concerning the Person and Work of the Lord Jesus Christ. However, if these 356 passages are based upon the Gnostic Critical Greek Words and their translations, you won't find the full and complete witness to God's Son in these false Bibles.

Nor will you find the witness of God to His Son in funny papers, movies, theaters, radio, television, Internet, or in any other of man's communication. It is only to be found in accurately-translated Bibles, though very few now, in all the languages of the world.

1 John 5:10

"He that believeth on the Son of God hath the witness in himself: he that believeth not God hath made him a liar; because he believeth not the record that God gave of his Son."

"He that believeth on the Son of God" includes only those who have trusted the Lord Jesus Christ as Deity. If this be the case, they have the witness in themselves.

> **Colossians 1:27** *"To whom God would make known what is the riches of the glory of this mystery among the Gentiles; which is **Christ in you, the hope of glory:"***

That is the witness in the hearts and minds of all genuine Christians.

> **CHRIST'S RECORD IS FOUND IN THE BIBLE**
> The record that God the Father gave concerning His Son is found in the teachings of the Bible. Those people who deny that the Lord Jesus Christ is the Son of God have made God a liar. They are saying that God is a liar.

> **Romans 3:4** *"God forbid: yea, **let God be true, but every man a liar**; . . ."*

It is man who is the liar, not God!

Titus 1:2 *"In hope of eternal life, which **God, that cannot lie**, promised before the world began;"*

All the religious apostates and liberals call God a liar and deny the truth of His Words in the Bible.

The Bible is quite clear that by truly trusting the Lord Jesus Christ as Saviour is the only way to get to the Bible's Heaven. The Lord Jesus said it clearly in John 14:6.

- **John 14:6**

"Jesus saith unto him, I am the way, **the truth**, and the life: no man cometh unto the Father, but by me."

That's the only way. That's why these liberal versions and the false Greek texts have taken out two words of John 6:47,

- **John 6:47**

"Verily, verily, I say unto you, He that believeth **on me** hath everlasting life."

GNOSTICS REMOVED "ON ME" IN JOHN 6:47

These false Gnostic Critical Text translations remove *"on me."* By so doing, they are calling the Lord Jesus Christ a liar! The religious apostates deny the truths of the Bible including the bodily, physical resurrection of the Lord Jesus Christ, His perfect Deity and sinless character, His miracles, and His virgin birth. All the other doctrines of Christology and many other Biblical doctrines are distorted as well.

Christology involves the doctrines of the Lord Jesus Christ. If someone comes to your home and rejects the Bible's complete teachings about the Lord Jesus Christ, you are not to bid them God speed. To do so is to be a partaker of their evil deeds.

- **2 John 1:11**

"For **he that biddeth him God speed is partaker of his evil deeds**."

Genuine Christians should not have any dealings with those who don't believe the Biblical doctrines concerning the Lord Jesus Christ.

1 John 5:11

"And this is the record, that God hath given to us eternal life, and this life is in his Son."

ETERNAL LIFE IS ONLY IN CHRIST

One of the clear teachings of the Bible is the fact that God has talked about eternal life. The words, "*eternal life*" occur in 26 verses in our King James Bible. The words "*everlasting life*" occur in 11 more verses in our King James Bible. The only way to receive either eternal or everlasting life is for people to genuinely believe on the Lord Jesus Christ as their Saviour. Eternal and everlasting life are centered in God's Son, the Lord Jesus Christ, and in Him alone.

John 3:16 "For God so loved the world, that he gave his only begotten Son, that **whosoever believeth in him should not perish, but have everlasting life**."

John 17:3 "*And this is **life eternal**, that they might **know thee** the only true God, **and Jesus Christ, whom thou hast sent**.*"

Romans 6:23 "*For the wages of sin is death; but **the gift of God is eternal life through Jesus Christ our Lord**.*"

"*And this is the record, that God hath given to us eternal life*" but eternal life is not dispensed to everyone in this world, sad to say. It's for everyone in this world. The invitation is there for everyone in this world. Only the lost people who sincerely trust in the Lord Jesus Christ, can receive eternal life. People must have God's Son as their Saviour in order to have eternal life. This life is only in God's Son, the Lord Jesus Christ.

ETERNAL LIFE BRINGS NO SEPARATION FROM GOD

Those who possess this eternal life by having genuinely believed on and received the Lord Jesus Christ as their Saviour will never be separated from God. They will die physically. When that happens, their spirit and soul are separated from their bodies, but they will never be separated from God. Eternal death, on the other hand, is the separation of the spirit, soul, and body from God in Hell. This will last for all eternity to come.

1 John 5:12

"He that hath the Son hath life; and he that hath not the Son of God hath not life."

HAVING CHRIST AS SAVIOUR MEANS ETERNAL LIFE
This is very simple for anyone to understand. If you have the Lord Jesus Christ as your Saviour by genuine faith, you have eternal life. Those who have not truly received Him by faith do not possess eternal life. They are living in spiritual death. Upon their physical death, they will receive eternal death and will be sent to the Lake of Fire called Hell.

- John 3:15

"That **whosoever believeth in him should not perish**, but have eternal life."

The Lord Jesus Christ told to the Pharisee Nicodemus exactly how to receive eternal life.

- John 6:68

"Then Simon Peter answered him, Lord, to whom shall we go? **thou hast the words of eternal life**."

CHRIST HAS THE WORDS OF ETERNAL LIFE
Simon Peter and the other disciples were asked by the Lord Jesus Christ if they were going to leave Him like the other people. Peter answered that only He had the "*words of eternal life.*" No other One in all the world has eternal life to give to those who sincerely believe on Him.

- John 10:28-29

"And **I give unto them eternal life; and they shall never perish**, neither shall any *man* pluck them out of my hand. My Father, which gave *them* me, is greater than all; and no *man* is able to pluck *them* out of my Father's hand."

The Lord Jesus Christ alone can give true believers eternal life. True Christians are secure and shall never perish.

- Romans 6:23

"For the wages of sin *is* death; but **the gift of God *is* eternal life through Jesus Christ our Lord**."

Eternal life cannot be gained by good works. It is a gift of God given by genuine faith in the Lord Jesus Christ.

- **Titus 3:7**
"That being **justified by his grace, we should be made heirs according to the hope of eternal life.**"
Only by God's grace can eternal life be received by true faith in God's Son.
- **John 1:4**
"**In him was life**; and the life was the light of men"
Only in the Lord Jesus Christ is there eternal life. It can be found in no other faith or religion, but only in Him.
- **John 5:26**
"For as the Father hath life in himself; so hath **he given to the Son to have life in himself**;"
The Lord Jesus Christ has eternal life in Himself as God the Son and the Son of God.
- **John 5:40**
"And ye will not **come to me, that ye might have life.**"
The Pharisees didn't want to come to the Lord Jesus Christ that they might receive eternal life by true faith in Him. Their jealousy, resentment, and loss of the control of some of their traditions kept them from receiving Him.
- **John 6:33-34**
"For the bread of God is **he which cometh down from heaven, and giveth life unto the world**. Then said they unto him, Lord, evermore give us this bread."
The Lord Jesus Christ came down from Heaven to provide eternal life for those who truly trust Him as their Saviour.
- **John 6:40**
"And this is the will of him that sent me, that **every one which seeth the Son, and believeth on him, may have everlasting life**: and I will raise him up at the last day."
This is how everlasting life is obtained–only by genuine faith in the Saviour.
- **John 6:47**
"Verily, verily, I say unto you, **He that believeth on me hath everlasting life.**"
The way of everlasting life by genuine faith in the Lord Jesus Christ is very clear here once again.
- **John 10:10**
"The thief cometh not, but for to steal, and to kill, and to destroy: **I am come that they might have life**, and that they might have *it* more abundantly."
The Lord Jesus Christ came from Heaven to earth to provide eternal life to those who truly trust Him as their Saviour.

- **John 11:25**

"Jesus said unto her, I am the resurrection, and the life: **he that believeth in me, though he were dead, yet shall he live**:"

Genuinely believing on the Lord Jesus Christ brings life everlasting.

- **John 14:6**

"Jesus saith unto him, **I am** the way, the truth, and **the life: no man cometh unto the Father, but by me**."

The Lord Jesus Christ is the only life and the only way to God the Father and Heaven.

- **Romans 6:23**

"For the wages of sin *is* death; but **the gift of God *is* eternal life through Jesus Christ our Lord**."

ETERNAL LIFE IS GOD'S GIFT THROUGH FAITH

Eternal life is God's gift only through faith in the Lord Jesus Christ.

- **1 John 5:20**

"And we know that the Son of God is come, and hath given us an understanding, that we may know him that is true, and we are in him that is true, *even* in his Son Jesus Christ. **This is the true God, and eternal life**."

One of the titles of the Lord Jesus Christ is "*eternal life*" which is found only through true faith in Him.

1 John 5:13

"These things have I written unto you that believe on the name of the Son of God; that ye may know that ye have eternal life, and that ye may believe on the name of the Son of God."

John wrote his letter to give the true Christians assurance that they have eternal life. The Greek Word for "*believe*" is in the Greek present tense. It emphasizes continuous belief and faith in the Lord Jesus Christ.

CONFIDENCE OF SALVATION IS IMPORTANT

The Greek verb used in the phrase, "*that ye may know,*" is in the Greek perfect tense. This emphasizes knowledge that began in the past, with results remaining into the present and future. It gives great confidence.

Verses On Assurance

- **Isaiah 32:17**

"And the work of righteousness shall be peace; and the effect of righteousness quietness and **assurance for ever**."

We must have assurance about our salvation and about many other things as well.

- **John 10:27-28**

"My sheep hear my voice, and I know them, and they follow me: And **I give unto them eternal life; and they shall never perish**, neither shall any *man* pluck them out of my hand."

> **SHALL NEVER PERISH BRINGS ASSURANCE**
>
> "*Shall never perish*"—that's assurance for those who have truly trusted in the Lord Jesus Christ as their Saviour. They possess "*eternal life.*"

- **Acts 2:36**

"Therefore let all the house of Israel **know assuredly, that God hath made that same Jesus**, whom ye have crucified, **both Lord and Christ**."

People can have assurance that God has made His Son both the Lord and Christ, the Anointed One. No other religious leader can truly say this.

- **1 Thessalonians 1:5**

"For **our gospel came** not unto you in word only, but also in power, and in the Holy Ghost, and **in much assurance**; as ye know what manner of men we were among you for your sake."

The Bible's gospel about the Lord Jesus Christ brings much assurance with it.

- **2 Timothy 3:14**

"But **continue thou** in the things which thou hast learned and **hast been assured** of, knowing of whom thou hast learned *them*;"

> **PASTOR TIMOTHY WAS GIVEN ASSURANCE**
>
> Pastor Timothy was led to the Lord Jesus Christ by Paul and was given assurance about the things he learned from Paul.

- **Hebrews 10:22**

"Let us draw near with a true heart **in full assurance of faith**, having our hearts sprinkled from an evil conscience, and our bodies washed with pure water."

Faith in the Lord Jesus Christ must be with a true heart and in full assurance to be victorious.

1 John 5:14

"And this is the confidence that we have in him, that, if we ask any thing according to his will, he heareth us:"

There is confidence about genuine Christians asking things that are according to God's will. He hears their prayers. The Greek Word for "ask" is in the Greek present tense, meaning a continuous action. We should ask according to His will.

ASKING ACCORDING TO GOD'S WILL

We are confident that if we ask anything according to His will, He hears. He doesn't always grant the requests that Christians have. He knows what is best for them, but He hears their prayers. If you go to a human judge, you have a hearing. That's all it is--a hearing. The judge listens to the case, both from the defense, and from the prosecution. Then the judge decides what to do.

Verses On The Will Of God

- Mark 3:35

"For **whosoever shall do the will of God**, the same is my brother, and my sister, and mother."

CHRIST'S BROTHERS, SISTERS, AND MOTHERS

Whosoever does the will of God, is related to the Lord Jesus Christ, as brothers, sisters, or mothers.

- Romans 1:10

"Making request, if by any means now at length I might have a prosperous journey **by the will of God to come unto you**."

Paul finally came to Rome in shackles as a prisoner. He wanted to visit the Romans, and God granted that request. Paul wanted to have the will of God. God got Paul to Rome. He didn't have to pay any money for the travel–the Roman government sent him on his way as a captive.

- Romans 8:27

"And he that searcheth the hearts knoweth what *is* the mind of the Spirit, because he maketh **intercession for the saints according to *the will of* God**."

The Holy Spirit makes intercession for all true Christians according to God's will. They often don't know what God's will is for their lives. The Spirit of God makes intercession for them according to the will of God.
- **Romans 12:2**
"And be not conformed to this world: but be ye transformed by the renewing of your mind, **that ye may prove what *is* that good, and acceptable, and perfect, will of God**."

> **GOD'S WILL FOUND IN GOD'S BIBLE WORDS**
> The will of God is following the Words of God in the Bible. True Christians must know Scriptures to know His will. Then they must want to follow that will. It's not enough to know it. The Scriptures must be followed.

- **Romans 15:32**
"That I may come unto you with joy **by the will of God**, and may with you be refreshed."

Again, Paul wanted to be in the will of God when he came to the churches in Rome.

- **Galatians 1:4**
"Who gave himself for our sins, **that he might deliver us** from this present evil world, **according to the will of God** and our Father:"

> **GOD'S WILL DELIVERS FROM THIS WICKED WORLD**
> The will of God is to deliver genuine Christians from this present wicked world.

- **Ephesians 6:6**
"Not with eyeservice, as menpleasers; but as the servants of Christ, **doing the will of God from the heart**;"

Servants should serve like they are doing the will of God from their hearts rather than pleasing men.

- **Colossians 4:12**
"Epaphras, who is *one* of you, a servant of Christ, saluteth you, always labouring fervently for you in prayers, **that ye may stand perfect and complete in all the will of God**."

This was an important prayer request. Every true Christian should stand complete in all of God's will.

- **1 Thessalonians 4:3**
"For **this is the will of God, *even* your sanctification**, that ye should abstain from fornication:"

God's will is for every true Christian to be separated from fornication and all other sins.
- **1 Thessalonians 5:18**
"In every thing **give thanks: for this is the will of God** in Christ Jesus concerning you."

God's will is for every genuine Christian to give thanks in every circumstance of their lives despite the hardships that might come their way.
- **1 John 2:17**
"And the world passeth away, and the lust thereof: but **he that doeth the will of God abideth for ever**."

GENUINE CHRISTIANS ABIDE FOREVER
Genuine Christians have trusted the Lord Jesus Christ as their Saviour and will abide forever.

Verses On Prayer
- **John 15:7**
"If ye abide in me, and my words abide in you, **ye shall ask what ye will**, and it shall be done unto you."

Abiding in Christ brings answers to prayer.
- **Ephesians 3:20**
"Now unto him that is able to do exceeding abundantly **above all that we ask** or think, according to the power that worketh in us,"

God is powerful in answering the prayers of true Christians.
- **James 1:5-6**
"If any of you lack wisdom, **let him ask of God**, that giveth to all *men* liberally, and upbraideth not; and it shall be given him. But let him ask in faith, nothing wavering. For he that wavereth is like a wave of the sea driven with the wind and tossed."

God wants genuine Christians in faith to ask Him for wisdom. He will answer them.
- **1 John 3:22**
"And **whatsoever we ask, we receive of him**, because we keep his commandments, and do those things that are pleasing in his sight."

1,050 NEW TESTAMENT COMMANDMENTS
I mentioned earlier in this book that there were 1,050 commandments and imperatives in the New Testament for true Christians to fulfill. Those who keep these orders will receive what they ask for.

1 John 5:15

"**And if we know that he hear us, whatsoever we ask, we know that we have the petitions that we desired of him.**"

God promises to hear the petitions of true Christians when they pray. These petitions get through to Him. When He hears these petitions, sometimes He answers "yes" to them and sometimes "no."

1 John 5:16

"**If any man see his brother sin a sin which is not unto death, he shall ask, and he shall give him life for them that sin not unto death. There is a sin unto death: I do not say that he shall pray for it.**"

SINS UNTO PHYSICAL DEATH

Genuine Christians should pray for fellow Christians who commit sins not unto physical death. However, there are sins that lead to the physical death of those who commit them. These sins are not to be prayed for.

There are at least eight different people in the Scriptures that committed sins unto death. Two of them were Christians and the rest are found in the Old Testament.

Those Who Committed The Sin Unto Physical Death

    1. Moses And Aaron Committed Sins Unto Death

- **Numbers 20:2-13**

"And there was no water for the congregation: and they gathered themselves together against Moses and against Aaron. And the people chode with Moses, and spake, saying, Would God that we had died when our brethren died before the LORD! And why have ye brought up the congregation of the LORD into this wilderness, that we and our cattle should die there? And wherefore have ye made us to come up out of Egypt, to bring us in unto this evil place? it is no place of seed, or of figs, or of vines, or of pomegranates; neither is there any water to drink. And Moses and Aaron went from the presence of the assembly unto the door of the tabernacle of the congregation, and they fell upon their faces: and the glory of the LORD appeared unto them. And the LORD

spake unto Moses, saying, Take the rod, and gather thou the assembly together, thou, and Aaron thy brother, and **speak ye unto the rock before their eyes; and it shall give forth his water**, *and thou shalt bring forth to them water out of the rock: so thou shalt give the congregation and their beasts drink. And Moses took the rod from before the LORD, as he commanded him. And Moses and Aaron gathered the congregation together before the rock, and he said unto them,* **Hear now, ye rebels; must we fetch you water out of this rock? And Moses lifted up his hand, and with his rod he smote the rock twice**: *and the water came out abundantly, and the congregation drank, and their beasts also. And the LORD spake unto Moses and Aaron,* **Because ye believed me not, to sanctify me in the eyes of the children of Israel, therefore ye shall not bring this congregation into the land which I have given them**. *This is the water of Meribah; because the children of Israel strove with the LORD, and he was sanctified in them."*

There were four steps in God's command to Moses:
  (1) Take your rod.
  (2) Assemble together.
  (3) Speak unto the rock.
  (4) Out of the rock will come forth water to be given to the congregation and to the animals.

MOSES' SIN UNTO PHYSICAL DEATH
Moses didn't speak to the rock. He lifted up his hand with the rod, and he smote the rock twice. Water came out. God delivered the people of their thirst.

The Lord said to both Moses and Aaron, *"Because ye believed me not, to sanctify me in the eyes of the children of Israel, therefore ye shall not bring this congregation into the land which I have given them."* And this is exactly what happened.

- **Deuteronomy 32:49-52**

"Get thee up into this mountain Abarim, *unto* mount Nebo, which *is* in the land of Moab, that *is* over against Jericho; and behold the land of Canaan, which I give unto the children of Israel for a possession: And die in the mount whither thou goest up, and be gathered unto thy people; as Aaron thy brother died in mount Hor, and was gathered unto his people: Because ye trespassed against me among the children of Israel at the waters of Meribah-Kadesh, in the wilderness of Zin;

because ye sanctified me not in the midst of the children of Israel. Yet thou shalt see the land before *thee*; but thou shalt not go thither unto the land which I give the children of Israel."
- **Psalms 106:32**

"<u>They angered *him*</u> also at the waters of strife, so that it went ill with Moses for their sakes:"
Moses and Aaron angered the Lord by their sins.
- **Psalms 106:33**

"Because they provoked his spirit, so that he spake unadvisedly with his lips."
<u>Moses spoke unadvisedly with his lips</u> and bragged that he was the one who could bring forth the water rather than the LORD.

2. Two Of Aaron's Sons Committed The Sin Unto Death.
- **Leviticus 10:10**

"And that ye may put difference between holy and unholy, and between unclean and clean;"

> **NADAB AND ABIHU'S SINS UNTO PHYSICAL DEATH**
> Nadab and Abihu, two of the sons of Aaron, took God's censor full of incense and went in offering strange fire to the Lord. Therefore the Lord slew them.

3. Uzzah Committed The Sin Unto Death.
- **2 Samuel 6:6-8**

"And when they came to Nachon's threshingfloor, <u>Uzzah put forth *his* hand to the ark of God, and took hold of it; for the oxen shook *it*. And the anger of the LORD was kindled against Uzzah; and God smote him there for *his* error; and there he died by the ark of God</u>. And David was displeased, because the LORD had made a breach upon Uzzah: and he called the name of the place Perezuzzah to this day."
They brought the ark in there; Ahio drove the cart and Uzzah put forth his hand. He was not supposed to touch the ark because it was holy.

4. Ananias And Sapphira Committed The Sin Unto Death.
Now in the New Testament, two Christian believers, Ananias and Sapphira, committed the sin unto physical death.

- Acts 5:1-5

"But a certain man named **Ananias, with Sapphira his wife, sold a possession, And kept back *part* of the price**, his wife also being privy *to it*, and brought a certain part, and laid *it* at the apostles' feet. But Peter said, Ananias, why hath Satan filled thine heart to lie to the Holy Ghost, and to keep back *part* of the price of the land? Whiles it remained, was it not thine own? and after it was sold, was it not in thine own power? why hast thou conceived this thing in thine heart? **thou hast not lied unto men, but unto God. And Ananias hearing these words fell down, and gave up the ghost**: and great fear came on all them that heard these things."

LYING TO GOD WAS A SIN UNTO PHYSICAL DEATH

There's nothing wrong about keeping back part of the money, but they lied about it. They implied to the apostles that the entire price of the land was given to the Lord. Ananias and Sapphira committed the sin unto physical death, because they seemed to be bragging about giving more than they really did.

- Acts 5:7-9

"And it was about the space of three hours after, when his wife, not knowing what was done, came in. And Peter answered unto her, **Tell me whether ye sold the land for so much? And she said, Yea, for so much**. Then Peter said unto her, How is it that ye have agreed together to tempt the Spirit of the Lord? behold, **the feet of them which have buried thy husband *are* at the door, and shall carry thee out**."

SAPPHIRA LIED AND DIED LIKE HER HUSBAND

Sapphira told the same lie her husband told. They didn't have to give anything to the Lord. They could have given a portion to the Lord; to say they were giving it all to the Lord and giving only a portion of it was a lie. Sapphira also committed the sin unto physical death.

5. Herod Committed The Sin Unto Death.

- Acts 12:21-24

"And upon a set day **Herod, arrayed in royal apparel, sat upon his throne**, and made an oration unto them. And the people gave a shout, *saying,* **It *is* the voice of a god, and not of a man. And immediately the angel of the Lord**

smote him, because he gave not God the glory: and he was eaten of worms, and gave up the ghost. But the word of God grew and multiplied."
Herod didn't correct the blasphemy of the people, so God smote him. Herod committed the sin unto physical death.

1 John 5:17

"All unrighteousness is sin: and there is a sin not unto death."

> **UNRIGHTEOUSNESS DEFINED BY THE BIBLE**
> Unrighteousness must be determined by how the Bible defines it. As such, unrighteousness is sin, but it does not necessarily lead to physical death.

Verses On Unrighteousness

- **Psalms 92:15**

"To shew that **the LORD *is* upright**: *he is* my rock, and ***there is* no unrighteousness in him**."
In God, there is no unrighteousness.

- **John 7:18**

"He that speaketh of himself seeketh his own glory: but he that seeketh his glory that sent him, the same is true, and **no unrighteousness is in him**."
The Lord Jesus Christ is speaking of Himself. There is no unrighteousness or sin in Him.

- **Romans 1:18**

"For the wrath of God is revealed from heaven against all ungodliness and **unrighteousness of men, who hold the truth in unrighteousness**;"
God's wrath is revealed, and He will judge the ones who are doing unrighteous acts.

- **Romans 6:13**

"Neither yield ye your members *as* instruments of unrighteousness unto sin: but yield yourselves unto God, as those that are alive from the dead, and your members *as* instruments of righteousness unto God."
Genuine Christians are no longer to yield themselves to unrighteousness.

- **2 Corinthians 6:14**

"Be ye not unequally yoked together with unbelievers: for **what fellowship hath righteousness with unrighteousness**? and what communion hath light with darkness?"

There is no fellowship between righteousness and unrighteousness.

- **2 Thessalonians 2:8-10**

"And then shall that Wicked be revealed, whom the Lord shall consume with the spirit of his mouth, and shall destroy with the brightness of his coming: *Even him*, whose coming is after the working of Satan with all power and signs and lying wonders, And **with all deceivableness of unrighteousness** in them that perish; because they received not the love of the truth, that they might be saved."

These verses speak of Antichrist, a deceiving "man of sin."

- **2 Thessalonians 2:12**

"That they all might be damned who believed not the truth, but **had pleasure in unrighteousness**."

Unbelievers have pleasure in all sorts of unrighteousness.

- **2 Peter 2:15**

"Which have forsaken the right way, and are gone astray, following the way of **Balaam** *the son* of Bosor, who **loved the wages of unrighteousness**;"

The false prophet, Balaam, loved unrighteousness and the wages that went with it.

- **1 John 1:9**

"If we confess our sins, he is faithful and just to forgive us *our* sins, and to **cleanse us from all unrighteousness**."

The Lord Jesus Christ is able to cleanse genuine Christians who follow this verse from all unrighteousness.

1 John 5:18

"We know that whosoever is born of God sinneth not; but he that is begotten of God keepeth himself, and that wicked one toucheth him not."

CONTINUING IN SIN IS FALSE CHRISTIANITY

"Whosoever is born of God", that is, who is born-again, *"sinneth not;"* To understand this verse, you must realize that the Greek verb for *"sinneth"* is in the Greek present tense. As such, it indicates someone who lives in continuous sin. These are true Christians who have God

the Holy Spirit living within them. As such, He restrains such genuine Christians from continuing in sinful behavior. This cannot be said for non-Christians who have only their sinful flesh without the indwelling Holy Spirit.

Verses On Satan, The Wicked One
- **Ephesians 6:16**

"Above all, taking the shield of faith, wherewith ye shall be able to **quench all the fiery darts of the wicked**."

God has given the genuine Christian a shield of faith which can quench Satan's fiery darts.

- **2 Thessalonians 2:7-11**

"For the mystery of iniquity doth already work: only he who now letteth *will let*, until he be taken out of the way. And **then shall that Wicked be revealed**, whom the Lord shall consume with the spirit of his mouth, and shall destroy with the brightness of his coming: *Even him*, whose coming is **after the working of Satan** with all power and signs and lying wonders, And with all deceivableness of unrighteousness in them that perish; because they received not the love of the truth, that they might be saved. And for this cause God shall send them **strong delusion, that they should believe a lie:**"

MANY BELIEVE SATAN'S DECEPTIONS
Because of his deception, Satan will be believed by many, especially during the seven-year Tribulation.

- **1 John 2:13**

"I write unto you, fathers, because ye have known him *that is* from the beginning. I write unto you, young men, because **ye have overcome the wicked one**. I write unto you, little children, because ye have known the Father."

The young men spoken of here have overcome Satan, the wicked one.

- **1 John 3:12**

"Not as **Cain, *who* was of that wicked one**, and slew his brother. And wherefore slew he him? Because his own works were evil, and his brother's righteous."

Cain, who murdered his brother Abel, was of Satan, the wicked one. He disdained God's blood offerings and brought vegetables instead. He didn't obey God.

1 John 5:19

"**And we know that we are of God, and the whole world lieth in wickedness.**"

Speaking of genuine Christians, John says that they are of God. They are on God's side, but "*the whole world lieth in wickedness.*"

> **THE MEANING OF THE GREEK WORD, "KEIMAI"**
>
> The Greek Word for "*lieth*" is KEIMAI. Some of the meanings of that Greek Word are:
>
> "*1) to lie; 1a) of an infant; 1b) of one buried; 1c) of things that quietly cover some spot; 1c1) of a city situated on a hill; 1d) of things put or set in any place, in ref. to which we often use "to stand"; 1d1) of vessels, of a throne, of the site of a city, of grain and other things laid up together, of a foundation; 2) metaph. 2a) to be (by God's intent) set, i.e. destined, appointed; 2b) of laws, to be made, laid down; 2c) lies in the power of the evil one, i.e. is held in subjection by the devil.*"

In a metaphorical sense, "*the world*" implies something that is "*in the power of the evil one, that is, held in subjection by the devil.*" The whole world is held in subjection to wickedness. The only way people can get out of that power and snap those shackles of power that the devil has, is to trust confidently in the Lord Jesus Christ as their Saviour. Believe on Him and accept Him. That cancels the power of the evil one. That's why the Lord Jesus Christ came--to deliver people from all unrighteousness.

Verses On Wickedness

- **Matthew 22:18**

"But **Jesus perceived their wickedness**, and said, Why tempt ye me, *ye* hypocrites?"

The Pharisees and the Herodians were wicked. The Lord Jesus Christ, by His omniscience, could see right into their hearts and perceive their wickedness.

- **Mark 7:22**

"Thefts, covetousness, **wickedness**, deceit, lasciviousness, an evil eye, blasphemy, pride, foolishness:"

Wickedness is one of the things that comes out of the heart of the human and sinful flesh.
- **Luke 11:39**
"And the Lord said unto him, Now do ye Pharisees make clean the outside of the cup and the platter; **but your inward part is full of ravening and wickedness**."

WICKEDNESS LIES WITHIN THE HEARTS
Filthy wickedness was deep within the hearts of these Pharisees. Though it was not politically correct to tell them this, the Lord Jesus Christ made it plain to them.

- **Acts 8:22**
"**Repent therefore of this thy wickedness**, and pray God, if perhaps the thought of thine heart may be forgiven thee."

Wickedness must be repented of. There must be a change of the mind, and forgiveness can be given through true faith in the Lord Jesus Christ.

- **Romans 1:29**
"**Being filled with all** unrighteousness, fornication, **wickedness**, covetousness, maliciousness; full of envy, murder, debate, deceit, malignity; whisperers,"

We have a world that is filled with wickedness and all the other things mentioned in this verse.

- **Ephesians 6:12**
"For we wrestle not against flesh and blood, but against principalities, against powers, against the rulers of the darkness of this world, against **spiritual wickedness in high places**."

There is not only material wickedness, but through the leading of the Devil himself, there is much "*spiritual wickedness*." Apostasy and false doctrines are some forms of that kind of wickedness.

1 John 5:20

"**And we know that the Son of God is come, and hath given us an understanding, that we may know him that is true, and we are in him that is true, even in his Son Jesus Christ. This is the true God, and eternal life.**"

CHRIST IS THE TRUE GOD AND ETERNAL LIFE
The Lord Jesus Christ, the Son of God, has come from Heaven into this wicked world. He came by the

> miracle of the virgin birth in His incarnation, becoming perfect Man and perfect God in One Person. The Lord Jesus Christ *"is the true God, and eternal life."*

Verses On The Deity Of Christ

- **John 1:1**

"In the beginning was the Word, and the Word was with God, and **the Word was God**."

From John 1:14, "*the Word*" is identified as the Lord Jesus Christ. He is and was God the Son and full Deity.

- **John 1:14**

"And the Word was made flesh, and dwelt among us, (and we beheld his glory, the glory as of the only begotten of the Father,) full of grace and truth."

The Lord Jesus Christ was the only begotten of the Father and, as such, was God the Son.

- **John 20:28**

"And Thomas answered and said unto him, **My Lord and my God**."

> **THOMAS CALLED CHRIST HIS LORD AND HIS GOD**
>
> This is another very clear verse that teaches clearly the Deity of the Lord Jesus Christ. Thomas didn't believe in His bodily resurrection. At first, Thomas said he wasn't going to believe Jesus's resurrection until he put his fingers into the prints of the nails, and his hand into Christ's side. He was Thomas the doubter from the beginning. We should be thankful that the Apostle Thomas finally realized that the Lord Jesus Christ was and is his Lord and his God.

- **Romans 9:5**

"Whose *are* the fathers, and of whom as concerning the flesh **Christ *came*, who is over all, God blessed for ever**. Amen."

> **CHRIST IS GOD AND IS BLESSED FOREVER**
>
> This verse makes it clear that the Lord Jesus Christ is God and is blessed forever. The new versions have perverted this truth. Instead of saying He is God who is blessed forever, they say "*may God be blessed forever.*" That is a false translation.

- **Hebrews 1:8**
"**But unto the Son he saith, Thy throne, O God**, is for ever and ever: a sceptre of righteousness is the sceptre of thy kingdom."
In Bishop Westcott's commentary on the book of Hebrews, he mistranslates this: "*God is thy throne*" thus denying the Deity of the Lord Jesus Christ.
- **John 3:15**
"That whosoever believeth in him should not perish, but **have eternal life**."
The Lord Jesus Christ is not only God, but only by genuine faith in Him can people receive eternal life.

1 John 5:21

"**Little children, keep yourselves from idols. Amen.**"

I wonder why the Apostle John told this to his little children in the faith. They were those who were probably only recently saved. They may have previously been worshipping idols. That word, "*idolatry*" comes from two Greek words meaning "*worshipping what can be seen.*"

I've said many times, there are not only objects that are idols, worshipping that which you see, but there are also people that are worshipped like idols.

IDOLS CAN BE HUMAN AS WELL AS INANIMATE
People often follow such human idols rather than the clear teachings of the Words of God. True Christians must follow the Bible's commands and principles rather than idols.

Some of those who have diverged from Biblical doctrines, yet are worshipped by many, include: (1) Billy Graham; (2) Bill Hybels; (3) Rick Warren; (4) Joel Osteen; (5) movie stars; (6) football players; (7) baseball players; (8) basketball players; (9) television stars; (10) Internet leaders and their sites; (11) presidents; (12) senators; (13) congressmen; (14) mayors; (15) governors, and many, many others.

Verses On Idols
- **1 Corinthians 12:2**
"Ye know that ye were **Gentiles, carried away unto these dumb idols**, even as ye were led."

The Corinthians came from Gentile backgrounds. They were to forsake idols.
- **2 Corinthians 6:16**
"And **what agreement hath the temple of God with idols**? for ye are the temple of the living God; as God hath said, I will dwell in them, and walk in *them*; and I will be their God, and they shall be my people."

God wants genuine Christians to stay away from every kind of idol.
- **1 Thessalonians 1:9**
"For they themselves shew of us what manner of entering in we had unto you, and how **ye turned to God from idols** to serve the living and true God;"

That's a wonderful testimony of what these Thessalonians did.
- **Revelation 9:20**
"And the rest of the men which were not killed by these plagues yet **repented not of the works of their hands, that they should not worship devils, and idols of gold, and silver, and brass, and stone, and of wood: which neither can see, nor hear, nor walk**:"

TRUE CHRISTIANS MUST FORSAKE ALL IDOLS

May the Lord grant everyone who names the Name of the Lord Jesus Christ to forsake all sorts of idols and worship only God the Father and His only begotten Son, the Lord Jesus Christ.

2 John
Chapter One

2 John 1:1

"The elder unto the elect lady and her children, whom I love in the truth; and not I only, but also all they that have known the truth;"

The apostle John refers to himself as *"the elder."* He's talking to the elect lady. There are different interpretations of who that might refer to. Maybe it's just one person. Many feel that it might refer to a local church and all the *"children"* or members of that church. He loves them all *"in the truth"* which is found in the Words of God.

> **GOD'S TRUTH IS FOUND ONLY IN THE PROPER BIBLE**
>
> In the Bible versions available today, the full "truth" is very difficult to find unless a person is reading the King James Bible. Other versions (in all the languages of the world) whose New Testaments are based upon the Gnostic Critical Greek Text differ from the Traditional Greek Text on which the King James Bible is based in over 8,000 places.

This includes over 356 doctrinal passages where the Gnostic Critical Greek text contains false and untrue doctrines. This false Greek text is found today in three places:

(1) The Westcott and Hort Greek Text
(2) The Nestle-Aland Greek Text
(3) the United Bible Societies Greek Text

All three of these false Greek texts are a very serious attack on God's Words and His truth.

Verses About The Truth

There are a number of verses we want to look at concerning the truth.

- **Psalms 25:5**

"**Lead me in thy truth**, and teach me: for thou *art* the God of my salvation; on thee do I wait all the day."

> **KING JAMES BIBLE IS AN ACCURATE TRANSLATION**
> Genuine Christians need to know and be led by the truth of God. The King James Bible is the accurate English translation of the original, inspired, and preserved Hebrew, Aramaic, and Greek Words.

- **Psalms 86:11**
"Teach me thy way, O LORD; <u>I will walk in thy truth</u>: unite my heart to fear thy name."

> **TRUTH MUST BE KNOWN AND FOLLOWED**
> It's not enough to have the truth or only to know the truth. True Christians must "*walk*" in, follow, and be obedient to that truth.

- **Psalms 100:5**
"For the LORD *is* good; his mercy *is* everlasting; and <u>**his truth *endureth* to all generations**</u>."

> **BIBLE PRESERVATION IS VITAL**
> <u>This enduring truth teaches Bible preservation.</u> It's important to have God's truth preserved to all generations. What would happen if the truth ceased in David's time? In Samuel's time? In Saul's time? In Paul's time? In Peter's time? In the other Apostles' time? If this were the case, genuine Christians would have no truth in our day and time. They would have nothing to read, to follow, or to preach.

- **John 4:23-24**
"But the hour cometh, and now is, when the **<u>true worshippers shall worship the Father in spirit and in truth</u>**: for the Father seeketh such to worship him. **<u>God *is* a Spirit: and they that worship him must worship *him* in spirit and in truth</u>**."

The Lord Jesus Christ told the woman at the well about worshipping God the Father in both the spirit and in "*the truth.*" <u>There can be no proper worship except in the truth. In English, that Bible truth is found in the King James Bible.</u>

- **John 8:32**
"And <u>**ye shall know the truth, and the truth shall make you free**</u>."

THE TRUTH CAN MAKE PEOPLE FREE
The Lord Jesus Christ told His disciples that only the truth would make them free.

- **John 8:44**

"Ye are of *your* father **the devil**, and the lusts of your father ye will do. He was a murderer from the beginning, and **abode not in the truth, because there is no truth in him**. When he speaketh a lie, he speaketh of his own: for he is a liar, and the father of it."

There is no truth in the devil. He is the father and promoter of all varieties of lies.

- **John 14:6**

"**Jesus saith unto him, I am the way, the truth**, and the life: no man cometh unto the Father, but by me."

The Lord Jesus Christ is the Truth. That is one of His Divine Names.

- **John 14:17**

"*Even* **the Spirit of truth**; whom the world cannot receive, because it seeth him not, neither knoweth him: but ye know him; for he dwelleth with you, and shall be in you."

THE HOLY SPIRIT IS "THE SPIRIT OF TRUTH"
God the Holy Spirit is called **the Spirit of truth** because He has communicated God's truth to the human writers.

- **John 15:26**

"But when the Comforter is come, whom I will send unto you from the Father, *even* **the Spirit of truth**, which proceedeth from the Father, he shall testify of me:"

A TRUE WITNESS TO CHRIST'S PERSON AND WORK
The Holy Spirit gives a true testimony about the Person and Work of the Lord Jesus Christ.

- **John 16:13-14**

"Howbeit when he, **the Spirit of truth**, is come, he will guide you into all truth: for he shall not speak of himself; [that is, from himself as to the source] but whatsoever he shall hear, *that* shall he speak: and he will shew you things to come. He shall glorify me: for he shall receive of mine, and shall shew *it* unto you."

These verses give the details of how the words of the Bible came into being. The Lord Jesus Christ was the Author of all the Words of the New Testament (and by extension, of the Old Testament also). The Holy Spirit was the One Who gave Christ's Words to the human writers.

- **John 17:17**
"Sanctify them through thy truth: **thy word is truth**."

GOD'S WORDS CAN SANCTIFY THOSE WHO OBEY
Only God's truth, which is found in His Words, can sanctify those who read and follow it.

- **Romans 1:25**
"**Who changed the truth of God into a lie**, and worshipped and served the creature more than the Creator, who is blessed for ever. Amen."

The ancient heathen world did this, but the contemporary heathen world is also doing it today.

- **2 Corinthians 6:4-7**
"But in all *things* approving ourselves as the ministers of God, in much patience, in afflictions, in necessities, in distresses, In stripes, in imprisonments, in tumults, in labours, in watchings, in fastings; By pureness, by knowledge, by longsuffering, by kindness, by the Holy Ghost, by love unfeigned, **By the word of truth**, by the power of God, by the armour of righteousness on the right hand and on the left."

MINISTERS MUST PREACH AND OBEY GOD'S WORDS
Ministers of God should preach and live "*by the word of truth.*"

- **Galatians 4:16**
"Am I therefore become your enemy, **because I tell you the truth**?"

Paul was telling and preaching the truth to the Galatian Christians, even though they didn't like it. Paul became their enemy because he told them the truth.

- **Ephesians 6:10-17**
"Finally, my brethren, be strong in the Lord, and in the power of his might. Put on the whole armour of God, that ye may be able to stand against the wiles of the devil. For we wrestle not against flesh and blood, but against principalities, against powers, against the rulers of the darkness of this world, against spiritual wickedness in high *places*. Wherefore take unto you the whole armour of God, that ye may be able to withstand in the evil day, and having done all, to stand. Stand

therefore, **having your loins girt about with truth**, and having on the breastplate of righteousness; And your feet shod with the preparation of the gospel of peace; Above all, taking the shield of faith, wherewith ye shall be able to quench all the fiery darts of the wicked. And take the helmet of salvation, and the sword of the Spirit, which is the word of God:"

One of the important pieces of armor that genuine Christians must make use of has to do with their loins. They should be "*girt about with truth*" which is the Word of God. <u>Without the truth of God and the Words of God, along with all the other armor of God, no Christian can be a good soldier for the Lord Jesus Christ and prepared for battles.</u>

- **1 Thessalonians 2:13**

"For this cause also thank we God without ceasing, because, when **ye received the word of God** which ye heard of us, ye received *it* not *as* the word of men, but **as it is in truth, the word of God**, which effectually worketh also in you that believe."

God's Words are not just the words of men. They are God's truth.

- **1 Timothy 2:4**

"**Who will have all men** to be saved, and **to come unto the knowledge of the truth**."

God is willing to have every person trust His Son as their Saviour and be saved. But everyone does not share God's willingness. They are in rebellion against Him and His Son. God would like everyone in the world to come "*to the knowledge of the truth*."

- **1 Timothy 3:15**

"But if I tarry long, that thou mayest know how thou oughtest to behave thyself in the house of God, which is **the church of the living God, the pillar and ground of the truth**."

SOUND CHURCHES–THE GROUND OF THE TRUTH

Sound, Biblically-based local churches are called the pillars and <u>ground of the truth</u>. There are very few of these kinds of churches that live up to these standards today.

- **2 Timothy 2:15**

"Study to shew thyself approved unto God, a workman that needeth not to be ashamed, **rightly dividing the word of truth**."

Knowing the Words of God and rightly dividing them are both necessary. Our local Baptist church divides the Bible into various dispensations in order to understand the Bible clearly.
- **2 Timothy 4:3-4**
"For the time will come when they will not endure sound doctrine; but after their own lusts shall they heap to themselves teachers, having itching ears; And **they shall turn away *their* ears from the truth, and shall be turned unto fables**."

These people will turn from the truth to fables and fairy tales. This is what we have today in most of these New Testament Bible translations which are based on the false Gnostic Critical Greek text.

2 John 1:2

"For the truth's sake, which dwelleth in us, and shall be with us for ever."

The promised preserved truth of God's Words dwelled with those Christians in John's day, and it still dwells with us in our day and on into eternity. The Bible shall be preserved forever, according to God's promises. The Lord Jesus Christ, the living Truth, will be with the true Christians forever.

Verses On Christ Being With Genuine Christians
- **Matthew 28:19-20**
"Go ye therefore, and teach all nations, baptizing them in the name of the Father, and of the Son, and of the Holy Ghost: Teaching them to observe all things whatsoever I have commanded you: and, lo, **I am with you alway, *even* unto the end of the world**. Amen."

The Lord Jesus Christ promised to be with His true Christians always to the end of the world.
- **John 14:23**
"Jesus answered and said unto him, If a man love me, he will keep my words: and **my Father will love him, and we will come unto him, and make our abode with him**."

THE INDWELLING OF THE FATHER AND THE SON

According to this verse, not only do the genuine Christians have God, the Holy Spirit, indwelling them, but God the Father and God the Son, also indwell them.

- **Hebrews 13:5-6**
"*Let your* conversation *be* without covetousness; *and be* content with such things as ye have: for **he hath said, I will never leave thee, nor forsake thee**. So that we may boldly say, The Lord *is* my helper, and I will not fear what man shall do unto me."
The Lord Jesus Christ will never leave or forsake the true Christians. He is with them and helps them.

Verses On Bible Preservation
- **Psalms 12:6-7**
"**The words of the LORD *are* pure words**: *as* silver tried in a furnace of earth, purified seven times. **Thou shalt keep them, O LORD, thou shalt preserve them from this generation for ever**."

BIBLE PRESERVATION-THE CORRECT POSITION

By many Christian pastors, Christian teachers, and other Christians, the doctrine of Bible preservation has been perverted in the past, is being perverted in the present, and it will continue to be perverted in the future. Here are two erroneous positions, and the only correct position on this important Bible doctrine.

1. Those Who Doubt Bible Preservation. All the apostate churches and schools deny Bible Preservation. Sad to say, many churches and schools that are otherwise Fundamentalist in doctrines have completely rejected the Bible Preservation by God of the Hebrew, Aramaic, and Greek Words.

2. Those Who Believe That Bible Preservation Refers To The King James Bible. Peter Ruckman and Gail Riplinger and their many followers wrongly place Bible Preservation and inspiration with the King James Bible. Gail Riplinger goes so far as to teach that the King James Bible has completely replaced what God gave us in Hebrew, Aramaic, and Greek, thus making the King James Bible a new and fresh Divine revelation.

3. Those Who Believe The Proper Doctrine Of Bible Preservation Of The Hebrew, Aramaic, and Greek Words. The Bible is very clear that it is the Words that God gave us in the Old and New Testaments which He has promised to preserve. It exclusively refers to the Hebrew, Aramaic, and Greek Words. The King James

> Bible has clearly and accurately translated those original inspired and preserved Words into the English language. When God says in verse 7, "thou shalt preserve them from this generation for ever" He is referring to the Hebrew, Aramaic, and by extension, to the New Testament Greek Words. It is not referring to some translation of these Words.

- Psalms 105:8

"He hath remembered his covenant for ever, **the word which he commanded to a thousand generations**."

> **BIBLE PRESERVATION FOR A 1,000 GENERATIONS**
>
> God did not want His Words to die out in a few years. He commanded them to be preserved for a *"thousand generations."* If a generation is 20 years, that would be Bible preservation for 20,000 years. If a generation is 30 years, that would be Bible preservation for 30,000 years. This is certainly Bible preservation, is it not!!

- Proverbs 22:20-21

"Have not I written to thee excellent things in counsels and knowledge, **That I might make thee know the certainty of the words of truth; that thou mightest answer the words of truth to them that send unto thee**?"

We have to have certainty of God's words that have been preserved so we can answer people. The only way that genuine Christians can have certainty of God's Words of truth is to have the original manuscripts preserved for us.

- Matthew 4:4

"But he answered and said, **It is written, Man shall not live by bread alone, but by every word that proceedeth out of the mouth of God**."

When confronted by the Devil, the Lord Jesus Christ, after forty days and forty nights, without food or drink, quoted from the preserved Words of God from the Old Testament. The Devil told the Lord Jesus Christ to turn stones into bread. The Devil knew the Lord Jesus Christ could do this, but He refused this miracle for His own profit. Instead, He quoted the preserved Words of God from the Old Testament and said:

> **Deuteronomy 8:3** *"And he humbled thee, and suffered thee to hunger, and fed thee with manna, which thou knewest not, neither did thy fathers know; that he might make thee*

*know that **man doth not live by bread only, but by every word that proceedeth out of the mouth of the LORD doth man live**.*"

"IT IS WRITTEN"—KEPT PAST, PRESENT & FUTURE

If God had not preserved these Words, the Saviour could not have quoted them and said *"it is written."* God has preserved His Words in the Hebrew, Aramaic, and Greek languages.

Many of our fundamentalist brethren at Bob Jones University, the former Calvary Baptist Seminary, and their sister schools do not believe that God even **promised** to preserve His Hebrew, Aramaic, and Greek Words, much less that He **has** preserved these Words. This is apostasy!

- Matthew 5:17-18

"Think not that I am come to destroy the law, or the prophets: I am not come to destroy, but to fulfil. For verily I say unto you, **Till heaven and earth pass, one jot or one tittle shall in no wise pass from the law, till all be fulfilled**."
Nothing will *pass* from the law or any other part of the Bible. Has heaven and earth yet *passed*? No. They are both still here.

JOTS AND TITTLES EXPLAINED

What's a jot? The Greek Word is IOTA. It's the smallest Hebrew letter. It looks like our English comma. The Greek Word for tittle is KERAIA. In the Hebrew text it is one of the punctuation marks looking like a small dot. In these verses, the Lord Jesus Christ was teaching Bible preservation of the original inspired inerrant Hebrew, Aramaic, and Greek Words.

- Matthew 24:35

"Heaven and earth shall pass away, but **my words shall not pass away**."
One day the heavens and the earth shall pass away. These are the largest objects in all the world. It includes all the galaxies and the millions and even billions of stars in them. The Lord Jesus Christ said that one day they will all *pass away*. He said there was something that was permanent that will not pass away–it is His Old and New Testament Words.

> **"OU ME"–THE STRONGEST GREEK NEGATIVE**
> The Greek Word for "not" is OU ME. It is the strongest negative in the Greek language. It means never, never, never!

I cannot understand why our otherwise fundamentalist brethren do not believe these spoken Words of the Lord Jesus Christ.

- **Mark 13:31**

"Heaven and earth shall pass away: but **my words shall not pass away**."

These are the same words as in Matthew 24:35.

- **Luke 21:33**

"Heaven and earth shall pass away: but **my words shall not pass away**."

These are also the same words as in Matthew 24:35. Bible preservation of the Hebrew, Aramaic, and Greek Words are very important.

- **Colossians 1:17**

"And he is before all things, and **by him all things consist**."

The Greek Word for "*consist*" is SUNISTAO.

> **THE MEANING OF THE GREEK WORD, "SUNISTAO"**
> Some of the meanings of this Greek Word are:
> "*1) to place together, to set in the same place, to bring or band together; 1a) to stand with (or near); 2) to set one with another; 2a) by way of presenting or introducing him; 2b) to comprehend; 3) to put together by way of composition or combination, to teach by combining and comparing; 3a) to show, prove, establish, exhibit; 4) to put together, unite parts into one whole; 4a) to be composed of, consist*"

This word can be applied to the Bible's preservation of its Hebrew, Aramaic, and Greek Words in the sense of "*placing together, setting in the same place,*" and "*establishing,*" and "*putting together, and uniting parts into one whole.*"

- **1 Peter 1:23-25**

"Being born again, not of corruptible seed, but of incorruptible, by the word of God, which liveth and abideth for ever. For all flesh *is* as grass, and all the glory of man as

¹the flower of grass. The grass withereth, and the flower thereof falleth away: But **the word of the Lord endureth for ever**. And this is the word which by the gospel is preached unto you."

This is Bible preservation. <u>If we don't have Bible preservation, we would not have the true gospel to preach to people.</u>

• **John 6:47**
"Verily, verily, I say unto you, He that believeth <u>**on me**</u> hath everlasting life."

Here's a verse that proves the need for the preservation of every one of the Bible's original Hebrew, Aramaic, and Greek Words. <u>Unless you have a King James Bible or some other Bible based upon the Received Greek Text, the words "*on me*" do not appear.</u> <u>If genuine faith is not placed in the Lord Jesus Christ, people cannot have "everlasting life" and will go into Hell's Lake of Fire.</u> <u>Bible preservation is necessary for truth to be in existence and in evidence.</u>

2 John 1:3

"Grace be with you, mercy, and peace, from God the Father, and from the Lord Jesus Christ, the Son of the Father, in truth and love."

GRACE, MERCY, AND PEACE

John greets his audience with three great doctrinal words of "grace," "mercy," and "peace" from God the Father and from the Lord Jesus Christ, the Son of the Father. All three of these things are possessed by every genuine Christian.

Verses On Grace

• **Genesis 6:8**
"But **Noah found grace in the eyes of the LORD**."

<u>Noah didn't deserve God's grace, but God selected him to build an ark to save himself</u>, seven others, and many animals from the universal flood; in order to preserve life upon the earth after God's judgment on men because of their evil, wickedness, and injustice, Noah experienced God's grace.

• **Romans 3:24**
"Being **justified freely by his grace through the redemption that is in Christ Jesus**:"

<u>The only way anyone can be justified today is by God's grace</u> through the redemption that is in the Lord Jesus Christ.

- 2 Corinthians 8:9

"For **ye know the grace of our Lord Jesus Christ**, that, though he was rich, yet **for your sakes he became poor, that ye through his poverty might be rich**."

GOD'S GRACE SENT THE SAVIOUR FROM HEAVEN
It was God's grace that the Lord Jesus Christ came from the riches of Heaven to become poor and put to death on the cross so that those who truly trust Him might be rich in eternal life and Heaven.

- 2 Corinthians 12:9

"And he said unto me, **My grace is sufficient for thee**: for my strength is made perfect in weakness. Most gladly therefore will I rather glory in my infirmities, that the power of Christ may rest upon me."

Paul was given a thorn in the flesh by the Lord. He prayed three times to have it removed, but the Lord did not answer his prayer. The Lord Jesus Christ said His grace was sufficient for him. So Paul rejoiced in this great provision.

Verses On Mercy

- Ephesians 2:3-4

"Among whom also we all had our conversation in times past in the lusts of our flesh, fulfilling the desires of the flesh and of the mind; and were by nature the children of wrath, even as others. But **God, who is rich in mercy**, for his great love wherewith he loved us,"

Every person on earth deserves Hell, but because of God's rich mercy, can be saved and go to God's Heaven.

- 1 Timothy 1:13

"Who was before a blasphemer, and a persecutor, and injurious: **but I obtained mercy**, because I did *it* ignorantly in unbelief."

Paul received abundant mercy from God, and he thanked God for it. He had many Christians killed, imprisoned, and stoned. Paul was a blasphemer, persecutor, and injurious, but he obtained mercy.

- Titus 3:5

"Not by works of righteousness which we have done, but **according to his mercy he saved us**, by the washing of regeneration, and renewing of the Holy Ghost;"

Salvation can come to truly-trusting sinners only by God's mercy because of what was accomplished by the Lord Jesus Christ on the cross at Calvary.

Verses On Peace

> ### A GOOD DEFINITION OF 'PEACE"
> Here is a good definition of *"peace"*:
> *"The tranquil state of a soul, assured of its salvation through Christ, and so fearing nothing from God and content with its earthly lot of whatsoever sort that is."*

- **Romans 5:1**

"Therefore being justified by faith, **we have peace with God** through our Lord Jesus Christ:"

Justified by genuine faith, a person can have peace with God only through what the Lord Jesus Christ accomplished at Calvary's cross.

- **Philippians 4:7**

"And **the peace of God**, which passeth all understanding, **shall keep your hearts and minds through Christ Jesus**."

That's what God's peace can do once a person truly believes on His Son, the Lord Jesus Christ.

- **Colossians 1:20**

"And, **having made peace through the blood of his cross**, by him to reconcile all things unto himself; by him, *I say*, whether *they be* things in earth, or things in heaven."

It was at Christ's cross of Calvary where God provided peace to those who have truly trusted in His Son.

- **Colossians 3:15**

"And **let the peace of God rule in your hearts**, to the which also ye are called in one body; and be ye thankful."

> ### GOD'S PEACE RULING THE HEARTS
> Once people become genuine Christians, they should let God's peace rule in their hearts.

2 John 1:4

"**I rejoiced greatly that I found of thy children walking in truth, as we have received a commandment from the Father.**"

The Apostle John rejoices because his readers are walking in the truth as found in God's Words. They not only have the truth, but are walking in it.

> **THE MEANING OF THE GREEK WORD, "PERIPATEO"**
>
> The Greek Word for "*walk*" is PERIPATEO. Some of the meanings of this Greek Word are:
>
> "*1) to walk; 1a) to make one's way, progress; to make due use of opportunities; 1b) Hebrew for, to live; 1b1) to regulate one's life; 1b2) to conduct one's self; 1b3) to pass one's life*"

Walking is not running. Walking is a step at a time. Walking is perfectly upright. Walking is not hurried. Walking is making progress, however slow.

Verses On Walking

- **Acts 9:31**

"Then had the churches rest throughout all Judaea and Galilee and Samaria, and were edified; and **walking in the fear of the Lord, and in the comfort of the Holy Ghost**, were multiplied."

They walked in the fear of the Lord and in the comfort of the Holy Spirit. They didn't have much money, much food, much clothing to wear, or large houses. Yet they walked in the fear of the Lord and comfort in God's Spirit.

- **2 Corinthians 4:2**

"But have renounced the hidden things of dishonesty, **not walking in craftiness**, nor handling the word of God deceitfully; but by manifestation of the truth."

Paul's walk with the Lord Jesus Christ was not in craftiness and deceit, but was manifesting God's truth.

- **2 Peter 3:3**

"Knowing this first, that there shall come in the last days scoffers, **walking after their own lusts**,"

> **MANY WALK AFTER THEIR OWN LUSTS**
> We are certainly in the last days' kind of activities. Many men and women are walking after their own wicked lusts rather than after the Bible's precepts and truths.

2 John 1:5

"And now I beseech thee, lady, not as though I wrote a new commandment unto thee, but that which we had from the beginning, that we love one another."

The Apostle John brings up once again the need for genuine Christians to have Christian love one for another. This doesn't mean that true Christians always agree with one another in matters of doctrines or practices, but, though very difficult to put into practice, they should have genuine love for all true Christians. It's just like in a family. I grew up with two sisters, one older and one younger. Though I didn't always agree with them, yet I have always loved them.

Verses Commanding True Christians
To Love One Another

- John 13:34

"**A new commandment** I give unto you, **That ye love one another; as I have loved you**, that ye also love one another."

> **LOVE ONE ANOTHER AS CHRIST LOVED US**
> That's an extremely high standard. The Lord Jesus Christ showed His love for all mankind by entering this world and by dying for the sins of every person who ever lived. They must truly trust Him, however, to take advantage of that great love and receive everlasting life.

- John 15:12

"**This is my commandment, That ye love one another, as I have loved you.**"
This is a very clear command for all genuine Christians. It is very difficult, but it must be the goal to aim at.

- John 15:17

"These things **I command you, that ye love one another**."
Again, this clear command is given.

- **Romans 13:8**
"**Owe no man any thing, but to love one another**: for he that loveth another hath fulfilled the law."
Paul reminded the Christians at Rome about this requirement.
- **1 Thessalonians 4:9**
"But as touching brotherly love ye need not that I write unto you: for **ye yourselves are taught of God to love one another**."

Love and respect for genuine Christians is taught by God Himself. It's true that we differ with many true Christians in points of doctrine, including the Bible versions they support and many other things, but we must still love them in the Lord, despite how soundly and strongly we differ with them on many other important things.
- **1 Peter 1:22**
"Seeing ye have purified your souls in obeying the truth through the Spirit unto **unfeigned love of the brethren, *see that ye* love one another with a pure heart fervently**:"

UNFEIGNED LOVE IS NECESSARY
Unfeigned love without hypocrisy is necessary. The words, "*one another*" demands that this love must be mutual rather than just one way. True Christians are required to love us back! It's not just a one-way street. But even if they don't love you back, still God demands that genuine Christians must love one another.

- **1 John 3:11**
"For this is the message that ye heard from the beginning, that **we should love one another**."
This was a message from the beginning of the New Testament books.
- **2 John 1:5**
"And now I beseech thee, lady, not as though I wrote a new commandment unto thee, but **that which we had from the beginning, that we love one another**."
This is one of John's themes that he repeats in all of his books.

2 John 1:6

"And this is love, that we walk after his commandments. This is the commandment, That, as ye have heard from the beginning, ye should walk in it."

OBEDIENCE MUST FOLLOW GENUINE LOVE

The result of love for the Lord Jesus Christ is that true Christians should walk in accord with what God commands them. Love must be followed by obedience to God's commands.

Verses On Obedience To God's Words

- John 14:15

"If ye love me, **keep my commandments**."

Several weeks ago, I referred to a list of 1,050 orders or commands found in the New Testament. The result of love for the Lord Jesus Christ is obedience to God's Words.

- John 14:23

"Jesus answered and said unto him, **If a man love me, he will keep my words**: and my Father will love him, and we will come unto him, and make our abode with him."

READING THE WHOLE BIBLE EACH YEAR

That's why we must know God's Words in order to keep His Words. You can't keep what you don't know. I encourage every reader to get a copy of our YEARLY BIBLE READING SCHEDULE and follow it daily, reading 85 verses per day. You will be able to finish the entire Bible in one year that way.

Obedience in keeping God's Words is a proof of people's love for the Lord Jesus Christ. No genuine obedience signals no genuine love.

- John 15:10

"**If ye keep my commandments, ye shall abide in my love**; even as I have kept my Father's commandments, and abide in his love."

The Lord Jesus Christ told His disciples that keeping His commandments would ensure their abiding in His love.

More Verses On Walking

- **John 8:12**

"Then spake Jesus again unto them, saying, I am the light of the world: **he that followeth me shall not walk in darkness**, but shall have the light of life."

The Lord Jesus Christ wants all true Christians to walk in the light of God's Words and not in the darkness and lies of this wicked world.

- **Romans 6:4**

"Therefore we are buried with him by baptism into death: that like as Christ was raised up from the dead by the glory of the Father, even so **we also should walk in newness of life**."

> **WALKING IN NEWNESS OF ETERNAL LIFE**
>
> When people become genuine Christians by receiving the Lord Jesus Christ as their Saviour, they are given a newness of life in which to walk. They should walk in that newness rather than in their old unsaved lives.

- **Romans 13:13**

"**Let us walk honestly**, as in the day; not in rioting and drunkenness, not in chambering and wantonness, not in strife and envying."

The true Christian's walk must be an honest walk.

- **2 Corinthians 5:7**

"(For **we walk by faith, not by sight**:)"

> **GENUINE CHRISTIANS MUST WALK BY FAITH**
>
> Genuine Christians walk by faith because they have never seen their Saviour face to face. They must walk in obedience to God's written Words.

- **Galatians 5:16**

"*This* I say then, **Walk in the Spirit**, and ye shall not fulfil the lust of the flesh."

The proper walk for all true Christians is in the power of God the Holy Spirit Who indwells them rather than in their sinful flesh.

- **Ephesians 2:10**

"For we are his workmanship, created in Christ Jesus unto **good works, which God hath before ordained that we should walk in them**."

> **WALKING IN GOOD WORKS AFTER SALVATION**
>
> Genuine Christians have been ordained by God to walk in good works.

- **Ephesians 5:2**
"And <u>walk in love</u>, as Christ also hath loved us, and hath given himself for us an offering and a sacrifice to God for a sweetsmelling savour."

The walk of true Christians should be a walk in love–love for the Lord Jesus Christ, and love for God's Words.

- **Colossians 2:6**
"<u>As ye have therefore received</u> Christ Jesus the Lord, <u>so walk ye in him</u>:"

Genuine Christians receive everlasting life by faith and should walk by faith daily.

- **1 John 1:7**
"But <u>if we walk in the light</u>, as he is in the light, we have fellowship one with another, and the blood of Jesus Christ his Son cleanseth us from all sin."

True Christians who walk in the light have fellowship with one another.

2 John 1:7

"For many deceivers are entered into the world, who confess not that Jesus Christ is come in the flesh. This is a deceiver and an antichrist."

THERE ARE MANY DECEIVERS AND ANTICHRISTS

The Apostle John states very clearly that there are "many deceivers" even in his day. Deceivers are those who lead people astray while seeming to lead them in the right way.

THE MEANING OF THE GREEK WORD, "PLANOS"

The Greek Word for "*deceiver*" is PLANOS. Some of the meanings of this Word are:

"1) wandering, roving; 2) misleading, leading into error; 2a) a vagabond, "tramp", imposter; 2b) corrupter, deceiver."

One of the most important deceptions of these deceivers is their denial of the incarnation, that "*Jesus Christ is come in the flesh.*" Their denial rejected the fact that perfect Deity became perfect Humanity by the miracle power of God.

APOSTATES AND GNOSTIC HERETICS
That deception is one of the many Gnostic heresies. This miracle is denied not only by the world religions, but also by apostate Protestant teachers who used to believe in it. The Apostle John called people who believe this error by two names: (1) deceivers and (2) antichrists.

Verses On Deceivers
- **Matthew 24:4**

"And Jesus answered and said unto them, **Take heed that no man deceive you**."

The Lord Jesus Christ warned His followers about deceivers. There are many deceiver even today.

- **Matthew 24:5**

"For many shall come in my name, **saying, I am Christ; and shall deceive many**."

Those pretending to be the Messiah are deceivers.

- **John 7:12**

"And there was much murmuring among the people concerning him: for some said, He is a good man: others said, Nay; but **he deceiveth the people**."

These people falsely charged the Lord Jesus Christ of being a deceiver of the people.

- **2 Timothy 3:13**

"But evil men and **seducers shall wax worse and worse, deceiving, and being deceived**."

God predicted through Paul, as he wrote to Pastor Timothy at the church in Ephesus, that seducers will become worse and worse, not only deceiving others, but being deceived themselves. Those that deceive themselves deny that the Lord Jesus Christ came in the flesh, denying His Deity, and many other Bible doctrines.

- **Revelation 12:9**

"And the great dragon was cast out, [that's one of the names for Satan] that old serpent, [that's a second name] called the Devil, [that's another name] and **Satan, which deceiveth the whole world**: he was cast out into the earth, and his angels were cast out with him."

Satan is the master deceiver.

- **Revelation 20:10**

"And **the devil that deceived them** was cast into the lake of fire and brimstone, where the beast and the false prophet *are*, and shall be tormented day and night for ever and ever."

Satan will be cast into the lake of fire forever.

Verses On Antichrist
Notice that an *"antichrist"* is defined here in 2 John 1:7. It includes many kinds of people in the definition. It is not limited only to the main Antichrist who will one day be revealed. Includes all . . .

> *"who confess not that Jesus Christ is come in the flesh. This is a deceiver and an antichrist."*

THE BIBLE'S DEFINITION OF AN "ANTICHRIST"
This is not only a definition of "the Antichrist" who will be manifested during the last half of the seven-year Tribulation; it is also a title that should be used for all people who do not confess and agree with the miracle of the incarnation that *"Christ is come in the flesh."* This *"antichrist"* definition can be applied to every apostate religious leader or follower who does not confess that the Lord Jesus Christ *"is come in the flesh"* in the incarnation.

- 1 John 2:22
"*Who is a liar but he that denieth that Jesus is the Christ?* **He is antichrist, that denieth the Father and the Son**."

Here is another part of the definition of *"antichrist."* It is applied to those who deny *"the Father and the Son."* This would mean a denial that the Lord Jesus Christ is equal to the Father and a member of the Divine Trinity.

- 1 John 4:3
"**And every spirit that confesseth not that Jesus Christ is come in the flesh is not of God: and this is that spirit of antichrist**, whereof ye have heard that it should come; and even now already is it in the world."

Again, this verse talks about *"that spirit of antichrist"* that denies that *"Jesus Christ is come in the flesh."* That spirit is not of God, but is of the antichrist.

2 John 1:8

"Look to yourselves, that we lose not those things which we have wrought, but that we receive a full reward."

Looking to ourselves would imply a self-examination. This should occur, but it does not happen as often as it should. Quite often Christians look to other people and criticize them without examining their own lives in the light of the Words of God.

Verses On Examination
- **1 Corinthians 11:28**

"But **let a man examine himself**, and so let him eat of *that* bread, and drink of *that* cup."

> **ONLY GENUINE CHRISTIANS AT THE LORD'S TABLE**
>
> Self-examination should be made to be sure a person is a genuine Christian before partaking of the Lord's table. Unsaved people have no right to partake of the Lord's table.

- **2 Corinthians 13:5**

"**Examine yourselves, whether ye be in the faith**; prove your own selves. Know ye not your own selves, how that Jesus Christ is in you, except ye be reprobates?"

It is of eternal importance for people to examine themselves to see if they are true Christians in the Biblical faith.

Verses On Rewards
- **Psalms 19:9-11**

"The fear of the LORD *is* clean, enduring for ever: **the judgments of the LORD *are* true *and* righteous altogether**. More to be desired *are they* than gold, yea, than much fine gold: sweeter also than honey and the honeycomb. Moreover by them is thy servant warned: *and* **in keeping of them *there is* great reward**."

The Words of God are true and righteous. They are compared to fine gold and honey. God gives a reward when people follow and keep them.

- **Matthew 5:11-12**

"Blessed are ye, when *men* shall revile you, and persecute *you*, and shall say all manner of evil against you falsely, for my sake. Rejoice, and be exceeding glad: for **great *is* your reward in heaven**: for so persecuted they the prophets which were before you."

When fierce persecution comes to true Christians for the sake of the Lord Jesus Christ, they should be exceeding glad, for great will be their reward in Heaven.

- **1 Corinthians 3:10-15**

"According to the grace of God which is given unto me, as a wise masterbuilder, I have laid the foundation, and another buildeth thereon. But let every man take heed how he buildeth thereupon. For other foundation can no man lay than that is laid, which is Jesus Christ. Now if any man build upon this foundation gold, silver, precious stones, wood, hay, stubble; Every man's work shall be made manifest: for the day shall declare it, because it shall be revealed by fire; and the fire shall try every man's work of what sort it is. **If any man's work abide which he hath built thereupon, he shall receive a reward.** If any man's work shall be burned, he shall suffer loss: but he himself shall be saved; yet so as by fire."

THE JUDGMENT SEAT OF CHRIST EXPLAINED

These verses explain the judgment seat of Christ where <u>every genuine Christian will appear for judgment by the Lord Jesus Christ</u>. Based on how they build on Christ the Foundation, they will either suffer loss, or *"receive a reward."*

- Revelation 22:12

"And, <u>**behold, I come quickly; and my reward** *is* **with me**</u>, to give every man according as his work shall be."
<u>The Lord Jesus Christ will bring with Him a reward for those true Christians</u> who have served Him faithfully in this wicked world.

2 John 1:9

"Whosoever transgresseth, and abideth not in the doctrine of Christ, hath not God. He that abideth in the doctrine of Christ, he hath both the Father and the Son."

<u>Abiding in the doctrines and teachings of and about the Lord Jesus Christ shows that you have both God the Father and God the Son as your Masters.</u>

<u>Verses On Doctrine</u>

- Matthew 7:28

"And it came to pass, when Jesus had ended these sayings, **the people were astonished at his doctrine**:"
People were amazed at the teachings and doctrines of the Lord Jesus Christ when He was on earth.

- Matthew 22:33

"And when **the multitude** heard *this*, they **were astonished at his doctrine**."
On this occasion <u>a great multitude of people were listening to the teachings of the Lord Jesus Christ</u> and were astonished at the doctrine that He taught them.

- **John 7:16-17**
"Jesus answered them, and said, **My doctrine is not mine, but his that sent me.** If any man will do his will, he shall know of the doctrine, whether it be of God, or *whether* I speak of myself."

CHRIST AND GOD THE FATHER–NO CONTRADICTION
The doctrine of the Lord Jesus Christ was from God the Father Who sent Him into the world. There was no contradiction between God the Father and God the Son.

- **Acts 2:42**
"And **they continued stedfastly in the apostles' doctrine** and fellowship, and in breaking of bread, and in prayers."

THE EARLY CHURCH KEPT SOUND DOCTRINES
The early church continued in the doctrine of the apostles. They didn't modify or corrupt any of these Biblical doctrines.

- **Acts 5:28**
"Saying, Did not we straitly command you that ye should not teach in this name? and, behold, **ye have filled Jerusalem with your doctrine**, and intend to bring this man's blood upon us."

THE APOSTLES TAUGHT SOUND DOCTRINES
The apostles taught faithfully the doctrines and teachings of the Lord Jesus Christ. Because of this, the godless Pharisees despised them.

- **Romans 16:17**
"Now I beseech you, brethren, **mark them which cause divisions and offences contrary to the doctrine which ye have learned; and avoid them**."

Those who teach against the doctrines of the Bible, "**mark them**" and expose them, then "**avoid them**."

- **2 Timothy 3:16-17**
"All scripture *is* given by inspiration of God, and *is* profitable for doctrine, for reproof, for correction, for instruction in righteousness: That the man of God may be perfect, throughly furnished unto all good works."

The Scripture must be used as the basis for all doctrine and teachings in our churches today. That's why God gave us the Bible.

- **2 Timothy 4:2-4**

"Preach the word; be instant in season, out of season; reprove, rebuke, **exhort with all longsuffering and doctrine**. For the time will come when **they will not endure sound doctrine**; but after their own lusts shall they heap to themselves teachers, having itching ears; And **they shall turn away *their* ears from the truth, and shall be turned unto fables**."

16 DOCTRINES ABOUT THE LORD JESUS CHRIST

Many of the doctrines about the Lord Jesus Christ–called Christology--have been, are being, and will be denied by millions of people on this earth–including many who call themselves preachers or teachers.

The Doctrines Of The Lord Jesus Christ

1. His Deity
2. His Eternal Sonship
3. His Virgin Birth
4. His Bodily Resurrection
5. His Miracles
6. His Truthfulness
7. His Omniscience
8. His Omnipresence
9. His Omnipotence
10. His Death On The Cross For The Sins Of All People
11. Salvation By Genuine Faith In Him Alone
12. His Mission To Seek And Save The Lost
13. His Preparing A Place In Heaven For True Christians
14. His Judgment Of Genuine Christians
15. His Great White Throne Judgment Of The Lost
16. His Thousand-Year Millennial Reign On Earth

This is only one category of doctrines that are being denied in our days. There are many other categories of doctrines that have also been trashed by the unbelievers of today.

2 John 1:10

"If there come any unto you, and bring not this doctrine, receive him not into your house, neither bid him God speed:"

John is talking about the "doctrine of Christ"–Christology–as listed above. If anyone comes to your house–like the Jehovah's Witnesses–and doesn't hold to these doctrines about the Lord Jesus Christ, don't receive them into your house. Don't let them try to teach you their false doctrines, and don't bid them God speed when they depart. This verse teaches that genuine Christians should not bring these heretics into their houses. They should shut them out.

KEEP JEHOVAH'S WITNESSES OUT OF YOUR HOUSE

Every time the Jehovah Witnesses knock on the door, people should refuse to let them into their houses. If they come in and teach their heretical doctrines, they might influence the husband, the wife, or the children to accept their lies. Genuine Christians must be separate from apostate and heretical doctrines that are not the Biblical doctrines about the Lord Jesus Christ.

Verses On Separation From False Doctrines

- **Ephesians 5:11**

"And **have no fellowship with the unfruitful works of darkness, but rather reprove** *them*."

THE MEANING OF THE GREEK WORD, "ELENCHO"

The Greek Word for *"reprove"* is ELENCHO. It means *"to reprove, shine the light on, and expose."* This is what I have been doing throughout my public ministry regarding false and unscriptural teachings.

- 2 Corinthians 6:14-18

"**Be ye not unequally yoked together with unbelievers**: for what **fellowship** hath righteousness with unrighteousness? and what **communion** hath light with darkness? And what **concord** hath Christ with Belial? or what **part** hath he that believeth with an infidel? And what **agreement** hath the temple of God with idols? for ye are the temple of the living God; as God hath said, I will dwell in them, and walk in *them*; and I will be their God, and they shall be my people. Wherefore **come out from among them,**

and be ye separate, saith the Lord, and touch not the unclean *thing*; and I will receive you, And will be a Father unto you, and ye shall be my sons and daughters, saith the Lord Almighty."
Between truth and error, there's no *"fellowship, communion, concord, part, or agreement."* For this reason, God is very clear that genuine Christians should "come out from among them" and be separate, without even touching any unclean thing. I have tried to practice such Biblical separation throughout my public ministry for the Lord Jesus Christ. It is not a popular or universal position, sad to say.

2 John 1:11
"For he that biddeth him God speed is partaker of his evil deeds."

DON'T BID "GOD SPEED" TO APOSTATE PEOPLE
Those who deny the Biblical doctrines of Christology, concerning the Person and Work of the Lord Jesus Christ, should not be admitted into genuine Christians' homes and certainly should never be bidden *"God speed"* as they go away. To do so would make the Christian a "partaker of" the *"evil deeds"* of these people.

Verses On Evil
- **Ezra 9:13**

"And after all that is come upon us **for our evil deeds**, and for our great trespass, seeing that thou our God hast punished us less than our iniquities *deserve*, and hast given us *such* deliverance as this;"
Ezra realized that the seventy years of captivity in Babylon was because of the southern kingdom's evil deeds.
- **Job 1:1**

"There was a man in the land of Uz, whose name *was* Job; and that man was perfect and upright, and one that feared God, and **eschewed evil**."
Job separated himself from evil and unto his God.
- **Psalms 1:1**

"Blessed *is* the man that walketh not in the counsel of the ungodly, **nor standeth in the way of sinners**, nor sitteth in the seat of the scornful."

> **DON'T STAND IN THE WAY WITH SINNERS**
> True Christians should follow the advice of the psalmist and not stand anywhere in the way of sinners. They should be separate from such evil.

- **Matthew 6:13**
"And lead us not into temptation, but **deliver us from evil**: For thine is the kingdom, and the power, and the glory, for ever. Amen."

The so-called disciples prayer includes a wish to be delivered from evil. That's very important.

- **John 17:15**
"I pray not that thou shouldest take them out of the world, but that thou shouldest **keep them from the evil**."

The Lord Jesus Christ, in His High Priestly prayer to God the Father, asked that He would keep his followers from evil. This is Biblical separation.

- **Romans 12:9**
"*Let* love be without dissimulation. **Abhor that which is evil**; cleave to that which is good."

Evil should be strongly hated while cleaving closely to what the Bible calls the good.

- **Romans 12:21**
"**Be not overcome of evil**, but overcome evil with good."

Genuine Christians should not be overcome with evil. It should not have a victory over them.

- **Romans 13:4**
"For he is the minister of God to thee for good. But **if thou do that which is evil, be afraid**; for he beareth not the sword in vain: for he is the minister of God, a revenger **to *execute* wrath upon him that doeth evil**."

> **BIBLICAL GOVERNMENT DEFINED IN ROMANS 13**
> Biblical government as defined in Romans 13:4, rewards the good and punishes those who do evil. A proper government is important because we have some improper governments all over the world. Under these governments, the gospel of Christ is restricted.

- **1 Corinthians 15:33**
"Be not deceived: **evil communications corrupt good manners**."

Evil associations and friends have a corrupting influence on the lives of true Christians. Such associations must be avoided.

- 1 Thessalonians 5:22
"Abstain from all appearance of evil."

> **ABSTAIN FROM EVEN THE APPEARANCE OF EVIL**
> Even the *"appearance"* of something that is evil must be stopped. This involves many areas of life. Though what is said or done might not be evil, if it might appear to be evil, it should be avoided.

- 2 Thessalonians 3:3
"But the Lord is faithful, who shall stablish you, and **keep you from evil**."

For genuine Christians who are walking in the power of the Holy Spirit Who indwells them, God is able to keep them from all evil. That's His promise here in this verse. But they must want to keep away from "evil."

- 2 Timothy 4:18
"And **the Lord shall deliver me from every evil work**, and will preserve *me* unto his heavenly kingdom: to whom *be* glory for ever and ever. Amen."

> **PAUL KEPT FROM EVIL EVEN WHILE FACING DEATH**
> Paul wrote this from a Roman prison. It was his last letter before he was executed. Even at this late date in his life, he believed that the Lord would deliver him from every evil work, even if it meant his death. He was not going to compromise with evil in order to escape execution as some might do.

- 1 Peter 3:11
"**Let him eschew evil**, and do good; let him seek peace, and ensue it."

Peter taught his readers that they were to separate and stay away from evil. This is what Job did as I mentioned above in Job 1:1.

2 John 1:12

"Having many things to write unto you, I would not write with paper and ink: but I trust to come unto you, and speak face to face, that our joy may be full."

Though John had many things to write, he wanted especially to see them face to face so that his joy and theirs might be full by this visit.

Verses On Joy

- **Psalms 16:11**

"Thou wilt shew me the path of life: **in thy presence *is* fulness of joy**; at thy right hand *there are* pleasures for evermore."

When genuine Christians are in Heaven, there will be fulness of joy in God's very Presence.

- **Psalms 51:12**

"**Restore unto me the joy of thy salvation**; and uphold me *with thy* free spirit."

David had repented of his sins of adultery, murder, and cover-up. He wanted the joy of God's salvation to be restored to him.

- **Jeremiah 15:16**

"Thy words were found, and I did eat them; and **thy word was unto me the joy and rejoicing of mine heart**: for I am called by thy name, O LORD God of hosts."

The Words of the God of the Bible can bring the true Christians who read and follow it joy and rejoicing.

- **Habakkuk 3:17-18**

"Although the fig tree shall not blossom, neither *shall* fruit *be* in the vines; the labour of the olive shall fail, and the fields shall yield no meat; the flock shall be cut off from the fold, and *there shall be* no herd in the stalls: **Yet I will rejoice in the LORD, I will joy in the God of my salvation**."

JOY EVEN IN THE MIDST OF CATASTROPHES
Habakkuk explained that even if bad things happened to his figs, his vines, his olives, his fields, his flocks, and his herds, yet he will joy in the God of his salvation.

- **Luke 2:10**

"And the angel said unto them, Fear not: for, behold, **I bring you good tidings of great joy, which shall be to all people**."

JOY CAME AT CHRIST'S COMING INTO THE WORLD
The announcement of the coming of the Lord Jesus Christ would bring joy to all people.

- **Luke 15:7**

"I say unto you, that likewise **joy shall be in heaven over one sinner that repenteth**, more than over ninety and nine just persons, which need no repentance."

JOY IN HEAVEN WHEN PEOPLE ARE SAVED
Heaven has great joy when lost sinners sincerely trust the Lord Jesus Christ as their Saviour.

- **John 16:22**

"And ye now therefore have sorrow: but I will see you again, and your heart shall rejoice, and your joy no man taketh from you."

The disciples were told that the Lord Jesus Christ was going to be crucified, but He told them they would see Him again and they would receive great joy once again.

- **John 16:24**

"Hitherto have ye asked nothing in my name: **ask, and ye shall receive, that your joy may be full**."

Answered prayer brings fullness of joy.

- **Acts 13:52**

"And **the disciples were filled with joy**, and with the Holy Ghost."

In spite of persecution and difficulties, the disciples were filled with the joy of the Lord.

- **Acts 20:24**

"But none of these things move me, neither count I my life dear unto myself, **so that I might finish my course with joy**, and the ministry, which I have received of the Lord Jesus, to testify the gospel of the grace of God."

PAUL WANTED TO FINISH HIS MISSION WITH JOY
Paul did not fear death by going to Jerusalem. He wanted to finish with joy the mission the Saviour gave to him when He saved him.

- **Romans 15:13**

"Now **the God of hope fill you with all joy** and peace in believing, that ye may abound in hope, through the power of the Holy Ghost."

Paul prayed that God would fill the genuine Christians at Rome with all joy.

- **Galatians 5:22**

"But **the fruit of the Spirit is love, joy**, peace, longsuffering, gentleness, goodness, faith,"

Joy is one of the fruits of God the Holy Spirit in true Christians who are controlled by Him.

- **Hebrews 12:2**
"Looking unto Jesus the author and finisher of *our* faith; who **for the joy that was set before him endured the cross**, despising the shame, and is set down at the right hand of the throne of God."

> **CHRIST'S JOY EVEN ON THE CROSS**
> The Lord Jesus Christ looked beyond the painful suffering on the cross to the joy of bringing multitudes into Heaven who would sincerely trust in Him.

- **1 Peter 1:8**
"Whom having not seen, ye love; in whom, though now ye see *him* not, yet **believing, ye rejoice with joy unspeakable and full of glory:**"

> **CHRIST–LOVED WITHOUT BEING SEEN**
> Though genuine Christians living today have never seen the Lord Jesus Christ, they can rejoice with unspeakable and glorious joy because of what He has done for them.

- **1 John 1:4**
"And **these things write we unto you, that your joy may be full**."

The purpose of the Apostle John's first epistle was to bring fullness of joy to those who would read it.

2 John 1:13

"**The children of thy elect sister greet thee Amen.**"

John is greeting those who are in the church he is addressing.
- **Philippians 4:21**
"Salute every saint in Christ Jesus. The brethren which are with me greet you."
- **3 John 1:14**
"But I trust I shall shortly see thee, and we shall speak face to face. Peace *be* to thee. *Our* friends salute thee. Greet the friends by name."

There should be greetings. John ends his second epistle in this way. Greet the friends. We've got to be greeting people.

> **THE MEANING OF THE WORD, "AMEN"**
> Then he ends the epistle with this one word "Amen." We've said it before but this word is a universal term. The word "Amen" is the most remarkable word,

> transliterated, letter for letter, directly from the Hebrew and the Greek in the New Testament. And then into Latin and into English and into other languages, so it is practically a universal word. It's been called the best known word in human speech. They have it in Korean, Spanish, French. The word is directly related, in fact, almost identical to the Hebrew word for believe.

So John closes his second letter with "Amen." The children and elect sister greet thee. As we look over this second letter, we praise the Lord that He wrote it. John the apostle wrote the Gospel of John, the book of Revelation, and 1 John, 2 John, and 3 John. He was one of the most prolific writers of the entire New Testament next to Paul.

3 John
Chapter One

3 John 1:1

"The elder unto the wellbeloved Gaius, whom I love in the truth."

The Apostle John was an elder, probably in the sense of a pastor/bishop/elder that I will describe below. He was writing to Gaius whom he loved in the truth.

Verses On Elders

- Acts 20:17

"And from Miletus he sent to Ephesus, and called the elders of the church."

> **MEANING OF THE GREEK WORD, "PRESBUTEROS"**
> The Greek Word for *"elder"* is PRESBUTEROS. Some of the meanings of this Greek word are:
>
> *"1) elder, of age; 1a) the elder of two people; 1b) advanced in life, an elder, a senior; 1b1) forefathers; 2) a term of rank or office; 2a) among the Jews; 2a1) members of the great council or Sanhedrin (because in early times the rulers of the people, judges, etc., were selected from elderly men); 2a2) of those who in separate cities managed public affairs and administered justice; 2b) among the Christians, those who presided over the assemblies (or churches) The NT uses the term bishop, elders, and presbyters interchange-ably 2c) the twenty four members of the heavenly Sanhedrin or court seated on thrones around the throne of God."*

That's what it means, an elder. The Presbyterian Church is called Presbyterian because it stresses elders. When Paul called the

elders at Ephesus, he told them what their duties were to be. Their duties involved the areas of being pastors, bishops, and elders in the local churches.
- **Acts 20:27-35**
"For I have not shunned to declare unto you all the counsel of God. Take heed therefore unto yourselves, and to all the flock, over the which the Holy Ghost hath made you **overseers, to feed the church of God**, which he hath purchased with his own blood. For I know this, that after my departing shall grievous wolves enter in among you, not sparing the flock. Also of your own selves shall men arise, speaking perverse things, to draw away disciples after them. Therefore watch, and remember, that by the space of three years **I ceased not to warn every one night and day** with tears. And now, brethren, I commend you to God, and to the word of his grace, which is able to build you up, and to give you an inheritance among all them which are sanctified. I have coveted no man's silver, or gold, or apparel. Yea, ye yourselves know, that these hands have ministered unto my necessities, and to them that were with me. I have shewed you all things, how that so labouring ye ought to support the weak, and to remember the words of the Lord Jesus, how he said, It is more blessed to give than to receive."

In the New Testament, the leader in each local church has three duties in one person. He must be a pastor, a bishop, and an elder. Paul left the pastors/bishops/elders at Ephesus and told them that they would see his face no more. He was going to Jerusalem and there would be taken as a prisoner to Rome for trial.

PASTORS MUST PREACH THE BIBLE FAITHFULLY
In their duty as pastors, they were to preach faithfully the Words of God to the congregation. In their duty as bishop or overseer, they were to take over-all charge of the church. In their duty as elder, they were to be mature Christians in all areas of their Christian life.

Paul reminded them that he had warned the elders from the church at Ephesus (Acts 20:29) about the grievous wolves who would enter their church from without after he left. He also predicted there would be false teachers from within their church who would also draw away many disciples after their perversions. Paul also commended them to the Words of God which were able to build them up and give them a godly inheritance.

- 1 Timothy 5:1

"**Rebuke not an elder**, but intreat *him* as a father; *and* the younger men as brethren;"
We are to have respect for older people as well and the younger men as brethren, so we are not to rebuke.

- 1 Timothy 5:17-20

"Let **the elders that rule well** be counted worthy of double honour, especially **they who labour in the word and doctrine**. For the scripture saith, Thou shalt not muzzle the ox that treadeth out the corn. And, The labourer *is* worthy of his reward. **Against an elder receive not an accusation, but before two or three witnesses**. Them that sin rebuke before all, that others also may fear."

TAKE CARE OF FAITHFUL PASTORS

Paul is talking about the preachers, the pastors, the bishops and elders of the local churches; they should be remunerated and paid for their services. **Their labour is worthy of their reward.** Against a pastor/bishop/elder, accusations should be well-founded in the testimony of at least two or three sound witnesses.

- Titus 1:5

"For this cause left I thee in Crete, that thou shouldest set in order the things that are wanting, and **ordain elders in every city**, as I had appointed thee:"
So pastors, bishops, and elders should be ordained and set in the ministry as they were supposed to be.

- 1 Peter 5:1-2

"**The elders which are among you I exhort**, who am also an elder, and a witness of the sufferings of Christ, and also a partaker of the glory that shall be revealed: **Feed the flock of God which is among you, taking the oversight *thereof*, not by constraint, but willingly; not for filthy lucre, but of a ready mind;**"

FEEDING THE FLOCK WITH THE WORDS OF GOD

So the pastor/bishop/elder is to feed the flock that he serves with the Words of God.
---

3 John 1:2

"Beloved, I wish above all things that thou mayest prosper and be in health, even as thy soul prospereth."

Now notice John wants his readers to be in health. Notice the extent of health he talks about. It is to the same extent as the soul prospers. If peoples' personal health would be as prosperous as their soul health, I wonder how healthy they would be. If this were the case, I believe that many true Christian people would be sick in bed because their souls are not prospering.

Verses On Prosperity

- **Joshua 1:8**

"This book of the law shall not depart out of thy mouth; but **thou shalt meditate therein day and night**, that thou mayest observe to do according to all that is written therein: for **then thou shalt make thy way prosperous**, and then thou shalt have good success."

Meditating on the Scriptures, the Words of God, will bring a prosperous way for those who do so.

- **Psalms 1:1-3**

"Blessed *is* the man that walketh not in the counsel of the ungodly, nor standeth in the way of sinners, nor sitteth in the seat of the scornful. But his delight *is* in the law of the LORD; and in his law doth he meditate day and night. And he shall be like a tree planted by the rivers of water, that bringeth forth his fruit in his season; his leaf also shall not wither; and **whatsoever he doeth shall prosper**."

Following these verses will bring spiritual prosperity in fulfillment of these promises.

- **Proverbs 28:13**

"**He that covereth his sins shall not prosper**: but whoso confesseth and forsaketh *them* shall have mercy."

There will be no prosperity with the Lord for those who cover their sins.

- **Isaiah 55:10**

"For as the rain cometh down, and the snow from heaven, and returneth not thither, but watereth the earth, and maketh it bring forth and bud, that it may give seed to the sower, and bread to the eater: **So shall my word** be that goeth forth out of my mouth: it shall not return unto me void, but it shall accomplish that which I please, and it shall **prosper *in the thing* whereto I sent it.**"

> **THE KING JAMES BIBLE HAS GOD'S PROPER WORDS**
> It must be the proper Words--all of the proper Words. These Words are absent, added to, or changed in the modern Bible versions. God has not promised to prosper that which are not His Words.

- 1 Corinthians 16:1

"Now concerning the collection for the saints, as I have given order to the churches of Galatia, even so do ye. Upon the first *day* of the week **let every one of you lay by him in store, as *God* hath prospered him**, that there be no gatherings when I come."

"Giving" by true Christians, should be as God has prospered them.

3 John 1:3

"For I rejoiced greatly, when the brethren came and testified of the truth that is in thee, even as thou walkest in the truth."

John rejoiced when the brethren came and testified of the truth that was in his friend, Gaius. <u>One thing is to have the truth, but Gaius continued to walk in that truth.</u> That is what is needed today in our genuine Christian churches. <u>We have our accurately translated King James Bible and we must walk in line with it.</u>

3 John 1:4

"I have no greater joy than to hear that my children walk in truth."

The Apostle John found no greater joy than to hear that his fellow Christians were walking in the truth of the Words of God.

Verses About Joy

- 1 Chronicles 29:1-9

"Furthermore David the king said unto all the congregation, Solomon my son, whom alone God hath chosen, *is yet* young and tender, and the work *is* great: for the palace *is* not for man, but for the LORD God. Now I have prepared with all my might for the house of my God the gold for *things to be made* of gold, and the silver for *things* of silver, and the brass for *things* of brass, the iron for *things* of iron, and wood for *things* of wood; onyx stones, and *stones* to be set, glistering stones, and of divers colours, and all manner of precious stones, and marble stones in abundance. Moreover, because I have set my affection to the house of my God, I have of mine own proper good, of gold and silver, *which* I have given to the house of my God, over and above all that I have prepared for the holy house, *Even* three thousand talents of gold, of the gold of Ophir, and seven thousand talents of refined silver, to overlay the walls of the houses *withal*: The gold for *things* of gold, and the silver for *things* of silver, and for all manner of work *to be made* by the hands of artificers. <u>And who *then* is willing to consecrate his service this day unto the LORD?</u> Then the chief of the fathers and princes of the tribes of Israel, and the captains of thousands and of hundreds, with the rulers of the king's work, offered willingly, And gave for the service of the house of God of gold five thousand talents and ten thousand drams, and of silver ten thousand talents, and of brass eighteen thousand talents, and one hundred thousand talents of iron. And they with whom *precious* stones were found gave *them* to the treasure of the house of the LORD, by the hand of Jehiel the Gershonite. Then **the people rejoiced**, for that they offered willingly, because with perfect heart they offered willingly to the LORD: and **David the king also rejoiced with great joy**."

- **Nehemiah 12:43**

"Also that day **they offered great sacrifices, and rejoiced: for God had made them rejoice with great joy: the wives also and the children rejoiced: so that the joy of Jerusalem was heard even afar off.**"
God made the Jews to rejoice greatly when they offered sacrifices in the rebuilt temple.

- **Matthew 2:10**

"When they saw the star, **they rejoiced with exceeding great joy.**"
At the birth of the Lord Jesus Christ, when the star appeared, those who saw it rejoiced with exceeding great joy.

- **Matthew 28:8**

"And **they departed quickly from the sepulchre with fear and great joy**; and did run to bring his disciples word."
Mary Magdalene and the other Mary had great joy when they saw the open tomb showing that the Lord Jesus Christ had been raised bodily from the dead.

- **Luke 2:10**
"And the angel said unto them, Fear not: for, behold, **I bring you good tidings of great joy**, which shall be to all people."
The shepherds were given great joy at the birth of the Lord Jesus Christ.
- **Luke 24:52**
"And they worshipped him, and **returned to Jerusalem with great joy**:"
The other disciples and apostles worshipped the bodily-resurrected Saviour, the Lord Jesus Christ, and returned to Jerusalem with great joy.
- **Acts 8:8**
"And **there was great joy in that city**."
When Philip preached about the Lord Jesus Christ, there was great joy in the city of Samaria.

3 John 1:5

"Beloved, thou doest faithfully whatsoever thou doest to the brethren, and to strangers;"

John commends Gaius for being faithful in what he does to the fellow Christians and to strangers.

Verses On Faithfulness

- **Deuteronomy 7:9**
"**Know therefore that the LORD thy God, he** *is* **God, the faithful God,** which keepeth covenant and mercy with them that love him and keep his commandments to a thousand generations;"
When the God of the Bible makes a promise, He keeps His promises. Genuine Christians should follow this pattern of faithfulness as well.
- **Nehemiah 7:1-2**
"Now it came to pass, when the wall was built, and I had set up the doors, and the porters and the singers and the Levites were appointed, That **I gave my brother Hanani, and Hananiah the ruler of the palace, charge over Jerusalem: for he** *was* **a faithful man**, and feared God above many."

A FAITHFUL MAN LED THE JEWS AFTER 70 YEARS
Only a faithful man should be in charge over Jerusalem as the Jews returned after 70 years of captivity in Babylon.

- **Nehemiah 9:7-8a**

"**Thou *art* the LORD the God, who didst choose Abram**, and broughtest forth out of Ur of the Chaldees, and gavest him the name of Abraham; **And foundest his heart faithful before thee**, . . . "

Abram was chosen by the LORD because his heart was faithful before God.

- **Psalms 119:138**

"**Thy testimonies** *that* thou hast commanded ***are* righteous and very faithful**."

God will never go back on His Words. His Words are always faithful.

- **Proverbs 14:5**

"**A faithful witness will not lie**: but a false witness will utter lies."

LYING HAS NO PART IN FAITHFUL WITNESSES

Lying will not be a part of those who are faithful witnesses. Truth must prevail always even when it is not "politically correct."

- **Proverbs 27:6**

"**Faithful *are* the wounds of a friend**; but the kisses of an enemy *are* deceitful."

A FRIEND'S WOUNDS ARE FAITHFUL

No one wants to be wounded in any way, but if a true friend says something that is true and wounds a true Christian, that Christian should be thankful for such a faithful wound that will help him in his life.

- **Matthew 25:21**

"His lord said unto him, **Well done, *thou* good and faithful servant: thou hast been faithful** over a few things, I will make thee ruler over many things: enter thou into the joy of thy lord."

If genuine Christians practice faithfulness in the little things, God will be able to trust them in larger and more important tasks.

- **Luke 16:10**

"**He that is faithful in that which is least is faithful also in much**: and he that is unjust in the least is unjust also in much."

This verse is similar to that in Matthew. Faithfulness in small things equips true Christians to be faithful also in more important things.

- **1 Corinthians 1:9**
"**God *is* faithful**, by whom ye were called unto the fellowship of his Son Jesus Christ our Lord."

God is always faithful to keep His Words and His promises to both the genuine Christians and to those who reject the Saviour.

- **1 Corinthians 4:2**
"Moreover **it is required in stewards, that a man be found faithful**."

STEWARDS MUST BE FAITHFUL TO THEIR MASTER

A steward is a person in charge of all that his master owns. It is required that he be faithful in that important office.

- **1 Corinthians 4:17**
"For this cause have I sent unto you **Timotheus, who is** my beloved son, and **faithful in the Lord**, who shall bring you into remembrance of my ways which be in Christ, as I teach every where in every church."

Paul sent Timothy to the true Christians in the church at Corinth because he knew him to be faithful in the Lord.

- **1 Corinthians 10:13**
"There hath no temptation taken you but such as is common to man: but **God *is* faithful**, who will not suffer you to be tempted above that ye are able; but will with the temptation also make a way to escape, that ye may be able to bear *it*."

Even in the midst of the greatest testings of genuine Christians, God is faithful in providing a way to escape so that they can bear them.

- **Ephesians 6:21**
"But that ye also may know my affairs, *and* how I do, **Tychicus, a beloved brother and faithful minister in the Lord**, shall make known to you all things:"

When Paul was a prisoner in Rome, he sent Tychicus to help the true Christians in Ephesus because he was a faithful minister.

- **Colossians 1:7**
"As ye also learned of **Epaphras** our dear fellowservant, **who is for you a faithful minister of Christ**;"

Epaphras was another genuine Christian whom Paul commended as a faithful minister of Christ.

- **Colossians 4:9**
"With **Onesimus, a faithful and beloved brother**, who is *one* of you. They shall make known unto you all things which *are done* here."

Onesimus could be added to the list of faithful brothers in the Lord that Paul commended.
- **1 Thessalonians 5:24**
"**Faithful *is* he that calleth you**, who also will do *it*."

God Himself is faithful to those whom He calls and who respond in genuine faith in the Lord Jesus Christ to that Divine call.
- **2 Thessalonians 3:3**
"But **the Lord is faithful**, who shall stablish you, and keep *you* from evil."

The Lord is faithful in establishing true Christians and keeping them from evil as they're being soundly established.
- **1 Timothy 1:12**
"And I thank Christ Jesus our Lord, who hath enabled me, for that **he counted me faithful**, putting me into the ministry;"

CHRIST FOUND PAUL FAITHFUL AS A MINISTER
Paul was glad that the Lord Jesus Christ put him into the ministry. The reason is that He reckoned that Paul would be faithful to that calling.

- **1 Timothy 3:11**
"Even so *must their* wives *be* grave, not slanderers, sober, **faithful in all things**."

LOCAL CHURCH DEACONS MUST BE MARRIED
Those who have been chosen as deacons in local churches must have wives. I believe it is assumed that not only must they have wives, but they must have wives who are faithful in all things.

- **2 Timothy 2:2**
"And the things that thou hast heard of me among many witnesses, the same **commit thou to faithful men, who shall be able to teach others also**."

Paul, before he was executed, in his last letter to Pastor Timothy, urged Timothy to commit the teachings he had learned from Paul to faithful men who would be able to teach others also. These truths were not to stop, but were to continue throughout time.
- **Titus 1:5-6**
"For this cause left I thee in Crete, that thou shouldest set in order the things that are wanting, and **ordain elders** in every city, as I had appointed thee: If any be blameless, the husband of one wife, **having faithful children** not accused of riot or unruly."

> **PASTORS/BISHOPS/ELDERS MUST BE MARRIED**
> One of the qualifications of the pastor-bishop-elder of a local church is that he should be married, being the *"husband of one wife,"* but also have children who are genuine Christians who are faithful to the Lord. Sadly, these standards are not followed in many local churches today.

- Titus 1:9

"<u>Holding fast the faithful word as he hath been taught</u>, that he may be able by sound doctrine both to exhort and to convince the gainsayers."

> **PROPER WORDS OF GOD MUST BE HELD**
> The pastor/bishop/elder of a local church should hold fast God's faithful Words. He must not add to them, subtract from them, or change them in any other ways. <u>The King James Bible has been accurately translated from the proper inspired and preserved Hebrew, Aramaic, and Greek Words.</u> Other versions, following a Gnostic Critical Greek Text in the New Testament, have changed the underlying Greek Words in over 8,000 places–356 places are important doctrinal passages.

- Hebrews 2:17

"Wherefore in all things it behoved him to be made like unto *his* brethren, that he might be a merciful and **faithful high priest** in things *pertaining* to God, to make reconciliation for the sins of the people."

<u>The Lord Jesus is a faithful High Priest in Heaven, helping all the genuine Christians on earth who call upon Him for assistance.</u>

- Hebrews 10:23

"Let us hold fast the profession of *our* faith without wavering; (for **he is faithful that promised**;)"

<u>God Himself is faithful to keep all that He has promised the true Christians in His Words. They should be faithful to Him as well.</u>

- 1 Peter 5:12

"By **Silvanus, a faithful brother** unto you, as I suppose, I have written briefly, exhorting, and testifying that this is the true grace of God wherein ye stand."

<u>Silvanus</u> is mentioned by Peter as being <u>a faithful brother in the Lord Jesus Christ.</u>

- **1 John 1:9**
"If we confess our sins, **he is faithful and just to forgive us *our* sins, and to cleanse us** from all unrighteousness."
When proper confession is made, God is faithful and just in forgiving these sins and cleansing them from all unrighteousness.
- **Revelation 1:5**
"And **from Jesus Christ, *who is* the faithful witness**, *and* the first begotten of the dead, and the prince of the kings of the earth. Unto him that loved us, and washed us from our sins in his own blood,"
The Lord Jesus Christ is the faithful witness who gave to the Apostle John the Words in the book of Revelation.

3 John 1:6

"**Which have borne witness of thy charity before the church: whom if thou bring forward on their journey after a godly sort, thou shalt do well:**"

True Christian brethren and strangers have borne witness of the love that Gaius showed to them. He was urged to help them with their journey as well.

Verses On Charity

- **1 Corinthians 8:1**
"Now as touching things offered unto idols, we know that we all have knowledge. Knowledge puffeth up, but **charity edifieth**."

> **CHARITY/LOVE NEEDED IN THE CHRISTIAN LIFE**
> Charity edifies and is needed in the Christian life. It is the opposite of knowledge which often puffs people up.

- **1 Corinthians 13:1-8**
"Though I speak with the tongues of men and of angels, and have not charity, I am become *as* sounding brass, or a tinkling cymbal. And though I have *the gift of* prophecy, and understand all mysteries, and all knowledge; and though I have all faith, so that I could remove mountains, and have not charity, I am nothing. And though I bestow all my goods to feed *the poor*, and though I give my body to be burned, and have not charity, it profiteth me nothing. **Charity suffereth long, *and* is kind; charity envieth not; charity vaunteth not itself, is not puffed up, Doth not behave itself unseemly, seeketh not her own, is not easily**

provoked, thinketh no evil; Rejoiceth not in iniquity, but rejoiceth in the truth; Beareth all things, believeth all things, hopeth all things, endureth all things. Charity never faileth: but whether *there be* prophecies, they shall fail; whether *there be* tongues, they shall cease; whether *there be* knowledge, it shall vanish away."

THE CHARACTERISTICS OF NEVER FAILING LOVE
The above things are the characteristics of charity or Christian love. It will never fail.

- **1 Corinthians 13:13-14**
"And now abideth faith, hope, charity, these three; but **the greatest of these is charity**. Let all your things be done with charity."

The strangers and the genuine Christian brethren were given love. Gaius is commended for this.

- **Colossians 3:14**
"And above all these things ***put on* charity, which is the bond of perfectness**."

Charity is something that can be put on like a garment. It is a bond of perfectness.

- **2 Thessalonians 1:3**
"We are bound to thank God always for you, brethren, as it is meet, because that your faith groweth exceedingly, and **the charity of every one of you all toward each other aboundeth**;"

The true Christians in Thessalonica were commended for having their love abounding toward one another.

- **1 Peter 4:8**
"And above all things **have fervent charity among yourselves: for charity shall cover the multitude of sins**."

PETER COMMANDED TO HAVE FERVENT CHARITY
Peter commands his readers to have fervent charity and love among themselves. Charity does not justify any sin, but it can shine through and work despite the sins that any person might have committed.

3 John 1:7

"**Because that for his name's sake they went forth, taking nothing of the Gentiles.**"

I believe this is referring here to those strangers and brethren that were missionaries to others. They went forth for the sake of the Name of the Lord Jesus Christ.

Verses On Name's Sake

- **Matthew 24:9**

"Then shall they deliver you up to be afflicted, and shall kill you: and ye shall be hated of all nations for my name's sake."

The apostles were to be afflicted and hated because of the Name of the Lord Jesus Christ.

- **John 15:21**

"But **all these things will they do unto you for my name's sake**, because they know not him that sent me."

PERSECUTED FOR CHRIST'S SAKE WAS PROMISED

The Lord Jesus Christ warned His followers that they would be persecuted for His Name's sake.

- **Acts 9:16**

"For I will shew him **how great things he must suffer for my name's sake**."

The Lord Jesus Christ told Paul when he was saved that he would have to suffer many things for His Name's sake.

- **1 John 2:12**

"I write unto you, little children, because your sins are forgiven you for his name's sake."

HOW SINS CAN BE FORGIVEN

For the sake of the Name of the Lord Jesus Christ and those who truly trust Him for salvation, their sins can be forgiven.

Refusing To Take Goods From The Heathen

In this verse, the genuine Christians went forth taking nothing of the non-Christian heathen Gentiles.

- **Genesis 14:21-24**

"And **the king of Sodom said unto Abram, Give me the persons, and take the goods to thyself**. And Abram said to the king of Sodom, I have lift up mine hand unto the LORD, the most high God, the possessor of heaven and earth, That **I will not *take* from a thread even to a shoelatchet, and**

1, 2, & 3 John–Preaching Verse-by-Verse

that I will not take any thing that *is* thine, lest thou shouldest say, I have made Abram rich: Save only that which the young men have eaten, and the portion of the men which went with me, Aner, Eshcol, and Mamre; let them take their portion."
Abraham refused to take anything from the wicked king of Sodom. He trusted in the Lord to take care of him.
- **Genesis 15:1**
"After these things **the word of the LORD came unto Abram** in a vision, saying, **Fear not, Abram: I *am* thy shield, *and* thy exceeding great reward**."

> **ABRAHAM REJECTED SODOM'S MONEY**
> Abraham was told by the Lord that He and He alone was his exceeding great reward. Abraham did not need any of the goods offered by the king of Sodom.

- **1 Corinthians 16:1-2**
"Now concerning the collection for the saints, as I have given order to the churches of Galatia, even so do ye. **Upon the first *day* of the week let every one of you lay by him in store, as *God* hath prospered him**, that there be no gatherings when I come."

> **MINISTRY FUNDS FROM TRUE CHRISTIANS**
> In the New Testament, the funds for the local churches and the missionary outreach of those churches was to come from the faithful giving of the genuine Christians within those churches–not from the unbelieving people of the world.

3 John 1:8

"We therefore ought to receive such, that we might be **fellowhelpers to the truth**."

John said before that he was sending some people to Gaius and that he was going to help them to travel. He told Gaius that he ought to receive these "*fellowhelpers to the truth*." He didn't want him to turn them away.

Other Verses Using "Fellow"
- **Matthew 18:28**
"But the same servant went out, and found **one of his fellowservants**, which owed him an hundred pence: and he laid hands on him, and took *him* by the throat, saying, Pay me that thou owest."

This man was a servant who mistreated one of his fellowservants.
John 11:16
"**Then said Thomas**, which is called Didymus, **unto his fellowdisciples**, Let us also go, that we may die with him."
These were other disciples like Thomas was.
- **Romans 16:7**
"Salute Andronicus and Junia, my kinsmen, and **my fellowprisoners**, who are of note among the apostles, who also were in Christ before me."
These two men were in prison with Paul.
- **2 Corinthians 8:23**
"Whether *any do enquire* of **Titus**, *he is* my partner and **fellowhelper** concerning you: or our brethren *be enquired of, they are* the messengers of the churches, *and* the glory of Christ."

> **TITUS WAS A FELLOWHELPER IN PAUL'S MINISTRY**
> **Titus was a helper along with Paul in the ministry for the Lord Jesus Christ.**

- **Ephesians 2:19**
"Now therefore ye are no more strangers and foreigners, but **fellowcitizens with the saints**, and of the household of God;"
These genuine Christians at Ephesus were citizens along with other true Christians in the household of God.
- **Ephesians 3:6**
"That **the Gentiles should be fellowheirs**, and of the same body, and partakers of his promise in Christ by the gospel:"
The true Christian Gentiles were heirs of God like the true Christian Jews.
- **Philippians 2:25**
"Yet I supposed it necessary to send to you **Epaphroditus**, my brother, and companion in labour, and **fellowsoldier**, but your messenger, and he that ministered to my wants."
Epaphroditus was a soldier for the Lord like Paul was.
- **Philippians 4:3**
"And I intreat thee also, true **yokefellow**, help those women which laboured with me in the gospel, with Clement also, and *with* other my fellowlabourers, whose names *are* in the book of life."
This person was yoked with Paul in laboring for the gospel of Christ.

- **Colossians 1:7**
"As ye also learned of **Epaphras our dear fellowservant**, who is for you a faithful minister of Christ;"
Epaphras served the Lord with Paul.
- **Colossians 4:7**
"All my state shall **Tychicus** declare unto you, *who is* a beloved brother, and a faithful minister and **fellowservant** in the Lord:"
Tychicus served the Lord along with Paul.
- **Colossians 4:10**
"**Aristarchus my fellowprisoner** saluteth you, and Marcus, sister's son to Barnabas, (touching whom ye received commandments: if he come unto you, receive him;)"
Aristarchus was also in prison as Paul was.
- **Colossians 4:11**
"And Jesus, which is called Justus, who are of the circumcision. These only *are* **my fellowworkers** unto the kingdom of God, which have been a comfort unto me."
They were workers together with one another.
- **1 Thessalonians 3:2**
"And sent Timotheus, our brother, and minister of God, and our **fellowlabourer in the gospel of Christ**, to establish you, and to comfort you concerning your faith:"
Timothy labored with Paul in the gospel of Christ.
- **Philemon 1:2**
"And to *our* beloved Apphia, and Archippus our **fellowsoldier**, and to the church in thy house:"
These were two more soldiers for the Lord fighting for the Lord along with Paul.
- **Philemon 1:23-24**
"There salute thee Epaphras, **my fellowprisoner** in Christ Jesus; Marcus, Aristarchus, Demas, Lucas, **my fellowlabourers**."
In this verse, Paul names both prisoners and laborers that were associated with him.
- **Revelation 6:11**
"And white robes were given unto every one of them; and it was said unto them, that they should rest yet for a little season, until their **fellowservants** also and their brethren, that should be killed as they *were*, should be fulfilled."
These servants of the Lord will be killed because of their faith in Christ.

- Revelation 19:10

"And I fell at his feet to worship him. And he said unto me, See *thou do it* not: I am **thy fellowservant**, and of thy brethren that have the testimony of Jesus: worship God: for the testimony of Jesus is the spirit of prophecy."

Only the Lord should be worshipped, not human servants.

3 John 1:9

"I wrote unto the church: but Diotrephes, who loveth to have the preeminence among them, receiveth us not."

The Apostle John wrote unto this local church. But a man named Diotrephes who loved to have the preeminence over all the others in that church refused to receive John.

DIOTREPHES WAS AN ARROGANT CHURCH BOSS

Diotrephes was a proud, arrogant professing Christian. John wanted the church to receive everyone who came, but this man refused to receive the Apostle John. He wanted John to stay away from his church. Why was this? It was because he loves to have the preeminence.

MEANING OF THE GREEK WORD, "PHILOPROTEUO"

The Greek Word for *"preeminence"* is PHILOPROTEUO. Some of the meanings of this Greek Word are:

"1) to aspire to pre-eminence, to desire to be first"

If John were permitted to come to the local church, perhaps Diotrephes would not be in first place in that church. He should not have refused to have John come to this local church. That was not a Christian action.

Verses On Preeminence

- Colossians 1:18

"And **he is the head of the body, the church**: who is the beginning, the firstborn from the dead; **that in all *things* he might have the preeminence.**"

PREEMINENCE BELONGS ONLY TO CHRIST

The Lord Jesus Christ should have the preeminence over every genuine Christian.

- **Exodus 9:17**
"**As yet exaltest thou thyself against my people**, that thou wilt not let them go?"
Pharaoh exalted himself against the Jewish people who were his captives in Egypt. He wanted the preeminence.
- **Exodus 15:2**
"The LORD *is* my strength and song, and he is become my salvation: he *is* my God, and I will prepare him an habitation; **my father's God, and I will exalt him**."
It is the God of the Bible Who must have the preeminence.
- **2 Samuel 22:47**
"The LORD liveth; and blessed *be* my rock; and **exalted be the God of the rock of my salvation**."

PREEMINENCE–NOT FOR HUMAN BEINGS
The LORD must be exalted and have the preeminence, not some human being.

- **1 Kings 1:5**
"Then **Adonijah the son of Haggith exalted himself, saying, I will be king**: and he prepared him chariots and horsemen, and fifty men to run before him."
This evil man wanted to be the king of Israel and have the preeminence.
- **Psalms 12:8**
"The wicked walk on every side, **when the vilest men are exalted**."
Wicked will be on every side when vile men have the preeminence.
- **Psalms 21:13**
"**Be thou exalted, LORD**, in thine own strength: *so* will we sing and praise thy power."
Our God must be exalted, not any human being.
- **Psalms 34:3**
"O magnify the LORD with me, and **let us exalt his name together**."
True Christians should join together in exalting God's Name.
- **Psalms 66:7**
"He ruleth by his power for ever; his eyes behold the nations: **let not the rebellious exalt themselves**."

REBELLIOUS EXALTATION LEADS TO CHAOS
If the rebellious exalt themselves and have the preeminence, only chaos will result.

- Isaiah 14:13

"For **thou hast said in thine heart, I will ascend into heaven, I will exalt my throne above the stars of God**: I will sit also upon the mount of the congregation, in the sides of the north:"

SATAN'S GOAL IS PREEMINENCE OVER GOD
Satan's main goal is to have the absolute preeminence over God and all of God's people.

- Daniel 11:36

"And **the king shall do according to his will; and he shall exalt himself, and magnify himself above every god**, and shall speak marvellous things against the God of gods, and shall prosper till the indignation be accomplished: for that that is determined shall be done."

The future Antichrist will exalt himself and take the preeminence over all others in the earth.

- Matthew 23:12

"And **whosoever shall exalt himself shall be abased**; and he that shall humble himself shall be exalted."

DIOTREPHESE–BAN HIM FROM CHURCHES
Genuine Christians and sound churches must get the sin of Diotrephes out of their system. The Lord Jesus Christ has promised to abase those who seek preeminence.

- Philippians 2:9

"Wherefore **God also hath highly exalted him, and given him a name which is above every name**:"

God the Father has highly exalted God the Son, the Lord Jesus Christ, and given Him the preeminence.

- Philippians 2:10

"That **at the name of Jesus every knee should bow**, of *things* in heaven, and *things* in earth, and *things* under the earth;"

Every knee should bow to the Lord Jesus Christ Who alone must have the preeminence.

- 2 Thessalonians 2:3-4

"Let no man deceive you by any means: for *that day shall not come*, except there come a falling away first, and **that man of sin be revealed, the son of perdition; Who opposeth and exalteth himself above all that is called God**, or that is worshipped; so that he as God sitteth in the temple of God, shewing himself that he is God."

THE ANTICHRIST WILL TAKE PREEMINENCE
The Antichrist will take the preeminence and exalt himself above all that is called God.

3 John 1:10

"Wherefore, if I come, I will remember his deeds which he doeth, prating against us with malicious words: and not content therewith, neither doth he himself receive the brethren, and forbiddeth them that would, and casteth them out of the church."

Notice the details of what this Diotrephes is doing. John says that he might come to this church. If he comes, John will remember the evil deeds of Diotrephes such as undermining John by prating against him with *"malicious words."*

THE MEANING OF THE GREEK WORD, "PHILUAREO"
The Greek Word for *"prating"* is PHLUAREO. Some of the meanings of this Greek Word are:

"1) to utter nonsense, talk idly, prate; 2) to bring forward idle accusations, make empty charges; 3) to accuse one falsely with malicious words"

This verb is in the Greek present tense and indicates a continual action of prating with malicious words. This indicates that Diotrephes is doing this against many people perpetually.

Not only is this church boss against John, but he is also against many other of the true Christian brethren. Against them, he tries to forbid them from coming to the local church and if they come, he casts them out of the church.

Verses On Malicious Words
- **Ephesians 4:31**

"Let all bitterness, and wrath, and anger, and clamour, and **evil speaking**, be put away from you, with all malice:"

PUT AWAY EVIL SPEAKING
The evil speaking should be put away from genuine Christians.

- **Colossians 3:8**
"But now ye also put off all these; anger, wrath, malice, blasphemy, **filthy communication out of your mouth**."
True Christians should put away such filthy communication and not be like Diotrephes.
- **1 Peter 2:1**
"Wherefore **laying aside** all malice, and all guile, and hypocrisies, and envies, and **all evil speakings**,"
Evil speaking should be laid aside and not used by genuine Christians. Diotrephes violated this command grievously.

3 John 1:11

"Beloved, follow not that which is evil, but that which is good. He that doeth good is of God: but he that doeth evil hath not seen God."

This negative command, "follow not," was given to the true Christians in John's day using the Greek present tense. As such, it indicates stopping an action or activity that was already in progress. These Christians were following evil and not that which was good. John told them to stop such wickedness.

THIS CHURCH ALLOWED DICTATOR DIOTREPHES

This church was allowing the evil of letting Diotrephes to throw people out of the church and not to receive others into the church. They were allowing Diotrephes to continue to be a dictator in that local church. He was the very personification of evil. If people continually follow evil, they have not seen God, no matter how much they might tell people they have.

Verses On Following

- **Romans 14:19**
"Let us therefore follow after the things which make for peace, and things wherewith one may edify another."

FOLLOW THINGS FOR PEACEFUL EDIFICATION

Paul was writing to genuine Christians. He told them to follow things making for peace and things that edify one another.

- **1 Thessalonians 5:15**
"See that none render evil for evil unto any *man*; but **ever follow that which is good**, both among yourselves, and to all *men*."

The following of that which is good, for the true Christians, must be a forever occupation. It must go on without any let up.
- **1 Timothy 6:11**
"But thou, O man of God, flee these things; and **follow after righteousness, godliness, faith, love, patience, meekness.**"
Paul instructed Pastor Timothy to follow all six of these virtues. All genuine Christians should also follow them.
- **2 Timothy 2:22**
"Flee also youthful lusts: but **follow righteousness, faith, charity, peace**, with them that call on the Lord out of a pure heart."
Paul repeated his instruction to Timothy about following righteousness and faith, but that he was also to follow charity and peace.
- **Hebrews 12:14**
"**Follow peace with all *men*, and holiness**, without which no man shall see the Lord:"
Peace and holiness must be followed with all.

3 John 1:12

"**Demetrius hath good report of all men, and of the truth itself: yea, and we also bear record; and ye know that our record is true.**"

Demetrius has a good report from all men, from the truth, and from John himself. He was the very opposite of Diotrephes. By following the Bible's instructions and being led by God the Holy Spirit, all genuine Christians today can also have a good report.

Verses On Good Report
- **Acts 22:12**
"And one **Ananias,** a devout man according to the law, **having a good report of all the Jews** which dwelt *there*,"
It was Ananias that caused Paul's eyesight to be restored after he met the Lord Jesus Christ on the road to Damascus. Ananias had a good report of all the Jews in that city.
- **Philippians 4:8**
"Finally, brethren, whatsoever things are true, whatsoever things *are* honest, whatsoever things *are* just, whatsoever things *are* pure, whatsoever things *are* lovely, **whatsoever things *are* of good report**; if *there* be any virtue, and if *there be* any praise, **think on these things.**"

> **PONDER THINGS OF GOOD REPORT**
> Things that are of good report must be thought about and pondered by true Christians.

- 1 Timothy 3:7

"Moreover he must have a good report of them which are without; lest he fall into reproach and the snare of the devil."

> **PASTORS/BISHOPS/ELDERS NEED A GOOD REPORT**
> Before being chosen as the pastor/bishop/elder of a local church, <u>the candidate must have a good report</u> of those outside the Christian faith, lest he fall into the snare of the Devil.

- Hebrews 11:1-2

"Now **faith** is the substance of things hoped for, the evidence of things not seen. For **by it the elders obtained a good report**."

<u>The Old Testament elders received a good report</u> by their genuine faith in God and His Words.

3 John 1:13

"I had many things to write, but I will not with ink and pen write unto thee:"

<u>John could have written many more things to this local church, but he decided not to do so at that time.</u> There are a number of Scriptures that talk about writing. Today, through the Divine preservation of God's original, verbally inspired, inerrant, and preserved Hebrew, Aramaic, and Greek Words, we have a Bible that is still in writing.

Verses On Writing

- Proverbs 22:20-21

"Have not I written to thee excellent things in counsels and knowledge, **That I might make thee know the certainty of the words of truth**; that thou mightest answer the words of truth to them that send unto thee?"

> **USE AND PREACH ONLY THE WORDS OF TRUTH**
> God wants His true Christians to have a certainty that His Words are the truth. That's why I follow, in English, the King James Bible which is the only accurate English translation of the Words of Truth which is based on the

original, verbally inspired, inerrant, and preserved Hebrew, Aramaic, and Greek Words.

- John 19:19

"And **Pilate wrote a title**, and put *it* on the cross. And **the writing was, JESUS OF NAZARETH THE KING OF THE JEWS.**"

PILATE WROTE ABOUT CHRIST BEING THE KING

Pilate put this title in writing so that all could see it and read it. It was written in three languages--Hebrew, Greek, and Latin. Those were the three languages current in that area in that time. When the unbelieving Jews complained to Pilate about this writing, Pilate said: *"What I've written I've written"* (John 19:22).

- Acts 15:20

"But **that we write unto them**, that they abstain from pollutions of idols, and *from* fornication, and *from* things strangled, and *from* blood."

THE LAW OF MOSES IS NOT FOR CHRISTIANS

The Jews and the Gentiles were having a problem. Should every Gentile who became a genuine Christian keep the law of Moses? No! James, Peter, and other leaders in the church wrote down four things from the law that they were to keep.

- 1 Corinthians 4:14

"**I write not these things to shame you**, but as my beloved sons I warn *you*."

Paul wrote to the Corinthian Christians to warn them, not shame them.

- 1 Corinthians 14:37

"If any man think himself to be a prophet, or spiritual, let him acknowledge that **the things that I write unto you are the commandments of the Lord.**"

Paul was writing to the church at Corinth the commandments of God.

- 2 Corinthians 2:9

"For **to this end also did I write**, that I might know the proof of you, **whether ye be obedient in all things.**"

Paul wrote to inquire concerning the obedience of the genuine Christians at Corinth.

- **2 Corinthians 13:2**
"I told you before, and foretell you, as if I were present, the second time; and **being absent now I write to them which heretofore have sinned**, and to all other, that, if I come again, I will not spare:"

Paul wrote to those who had sinned in this church.
- **2 Corinthians 13:10**
"Therefore **I write these things being absent**, lest being present I should use sharpness, according to the power which the Lord hath given me **to edification, and not to destruction**."

Paul wanted to edify rather than destroy. Because of this, he wrote to them rather than speaking to them in person.
- **Galatians 1:20**
"Now **the things which I write unto you**, behold, before God, I lie not."

Paul's writing was not a lie. It was the truth.
- **Philippians 3:1**
"Finally, my brethren, rejoice in the Lord. **To write the same things to you**, to me indeed *is* not grievous, but **for you *it is* safe**."

Paul wrote to the church at Philippi that they might be safe, not grieved.
- **2 Thessalonians 3:17**
"**The salutation of Paul with mine own hand**, which is the token **in every epistle: so I write**."

When Paul wrote a letter, usually he would sign it. Sometimes he used a stenographer.
- **1 Timothy 3:14**
"**These things write I unto thee**, hoping to come unto thee shortly:"

Paul wrote to Pastor Timothy hoping to see him soon.
- **2 Peter 3:1**
"**This second epistle, beloved, I now write unto you**; in *both* which I stir up your pure minds by way of remembrance:"

Peter wrote in order to stir up their minds to remember.
- **1 John 1:4**
"And **these things write we unto you**, that your joy may be full."

John wanted the people to whom he was writing to have fullness of joy.

- 1 John 2:1

"My little children, **these things write I unto you, that ye sin not**. And if any man sin, we have an advocate with the Father, Jesus Christ the righteous:"

John wrote to this local church so they wouldn't sin.

- 1 John 2:12

"**I write unto you, little children, because your sins are forgiven** you for his name's sake."

FORGIVEN ONLY THROUGH TRUE FAITH IN CHRIST

John wrote to this group of genuine Christians because their sins were forgiven through faith in the Lord Jesus Christ.

3 John 1:14

"But I trust I shall shortly see thee, and we shall speak face to face. Peace be to thee. Our friends salute thee. Greet the friends by name."

John wanted to visit this local church shortly so that he could speak with them face to face. When you have a face to face meeting, either one of you will appreciate one another more, or possibly you may get upset with one another and have an argument. John was coming to see this leader in this church, speaking with him face to face. I'm sure things went well with their meeting.

Verses On Face To Face

- Exodus 33:11

"And **the LORD spake unto Moses face to face**, as a man speaketh unto his friend. And he turned again into the camp: but his servant Joshua, the son of Nun, a young man, departed not out of the tabernacle."

THE LORD AND MOSES–A PERSONAL RELATIONSHIP

The LORD had a very personal face to face relationship with Moses, as a man speaks to his friend. That was indeed a sacred and holy privilege.

- Acts 25:16

"To whom I answered, It is not the manner of the Romans to deliver any man to die, **before that he which is accused have the accusers face to face**, and have licence to answer for himself concerning the crime laid against him."

Paul believed it was his right under Roman law to confront his accusers face to face.

- 1 Corinthians 13:12

"For **now we see through a glass, darkly; but then face to face**: now I know in part; but then shall I know even as also I am known."

IN HEAVEN--FACE TO FACE WITH CHRIST

When genuine Christians get to Heaven, there will be a face to face fellowship with the Lord Jesus Christ.

- 2 John 1:12

"Having many things to write unto you, I would not *write* with paper and ink: but **I trust to come unto you, and speak face to face, that our joy may be full**."

JOHN WANTED TO VISIT THIS CHURCH PERSONALLY

John wanted to come to this local church so he could speak to them face to face. This would help bring them fullness of joy.

1, 2, & 3 John–Preaching Verse-by-Verse   261

Index Of Words And Phrases

1 John Chapter Five. iv
1 John Chapter Four. iv
1 John Chapter One. iv
1 John Chapter Three. iv
1 John Chapter Two. iv
1,050 NEW TESTAMENT COMMANDMENTS. 186
16 DOCTRINES ABOUT THE LORD JESUS CHRIST
. . . . 223
2 John. . . . . iv, 6, 21, 85, 137, 139, 142,
178, 199, 204, 209, 212-215,
217, 219, 221, 224, 225, 227,
230, 231, 260
3 John. 1-iv, 1, 6, 21, 30, 51, 65, 103,
133, 169, 230, 231, 233, 236,
237, 239, 244, 246, 247, 250,
253-256, 259
90 A.D. 1, 139
A CENTURION DENIED CHRIST AS THE SON OF GOD. 156
A FAITHFUL MAN LED THE JEWS AFTER 70 YEARS. 239
A FRIEND'S WOUNDS ARE FAITHFUL. 240
A GOOD DEFINITION OF 'PEACE". 211
A TRUE WITNESS TO CHRIST'S PERSON AND WORK. 201
A Verse On The Lust Of The Eyes. 81
Abel. 74, 119, 120, 193
abide. 23, 25, 44, 59, 61-63, 67, 82, 90,
96, 105, 128, 140, 186, 215,
221
abiding. 62, 63, 97, 111, 122, 123, 140,
186, 215, 221
ABIDING IN CHRIST FORSAKES SINS. 111
ABIDING IN CHRIST, NOT BE ASHAMED OF HIM. 97
About the Author. iv
ABRAHAM BELIEVED IN A SON THROUGH SARAH 92
ABRAHAM REJECTED SODOM'S MONEY. 247
ABSTAIN FROM EVEN THE APPEARANCE OF EVIL. 227
Acknowledgments. . . . . ii, iv
ADAM'S SIN MADE ALL PEOPLE SINNERS. 40
ADULTERY OF THE HEART. 81
AGAIN, THE GREEK WORD, TIS, IS FOR ANY HUMAN. 57
agapao. 122

airo. 109
aletheia. 86
allelon. 148
Amen. 36, 151, 154, 196, 197, 202, 204,
                                        226, 227, 230, 231
Ananias And Sapphira Committed The Sin Unto Death. 189
ANIMALS WILL BE DELIVERED IN THE MILLENNIUM. 84
Antichrist. 82-85, 87, 137-140, 192, 217,
                                              219, 252, 253
Antichrists. 82-85, 87, 137-140, 217,
                                                         218
ANTICHRISTS AND LIARS ARE DEFINED BY JOHN. 138
ANTICHRISTS ARE OF THIS WORLD. 140
ANTICHRISTS DENY CHRIST'S INCARNATION. 85
ANTICHRISTS SHOULD LEAVE SOUND CHURCHES. 85
APHIEMI. 47, 48, 69, 70
apostate. 4, 83, 137, 138, 176, 205, 218,
                                                219, 224, 225
APOSTATE ANTICHRIST PREACHERS. 137
APOSTATES AND GNOSTIC HERETICS. 218
appearance. 227
ashamed. 96, 97, 99-101, 105, 128-130,
                                                    161, 203
ASKING ACCORDING TO GOD'S WILL. 184
assurance. 94, 99, 126, 127, 159, 160,
                                                     182-184
ASSURANCE OF SALVATION NEEDED. 159
assure. 126
AT THE RAPTURE, CHRISTIANS GET NEW BODIES.. 98
barus. 171
being strong. 75
BFT #4155.. i
BFT Phone: 856-854-4452. i
Bible For Today Baptist Church.. .... i, iii
Bible preservation. 200, 205-209
BIBLE PRESERVATION FOR A 1,000 GENERATIONS. 206
BIBLE PRESERVATION IS VITAL. 200
BIBLE PRESERVATION-THE CORRECT POSITION. 205
Bible reading. 215
BIBLE VERSES ON THE SIN NATURE.. 39
Biblical government. 226
BIBLICAL GOVERNMENT DEFINED IN ROMANS 13. 226
blood of Christ. 11, 32-37

bodily resurrection.. . . . . 1, 4, 5, 8, 90, 163,
173, 176, 196, 223
bold. 99, 160
boldness. 36, 99, 100, 128, 159-161
BOLDNESS IN CHRIST THOUGH UNLEARNED. 160
BORN OF GOD DEFINED CLEARLY.. 169
born-again.. . . . . 9, 12, 13, 19, 29, 64, 74,
96, 102, 112, 114-116, 118, 120,
123, 141, 167, 171, 192
boss. 250, 253
BY CHRIST ALL THINGS WERE CREATED. 7
Cain. 74, 119, 120, 193
CAIN HATED HIS BROTHER, ABEL.. 119
CAIN MURDERED ABEL AND LIED ABOUT IT. 120
Calvinism. 54, 58
Calvinists.. . . . . 54-57, 110, 119, 147, 152
Canter. iii
chaos. 251
charity. 107, 244, 245, 255
CHARITY/LOVE NEEDED IN THE CHRISTIAN LIFE.. 244
CHRIST AND GOD THE FATHER–NO CONTRADICTION. . . . 222
CHRIST AS LIGHT SHINES OUT OF DARKNESS. 66
Christ Coming In The Flesh. 136
CHRIST COMMANDED MUTUAL CHRISTIAN LOVE.. 141
CHRIST DELIVERS CHRISTIANS FROM DARKNESS.. 26
CHRIST DIED FOR ALL LOST SHEEP OF THE WORLD. 124
CHRIST DIED FOR ALL PEOPLE. 58
CHRIST DIED FOR ALL UNGODLY, NOT JUST ELECT. 110
CHRIST DIED FOR THE SINS OF THE WHOLE WORLD.. . . . 110
CHRIST DIED FOR THE SINS OF THE WORLD.. . . . . 108, 126
CHRIST ENDURED THE CROSS FOR FUTURE JOY. 21
CHRIST FORGAVE THOSE WHO CRUCIFIED HIM. 46
CHRIST FOUND PAUL FAITHFUL AS A MINISTER. 242
CHRIST HAD PART IN THE CREATION. 7
CHRIST HAS A BODILY RESURRECTION.. 8
CHRIST HAS THE WORDS OF ETERNAL LIFE. 180
CHRIST IS CALLED "THE TRUE GOD". 94
CHRIST IS GOD AND IS BLESSED FOREVER. 196
CHRIST IS THE ONLY "JUST ONE" THAT EVER LIVED. 44
CHRIST IS THE TRUE GOD AND ETERNAL LIFE. 195
CHRIST IS THE "HEIR OF ALL THINGS". 7
CHRIST JUDGED SATAN AT THE CROSS. 76
CHRIST NOW INTERCEDING FOR TRUE CHRISTIANS. 53

Christ Showed What Eternal Life Is. 11
CHRIST THE LIFE AND THE LIGHT. 22
Christ The Life Was Manifested.. 9
CHRIST THE LIGHT OF LIFE. 67
CHRIST THE LIGHT OF THE WORLD.. .... 25, 62
CHRIST THE ONLY LIGHT IN THIS DARK WORLD.. 23
CHRIST WANTS GOD'S LOVE IN TRUE CHRISTIANS. 130
CHRIST WANTS TO DELIVER FROM THE EVIL WORLD..... 77
CHRIST WAS AND IS THE ETERNAL SON OF GOD. 157
CHRIST WAS ETERNALLY WITH HIS FATHER. 13
CHRIST WAS GIVEN ALL JUDGMENT BY THE FATHER..... 89
CHRIST WAS GOD MANIFEST IN THE FLESH. 136
CHRIST WAS PERFECT GOD AND PERFECT MAN. 6, 10
Christ Was With The Father.. 13
CHRIST, THE SUBSTITUTE FOR EVERYONE. 110
Christian Brethren.. .... 147, 148, 244, 245, 253
CHRISTIANS CAN BE CLEANSED BY THE BIBLE. 47
CHRISTIANS MUST CARE FOR ONE ANOTHER. 165
CHRISTIANS MUST STUDY GOD'S WORDS.. 101
CHRISTIANS SHOULD LOVE CHRIST'S APPEARING. 98
CHRISTIANS SHOULD LOVE NOT THE WORLD. 76
CHRISTIANS SHOULD LOVE ONE ANOTHER. 66, 118, 141, 149
CHRISTIANS SHOULD WAIT FOR GOD'S PROMISES........ 93
CHRISTIANS WILL BE TAKEN IN THE RAPTURE. 83
CHRISTIANS' TWO NATURES–FLESH & HOLY SPIRIT. 79
Christology. 178, 223, 225
CHRIST–LOVED WITHOUT BEING SEEN. 230
CHRIST'S BODILY RESURRECTION REMOVED FEAR. 163
CHRIST'S BROTHERS, SISTERS, AND MOTHERS. 184
CHRIST'S ETERNAL DEITY. 6
CHRIST'S FACE SHOWN AS THE SUN. 3
CHRIST'S FIRST NEW TESTAMENT MIRACLE.. 10
CHRIST'S GAVE THE WORDS OF THE BIBLE. 141
CHRIST'S GREATER LOVE–DYING FOR EVERYONE. 124
CHRIST'S INCARNATION BY WATER AND BLOOD. 173
CHRIST'S INVITATION IS FOR ALL, NOT JUST SOME. 55
CHRIST'S JOY EVEN ON THE CROSS. 230
CHRIST'S RECORD IS FOUND IN THE BIBLE.. 177
CHRIST'S TITLE "I AM" SHOWS HIS ETERNAL DEITY.. 7
church boss.. .... 250, 253
CHURCH OFFICERS SHOULD NOT BE PRIDEFUL. 82

Church Phone: 856-854-4747. i
churches. 27, 37, 38, 85, 118, 162, 185,
203, 205, 212, 222, 233-235,
237, 242, 243, 247, 248, 252
cleansing. 35, 46-48, 112, 244
CLEANSING NEEDED FOR FLESH AND SPIRIT............. 47
Collingswood. .... i, iii
Collingswood, New Jersey. .... i, iii
coming of Christ... 97
commandments. 59, 60, 63, 129, 131, 170,
171, 186, 215, 239, 249, 257
commit. 44, 96, 114, 115, 155, 187, 242
confess............................ 42, 43, 47, 48, 85, 114, 127,
137, 139, 154, 169, 192, 217,
219, 244
CONFESS "FAULTS," TO OTHERS, NOT "SINS.".............. 43
confession... 42, 244
confidence......................... 81, 96, 97, 99, 105, 127-129,
160, 161, 182, 184
CONFIDENCE IN GOD AND HIS WORDS.................. 128
CONFIDENCE OF SALVATION IS IMPORTANT. 182
CONFIDENCE TOWARD GOD......................... 99, 127
CONSTITUTIONALISTS NOW CALLED TERRORISTS........ 24
CONTINUING IN SIN IS FALSE CHRISTIANITY............ 192
CONTINUING IN SIN IS THE DEVIL'S DESIRE............. 114
CORRUPTIBLE TO INCORRUPTIBLE BODIES. 105
CURRENT ANTICHRISTS DENY CHRIST'S DEITY........... 83
darkness. 16, 22-29, 62, 64, 66-69, 77,
117, 162, 192, 195, 202, 216,
224
DARKNESS BLINDS THE EYES OF CHRISTIANS............ 69
DARKNESS SHOULD BE REPROVED AND EXPOSED........ 26
DARKNESS TURNED TO LIGHT BY GOD'S CREATION....... 22
DAVID RESTORED FROM ADULTERY AND MURDER. 18
daysman. 52, 53
DEATH PASSED ON ALL PEOPLE THROUGH ADAM. 40
deceive......................... 32, 38, 40, 41, 83, 95, 112-114,
135, 136, 218, 252
deceived........................ 41, 76, 95, 112, 113, 135, 218,
226
deception........................ 40, 41, 113, 135, 176, 193,
218
DECEPTION COMES WITH EMPTY WORDS. 41

DECEPTION IS THE DEVIL'S KEY METHOD............... 135
Defined King James Bible Orders............................ iv
Deity of Christ.. 173, 196
DENIAL OF THE SON IS A DENIAL OF THE FATHER........ 88
DESTROYING THE WORKS OF THE DEVIL................. 158
Devil............................ 11, 27, 30, 31, 49, 52, 59, 60,
         76, 82, 114, 116, 117, 123, 158,
         163, 172, 194, 195, 201, 202,
         206, 218, 256
dictator.. 254
Diotrephes.. 250, 252-255
DIOTREPHES WAS AN ARROGANT CHURCH BOSS........ 250
DIOTREPHESE–BAN HIM FROM CHURCHES............. 252
DISTINCT PERSONS IN THE TRIUNE GODHEAD........... 89
DIVINE LOVE FOR TRUE FELLOW CHRISTIANS.......... 167
doctrine............................ 15, 27, 38, 41, 88, 95, 113,
         118, 119, 133, 136, 139, 142,
         167, 204, 205, 214, 221-224,
         235, 243
Doctrines Of The Lord Jesus Christ....................... 178,
         221, 223
DON'T BID "GOD SPEED" TO APOSTATE PEOPLE........... 225
DON'T STAND IN THE WAY WITH SINNERS.............. 226
edification.. 254, 258
edify... 254, 258
elder......................... 107, 199, 233-235, 243, 256
elect........................ 54-58, 110, 119, 136, 147, 199,
         230, 231
elencho... 224
entire world......................... 10, 19, 54, 57-59, 110,
         111, 143, 146, 147, 152
eternal life........................... 8-13, 19, 22, 31, 40, 56,
         58, 60, 82, 90, 92-94, 103, 109,
         122, 123, 130, 141, 144, 145,
         157, 158, 169, 178-183, 195-197,
         210, 216
ETERNAL LIFE BRINGS NO SEPARATION FROM GOD..... 179
ETERNAL LIFE GIVEN TO THOSE TRUSTING CHRIST...... 12
ETERNAL LIFE IS A GIFT FROM GOD..................... 13
ETERNAL LIFE IS GOD'S GIFT THROUGH FAITH.......... 182
ETERNAL LIFE IS ONLY IN CHRIST...................... 179
ETERNAL LIFE THROUGH FAITH IN THE SON OF GOD.... 157
EVERY PERSON HAS A SIN NATURE...................... 38

evil............... 15, 23, 24, 28, 43, 49, 64, 66, 67,
73, 74, 77, 79, 80, 82, 95, 96,
110, 119, 121, 127, 135, 166,
172, 173, 178, 183, 185, 187,
193, 194, 202, 209, 218, 220,
225-227, 242, 245, 251, 253,
254
EVIL MEN WILL BECOME WORSE AND WORSE........... 96
evil speaking....................................... 253, 254
evil spirits... 135
e-mail: BFT@BibleForToday.org........................... i
face to face........................... 21, 149, 216, 227, 230,
259, 260
faithful.......................... ii, 15, 27, 35, 42-44, 47, 48,
52, 59, 92, 93, 98, 114, 127,
169, 174, 192, 227, 235, 239-
244, 247, 249
faithful pastors................................... 98, 235
faithfulness............................... 43, 44, 239, 240
false prophets........................... 41, 58, 95, 133, 135,
136
FALSE TEACHERS TODAY GO IN CAIN'S WAYS............ 120
FAX: 856-854-2464... i
fear.......................... 2, 19, 22, 47, 80, 99, 126, 128,
162, 163, 190, 200, 205, 212,
220, 228, 229, 235, 238, 239,
247
FEEDING THE FLOCK WITH THE WORDS OF GOD......... 235
fellow............... 67-69, 72, 107, 108, 116, 121-
126, 130, 142, 143, 148, 159,
165-167, 170, 187, 237, 239,
248
Fellowship.................. 7, 12, 14-16, 23, 25-28, 32,
34, 35, 43, 62, 78, 85, 112,
127, 148, 159, 169, 192, 217,
222, 224, 241, 260
FELLOWSHIP WITH BOTH THE FATHER AND SON......... 15
FILLED WITH JOY DESPITE PERSECUTIONS.............. 20
first day...................................... 162, 237, 247
flesh.......................... 6, 8, 10, 12, 13, 26, 28, 29, 33,
45, 47, 48, 51, 52, 59, 64, 72,
74, 77, 79-81, 84, 85, 88, 92,
99, 102, 110, 112, 115, 128,

follow............................ 131, 136-139, 145, 150, 151, 158, 163, 165, 172, 193, 195, 196, 202, 208, 210, 216-219, 2, 7, 12, 24, 78, 93, 94, 96, 97, 107, 124, 136, 138, 145, 172, 183, 185, 192, 197, 200, 202, 215, 220, 226, 228, 239, 254-256
FOLLOW THINGS FOR PEACEFUL EDIFICATION.......... 254
FOLLOWING THE WORLD SPOILS CHRISTIANS 78
Foreword... iii, iv
forgive.......................... 40, 42, 44-47, 69-72, 114, 127, 169, 192, 244
forgiven......................... 46, 69-72, 147, 195, 246, 259
FORGIVEN ONLY THROUGH TRUE FAITH IN CHRIST..... 259
forgiveness........................ 10, 25, 33, 34, 45, 46, 48, 58, 70, 109, 117, 153, 157, 195
friend................................. ii, 78, 149, 237, 240, 259
FULL JOY DESIRED FOR TRUE CHRISTIANS............... 21
gennao.. 169, 171
GENUINE CHRISTIANS ABIDE FOREVER................. 186
GENUINE CHRISTIANS CALLED OUT OF DARKNESS....... 26
GENUINE CHRISTIANS MUST WALK BY FAITH........... 216
GENUINE CHRISTIANS' FELLOWSHIP WITH CHRIST. 15
Gnostic........................... 7, 10, 12, 26, 27, 43, 65, 66, 93, 136, 138, 145, 157, 172, 174-178, 199, 204, 218, 243
Gnostic Greek...................................... 10, 145, 176
GNOSTIC TEXTS ALTER 356 DOCTRINAL PASSAGES. 172
GNOSTIC VERSIONS DENY CHRIST'S INCARNATION...... 138
Gnostics. 7, 12, 145, 175, 178
GNOSTICS REMOVED "ON ME" IN JOHN 6:47............ 178
GOD IS ALWAYS JUST AND TRUE........................ 45
GOD IS NOT A LIAR ABOUT PEOPLE'S SINS............... 48
GOD LOVES RIGHTEOUSNESS AND HATES SIN........... 159
GOD MADE PROVISION FOR THE WHOLE WORLD......... 58
GOD PROTECTED CAIN, THE MURDERER................ 120
GOD SENT HIS SON AT HIS OWN PROPER TIME. 10
GOD SEPARATED THE LIGHT FROM THE DARKNESS. 24
God speed................................... 178, 224, 225
God the Father....................... 7, 9, 10, 13, 15, 19, 43, 45, 51-54, 58, 63, 73, 76, 84,

87-90, 92, 103, 121, 130, 131, 137, 140, 144, 147, 152, 153, 157, 161, 173, 177, 182, 198, 200, 204, 209, 221, 222, 226, 252
GOD THE FATHER AND GOD THE SON ARE DISTINCT...... 88
God the Holy Spirit. 13, 20, 29, 31, 38, 64, 86, 88, 89, 91, 92, 96, 112, 116, 128, 131, 139-141, 151, 174, 193, 201, 216, 229, 255
GOD THE HOLY SPIRIT INDWELLS TRUE CHRISTIANS.... 131
GOD WANTS ALL TO TRULY TRUST IN HIS SON........... 130
GOD WAS JUST IN FORGIVING SINNERS.................. 45
GOD WAS PROPITIATED BY CHRIST'S SACRIFICE......... 146
GOD WENT WITH MOSES IN THE WILDERNESS. 150
GOD'S CHILDREN MANIFESTED........................ 116
GOD'S DEFINITION OF A "LIAR"........................ 165
GOD'S ETERNAL PLAN OF REDEMPTION BY BLOOD. 11
GOD'S FORGIVENESS OF SINS THROUGH CHRIST. 70
GOD'S FULNESS HAS NOT BEEN SEEN................... 149
GOD'S GRACE SENT THE SAVIOUR FROM HEAVEN. 210
GOD'S LOVE EXPRESSED IN CHRIST'S DEATH............ 164
GOD'S LOVE SENT HIS SON TO DIE FOR US............... 103
GOD'S LOVE SHOWN BY SENDING HIS SON. 143
GOD'S LOVE WAS FIRST. 164
GOD'S PEACE RULING THE HEARTS..................... 211
GOD'S SEED IS THE HOLY SPIRIT....................... 115
GOD'S TRUTH IS FOUND ONLY IN THE PROPER BIBLE.... 199
GOD'S TRUTH IS UNCHANGEABLE. 90
God's will.............................. 82, 93, 144, 184-186
GOD'S WILL DELIVERS FROM THIS WICKED WORLD. 185
GOD'S WILL FOUND IN GOD'S BIBLE WORDS............. 185
GOD'S WORDS CAN SANCTIFY THOSE WHO OBEY
.... 202
good report....................................... 255, 256
grace.......................... 6, 14, 16, 20, 28, 33, 34, 36, 58, 65, 75, 88, 120, 149, 151, 153, 154, 170, 181, 196, 209, 210, 220, 229, 234, 243
GRACE, MERCY, AND PEACE. 153, 209
Greek present tense........................... 17, 75, 111, 112, 114-116, 121-123, 125, 133, 148, 182, 184, 192, 253, 254

GREEK PRESENT TENSE IS CONTINUOUS ACTION......... 111
hate............................. 23, 67-69, 120-123, 165-167
HATED FOR CHRIST'S SAKE.............................. 166
HATRED FOR CHRIST AND HATRED FOR CHRISTIANS.... 166
HAVING CHRIST AS SAVIOUR MEANS ETERNAL LIFE..... 180
heathen.................................. 16, 28, 202, 246
Heaven. 7, 9, 11, 13, 18, 19, 21, 22, 24,
34, 35, 44, 53, 62, 67, 82, 83,
85, 93, 97, 98, 105, 106, 111,
143, 145, 147, 149, 153, 158,
161, 174-178, 181, 182, 191,
195, 207, 210, 211, 220, 223,
228-230, 236, 243, 246, 252,
260
Hell. 12, 13, 24, 26, 27, 93, 102, 115,
117, 122, 146, 179, 180, 210
HELL WAS PREPARED FOR THE DEVIL. 117
heretic........................... 10, 32, 41, 54-58, 65, 88, 95,
110, 113, 152, 218, 224
Herod Committed The Sin Unto Death. 190
High Priest........................... 4, 52, 53, 121, 127, 155,
158, 174, 176, 243
hilasmos.. 54, 146
Holy Spirit. 7, 13, 20, 21, 29, 31, 38,
51, 63, 64, 73, 79, 80, 86, 88,
89, 91, 92, 96, 108, 112, 114-
116, 122, 128, 130-132, 139-141,
151, 161, 163, 173, 174, 185,
193, 201, 202, 204, 212, 216,
227, 229, 255
HOMOLOGEO.................................. 42, 114, 137
hope............................. iii, 12, 20, 31, 32, 60, 92, 98,
100, 106, 130, 149, 153, 161,
177, 178, 181, 229, 245
HOPE IS FUTURE YET ASSURED........................ 106
HOW SINS CAN BE FORGIVEN.......................... 246
Hyper-Calvinism....................................... 54, 58
HYPER-CALVINISM IS HERESY!........................ 58
hyper-Calvinists......................... 54-57, 110, 119, 147,
152
idol.. 80, 198
idols............................. 96, 197, 198, 224, 244, 257
IDOLS CAN BE HUMAN AS WELL AS INANIMATE. 197

IN HEAVEN--FACE TO FACE WITH CHRIST.	260
IN TESTINGS, A WAY TO ESCAPE BY GOD.	43
incarnation.	10, 85, 136-139, 173, 176, 196, 217, 219
Index of Words and Phrases..	iv, 261
indwell.	132
indwelling.	29, 79, 80, 108, 114, 116, 131, 132, 140, 151, 193, 204
indwelling Holy Spirit.	79, 80, 108, 114, 131, 132, 140, 151, 193
INDWELLING OF THE HOLY SPIRIT IN THE SAVED.	116
Intercessor.	51-53
Island of Patmos.	1
it is written.	42, 49, 155, 206
Jehovah's Witnesses.	224
John.	1, i-iv, 1-9, 11-14, 16, 17, 19, 21-25, 27, 28, 30-32, 35-40, 42, 47-49, 51, 53-63, 65-70, 72-76, 79, 82, 84-90, 93-96, 98, 99, 102-106, 108, 109, 111, 112, 114-131, 133, 135-154, 156-162, 164-167, 169-171, 173-184, 186, 187, 191-197, 199-202, 204, 209, 212-219, 221, 222, 224-227, 229-231, 233, 236, 237, 239, 244, 246-248, 250, 253-260
JOHN AND TWO OTHERS HEARD GOD'S VOICE.	3
JOHN CARED FOR JESUS' MOTHER, MARY.	5
John Handled And Touched Christ..	8
JOHN HANDLED THE LORD JESUS CHRIST.	8
John Heard And Looked Upon Christ..	8
JOHN LEANED ON CHRIST AT THE LAST SUPPER	8
JOHN PREPARED CHRIST'S LAST PASSOVER.	4
JOHN SAW CHRIST'S EMPTY TOMB.	4
JOHN SHOULD NOT HAVE FOLLOWED PETER HERE.	5
JOHN THE BAPTIST WAS A WITNESS TO CHRIST.	14
JOHN WANTED TO VISIT THIS CHURCH PERSONALLY.	260
John was an excellent firsthand witness.	1
JOHN WAS EXILED TO PATMOS FOR GOD'S WORDS.	6
John Wrote Of Christ As The Eternal Creator.	6
John's Banishment To The Isle Of Patmos..	5
John's Belief In Christ's Bodily Resurrection..	4

272 1, 2, & 3 John–Preaching Verse-by-Verse

John's Call To Be Christ's Follower........................... 2
John's Commission To Preach.............................. 2
John's Presence At Christ's Transfiguration.................. 3
John's Presence At Christ's Trial............................ 4
John's Presence At The Cross............................... 5
JOHN'S PURPOSE IN WRITING HIS GOSPEL.............. 138
John's Return To Fishing With Peter........................ 5
John's Special Assignment.................................. 4
John's Writing Of Many Bible Books........................ 6
JOTS AND TITTLES EXPLAINED......................... 207
joy. 17-22, 30, 65, 150, 185, 227-230, 237-240, 258, 260
JOY CAME AT CHRIST'S COMING INTO THE WORLD...... 228
JOY EVEN IN THE MIDST OF CATASTROPHES............ 228
JOY IN HEAVEN WHEN PEOPLE ARE SAVED............. 229
JOY, EVEN THROUGH MUCH AFFLICTION................ 21
judgment........................ 24, 42, 52, 76, 88, 89, 134, 144, 159-162, 209, 221, 223
just........................... 7, 8, 19, 32, 42, 44, 45, 47, 48, 55-58, 82, 103, 110, 112, 114, 123, 125, 127, 141, 144, 145, 152, 169, 170, 192, 199, 203, 213, 214, 228, 244, 255
KEEP JEHOVAH'S WITNESSES OUT OF YOUR HOUSE..... 224
KEEPING IN FELLOWSHIP WITH THE LORD............. 127
keimai... 194
King James Bible........................ i, iv, 17, 22, 23, 57, 62, 65, 67, 88, 91, 100, 106, 172, 174, 175, 177, 179, 199, 200, 205, 206, 209, 237, 243, 256
KING JAMES BIBLE IS AN ACCURATE TRANSLATION..... 200
know......................... 9, 11-13, 21, 26, 33, 45, 46, 59, 61, 69, 74, 78, 79, 82, 83, 86, 87, 89, 94, 96, 98, 101, 102, 104, 109, 116, 118, 119, 121-124, 126, 130-132, 134, 136-138, 140, 143, 149-151, 153, 158, 165, 166, 170, 174, 179, 182, 183, 185, 187, 192, 194, 195, 197, 200, 201, 203, 206, 207, 210, 215, 220, 222, 234, 241, 244, 246, 255-257, 260

knowing........................ 13, 21, 67, 86, 126, 141, 143,
183, 190, 204
LACK OF LOVE=NOT KNOWING GOD. 143
Lake of Fire......................... 24, 76, 123, 180, 209, 218
last days... 7, 83, 84, 212
last time... 82-84, 138
LAYING DOWN YOUR LIFE FOR FELLOW CHRISTIANS.... 124
liar............................ 31, 48, 49, 59, 60, 84, 87, 117,
123, 138, 139, 165, 177, 178,
201, 219
liars................................. 27, 49, 59, 60, 87, 138
light............................ 3, 9, 14, 16, 22-26, 29, 32, 35,
62, 64, 66-69, 77, 117, 153,
162, 181, 192, 216, 217, 220,
224
local church........................ 28, 82, 199, 234, 242, 243,
250, 253, 254, 256, 259, 260
LOCAL CHURCH DEACONS MUST BE MARRIED............ 242
LOOKING ALL AROUND IN OUR WALK.................... 30
LOST PEOPLE CAN'T UNDERSTAND GOD'S WORDS........ 86
love........................ 13, 20, 21, 29, 54, 59, 61, 63-66,
68, 69, 71, 75, 76, 85, 93, 98,
103, 107, 108, 110, 116, 118-
122, 124-126, 129, 130, 141-143,
146-150, 159, 160, 162-167, 169,
170, 192, 193, 199, 202, 204,
209, 210, 213-215, 217, 226,
229, 230, 233, 239, 244, 245,
255
LOVE AS CHRIST LOVED IS THE STANDARD............... 66
LOVE IN DEED AND TRUTH, NOT IN WORD ONLY........ 125
LOVE IS A GREAT MOTIVATOR......................... 164
LOVE ONE ANOTHER AS CHRIST LOVED US.............. 213
LOVE REGARDLESS OF DISAGREEMENTS................. 118
LOVING FELLOW CHRISTIANS................... 142, 167, 170
LOVING FELLOW-CHRISTIANS TAUGHT BY GOD......... 142
LOVING GOD AND LOVING FELLOW CHRISTIANS........ 170
lust............................ 28, 29, 48, 64, 79-82, 186, 216
lust of the eyes.. 79, 81
lying........................ 4, 31, 32, 60, 70, 190, 192, 193,
240
LYING HAS NO PART IN FAITHFUL WITNESSES.......... 240
LYING TO GOD WAS A SIN UNTO PHYSICAL DEATH....... 190

MAINTAINING LOVE DESPITE DIFFERENCES. 122
malicious. 253
MANY BELIEVE SATAN'S DECEPTIONS. 193
MANY PROTESTANT AND CATHOLIC ANTICHRISTS!. 85
MANY WALK AFTER THEIR OWN LUSTS. 213
married. 242, 243
Matthias. 91
MEANING OF THE GREEK WORD, "PARAKLETOS". 51
MEANING OF THE GREEK WORD, "PHILOPROTEUO". 250
MEANING OF THE GREEK WORD, "PRESBUTEROS". 233
MEANING OF THE GREEK WORD, "SPLANCHNON". 125
MEANING OF THE PRESENT TENSE OF "COMMIT". 115
MEETING ON THE FIRST DAY OF THE WEEK. 162
mercy. 37, 101, 108, 125, 150, 153, 164,
200, 209, 210, 236, 239
Messiah. 55, 68, 84, 87, 113, 137, 138,
218
metabaino. 122
MINISTERS MUST PREACH AND OBEY GOD'S WORDS. . . . 202
ministry. 1, 8, 16, 20, 78, 140, 224,
225, 229, 235, 242, 247, 248
MINISTRY FUNDS FROM TRUE CHRISTIANS. 247
More Verses On Walking. 216
Moses And Aaron Committed Sins Unto Death. 187
MOSES' SIN UNTO PHYSICAL DEATH. 188
murder. 18, 123, 165, 195, 228
murderer. 31, 44, 49, 60, 117, 120, 123,
201
MUSLIMS MURDER THEIR ENEMIES. 165
NADAB AND ABIHU'S SINS UNTO PHYSICAL DEATH. 189
Name's sake. 246
New International Version. 54, 146
New Testament commandments. 170, 186
nikao. 72, 139, 171
nike. 171
NIV. 93, 136, 138, 172
NO FEAR IN TRUE CHRISTIAN LOVE. 162
NO FELLOWSHIP WITH THE DEVIL OR HIS PEOPLE. 27
NO ONE SHOULD BE ASHAMED OF GOD'S WORDS. 100
NON-CHRISTIANS CALLED WANDERING STARS. 26
NOT ASHAMED BEFORE HIM AT HIS COMING. 105
NOT ASHAMED EVEN IN SUFFERING FOR CHRIST. 101
obedience. 215, 216, 257

OBEDIENCE MUST FOLLOW GENUINE LOVE............ 215
obey......................... 39, 129, 141, 165, 170, 172, 193, 202
ONE DAY EVERY KNEE SHALL BOW TO CHRIST........... 42
ONLY CHRIST CAN FORGIVE SINS........................ 46
ONLY CHRIST HAS ATONED FOR ALL SINS................. 39
ONLY GENUINE CHRISTIANS AT THE LORD'S TABLE..... 220
ONLY TRUE CHRISTIANS CAN WALK IN THE SPIRIT....... 29
Order Blank Pages....................................... iv
Orders: 1-800-John 10:9. i
Other Verses On Propitiation............................ 54
Other Verses Using "Fellow". 247
OU ME... 208
overcome......................... 49, 69, 72, 73, 75, 78, 139, 154, 171-173, 193, 226
overcoming... 73
PARAKLETOS... 51
paresia... 160
parresia.. 99
Pas... 106
Pastor D. A. Waite, Th.D.,Ph.D............................ 1
PASTOR TIMOTHY WAS GIVEN ASSURANCE.............. 183
pastor/bishop/elder. 233, 235, 243, 256
pastors........................... 98, 107, 205, 234, 235, 243, 256
PASTORS MUST PREACH THE BIBLE FAITHFULLY........ 234
pastors/bishops/elders........................ 234, 243, 256
PASTORS/BISHOPS/ELDERS MUST BE MARRIED......... 243
PASTORS/BISHOPS/ELDERS NEED A GOOD REPORT...... 256
Patmos... 1, 5, 6
Patricia Canter... iii
Paul......................... 15, 16, 20, 25, 31, 60, 66, 71, 75,
78, 81, 82, 91, 96, 100, 101,
106, 107, 110, 113, 117-119,
126-128, 151, 158, 161, 183-185,
202, 210, 214, 218, 227, 229,
231, 233-235, 241, 242, 246,
248, 249, 254, 255, 257, 258, 260
PAUL KEPT FROM EVIL EVEN WHILE FACING DEATH.... 227
PAUL PREACHED CHRIST AS THE SON OF GOD........... 158
PAUL WANTED CHRIST TO BE MAGNIFIED................ 100
PAUL WANTED TO FINISH HIS MISSION WITH JOY....... 229

PAUL WAS NOT ASHAMED OF CHRIST.................. 101
peace............................. 20, 34-36, 55, 71, 73, 91, 95,
107, 108, 126, 153, 155, 162,
163, 183, 203, 209, 211, 227,
229, 230, 254, 255, 259
perfect............................ 6, 10, 11, 17, 23, 36, 51, 53,
61, 71, 76, 83, 109, 111, 115,
122, 149, 156, 159, 162, 169,
171, 173, 174, 178, 182, 185,
196, 210, 217, 222, 225, 238
perfect tense............................. 17, 122, 169, 171, 182
PERIPATEO..................................... 28, 63, 212
perish............................ 11-13, 56, 62, 93, 94, 103, 130,
143, 145, 179, 180, 183, 192,
193, 197
persecute... 165, 220
PERSECUTED FOR CHRIST'S SAKE WAS PROMISED....... 246
persecution................................. 1, 20, 220, 229
Peter............................. 2-5, 8, 11, 12, 21, 26, 31, 33,
44, 45, 58, 60, 66, 73, 74, 78,
81, 84, 91, 93, 95, 98, 101,
105, 108, 111, 116, 119, 123,
124, 135-137, 142, 146, 148,
150, 151, 154, 160, 161, 167,
180, 190, 192, 205, 208, 212,
214, 227, 230, 235, 243, 245,
254, 257, 258
PETER COMMANDED TO HAVE FERVENT CHARITY....... 245
PETER'S READERS HAD NOT SEEN CHRIST.............. 150
philoproteuo.. 250
PILATE WROTE ABOUT CHRIST BEING THE KING........ 257
PLANAO... 40, 95, 112
planos.. 217
please.. 29, 129, 237
pleasing................................. 30, 36, 129, 185, 186
PLEROO... 17
PONDER THINGS OF GOOD REPORT..................... 256
prayer......................... 15, 43, 121, 129, 160, 185, 186,
210, 226, 229
PRAYING FOR LABORERS IN GOD'S HARVEST............. 3
preaching Verse-By-Verse................................. 1
preeminence... 250-253
PREEMINENCE BELONGS ONLY TO CHRIST.............. 250

PREEMINENCE–NOT FOR HUMAN BEINGS. 251
presbuteros. 233
pride. 79, 81, 82, 194
promise. 42, 63, 73, 75, 90-93, 104, 137,
153, 227, 239, 248
promises. 17, 44, 47, 55, 70, 80, 90-93,
187, 204, 236, 239, 241
proper Bible. 65, 199
PROPER WORDS OF GOD MUST BE HELD. 243
propitiation. 34, 53, 54, 146, 147, 165
PROPITIATION FOR THE SINS OF THE WORLD. 54
prosper. 236, 237, 252
prosperity. 236
Publisher's Data. iv
pure. 22, 38, 39, 106-108, 127, 142, 148,
167, 183, 205, 214, 255, 258
purity. 107, 108
PUT AWAY EVIL SPEAKING. 253
READING THE WHOLE BIBLE EACH YEAR. 215
rebellious. 251
REBELLIOUS EXALTATION LEADS TO CHAOS. 251
RECIPROCAL LOVE NOT PRACTICED MUCH TODAY. 167
RECONCILIATION FOR THE WHOLE WORLD. 57
Refusing To Take Goods From The Heathen. 246
REJOICE IN THE LORD ALWAYS. 19
REPROVE MEANS TO EXPOSE TO THE LIGHT. 16
RETURN TO THE LORD'S WAYS. 134
reward. 99, 120, 219-221, 235, 247
RIGHT HANDS OF FELLOWSHIP GIVEN IN THE BIBLE. 28
RIGHTEOUS AND UNRIGHTEOUS--NO FELLOWSHIP. 16
Romans 13. . . . . 25, 28, 64, 80, 142, 148, 166,
214, 216, 226
SALVATION FOR ALL WHO ACCEPT CHRIST. 152
SALVATION FOR AS MANY AS RECEIVE CHRIST. 55
SALVATION OFFERED TO THE ENTIRE WORLD. 152
SAPPHIRA LIED AND DIED LIKE HER HUSBAND. 190
SARAH BELIEVED GOD'S PROMISE OF A SON. 93
Satan. 12, 25, 31, 37, 60, 73, 74, 76,
77, 113, 114, 117, 118, 155,
190, 192, 193, 218
SATAN IS A LIAR AND A MURDERER. 117
SATAN LOOSED FOR WAR AFTER THE MILLENNIUM. 114
SATAN THE MASTER DECEIVER. 113

SATAN'S GOAL IS PREEMINENCE OVER GOD............. 252
second coming of Christ.................................. 97
SHALL NEVER PERISH BRINGS ASSURANCE............. 183
sin. 10-12, 16, 19, 22-25, 27, 28, 31,
32, 35, 38-42, 45, 47, 48, 51-
53, 56, 59, 62, 66, 68, 70, 71,
73, 75, 83, 93-95, 104, 108,
109, 111-115, 119, 127, 142,
158, 159, 164, 172, 173, 175,
179, 180, 182, 187-192, 217,
229, 230, 235, 245, 252, 259
SIN NEEDS TO BE CONFESSED AND FORSAKEN.......... 112
sin unto death................................ 187, 189, 190
sinless............................. 38, 53, 111, 112, 173, 178
sinlessness.. 111
sins of the whole world....................... 53, 54, 109-111,
147
SINS UNTO PHYSICAL DEATH....................... 187, 189
skandalon.. 68
Sodom... 246, 247
SOME OF THE FALSE DOCTRINAL SEDUCERS............. 95
Son of God. 7, 9, 11, 13, 36, 53, 56, 73,
88, 94, 110, 111, 114, 137, 138,
146, 154-159, 173, 177, 180-182,
195
sound churches.. 85, 252
SOUND CHURCHES–THE GROUND OF THE TRUTH........ 203
sound doctrine................................ 204, 223, 243
SPIRITS MUST BE TESTED FOR ERRORS. 133
splanchnon... 125
STEWARDS MUST BE FAITHFUL TO THEIR MASTER...... 241
STOP BEING DECEIVED................................. 112
STOP MARVELING AT THE WORLD'S HATRED........... 121
strong. 15, 31, 32, 60, 66, 75, 92, 99,
128, 141, 193, 202
STRONG DELUSION IN THE TRIBULATION PERIOD........ 31
sunistao.. 208
Table of Contents... iv
TAKE CARE OF FAITHFUL PASTORS...................... 235
teleioo... 61, 159
tereo... 59, 61, 170
testing.. 134
the Antichrist............................... 83, 84, 219, 253

THE APOSTLE JOHN RESPONDED TO CHRIST'S CALL.	2
THE APOSTLES TAUGHT SOUND DOCTRINES.	222
THE APOSTLES WERE TO WAIT FOR THE SPIRIT.	92
THE BIBLE FOR TODAY PRESS.	i
THE BIBLE'S DEFINITION OF AN "ANTICHRIST".	219
THE BRAZEN SERPENT--A PICTURE OF THE CROSS.	12
THE CHARACTERISTICS OF NEVER FAILING LOVE.	245
THE CHRISTIANS' INDWELLING HOLY SPIRIT.	151
THE CONTINUOUS GREEK IMPERFECT TENSE.	7
THE DARK WALK OF THE DEVIL'S CHILDREN.	29
THE DEAD IN CHRIST RISE FIRST.	106
THE DEVIL IS THE LEADING MURDERER OF ALL TIME.	123
THE DEVIL WILL BE SENT TO THE LAKE OF FIRE.	76
THE DOCTRINE OF THE INCARNATION OF CHRIST.	136
THE EARLY CHURCH KEPT SOUND DOCTRINES.	222
THE EFFECTS OF THE SPIRIT OF GOD.	163
THE ELECTION OF MATTHIAS WAS DISOBEDIENCE.	91
the faith.	75, 107, 110, 128, 135, 158, 161, 173, 197, 220
THE GNOSTIC GREEK TEXT REMOVES "GOD" HERE.	10
THE GREEK WORD, TIS, IS FOR ANY HUMAN.	57
THE HERETICAL TEACHINGS OF HYPER-CALVINISM.	54
THE HOLY SPIRIT CAN GUIDE CHRISTIANS.	96
THE HOLY SPIRIT INDWELLS TRUE CHRISTIANS.	63, 131
THE HOLY SPIRIT IS "THE SPIRIT OF TRUTH".	201
THE HOLY SPIRIT WITNESSES ABOUT CHRIST.	174
THE HOLY SPIRIT WOULD BE IN THE DISCIPLES.	131
THE HOLY SPIRIT'S COMING WAS PROMISED.	92
THE HYPER-CALVINISTS' ERRORS OF THE CROSS.	147
THE INDWELLING HOLY SPIRIT OF GOD.	132
THE INDWELLING OF THE FATHER AND THE SON.	204
THE JOY OF THE LORD GIVES STRENGTH.	18
THE JUDGMENT SEAT OF CHRIST EXPLAINED.	221
THE JUDGMENT SEAT OF CHRIST'S TEST OF WORKS.	134
THE KING JAMES BIBLE HAS GOD'S PROPER WORDS.	237
THE LAW OF MOSES IS NOT FOR CHRISTIANS.	257
THE LORD AND MOSES–A PERSONAL RELATIONSHIP.	259
The Lord Jesus Christ Is Called The Life.	8
THE MEANING OF THE GREEK WORD, "AGAPAO".	122
THE MEANING OF THE GREEK WORD, "AIRO".	109
THE MEANING OF THE GREEK WORD, "ALETHEIA".	86
THE MEANING OF THE GREEK WORD, "ALLELON".	148
THE MEANING OF THE GREEK WORD, "APHIEMI".	47, 48, 69

THE MEANING OF THE GREEK WORD, "BARUS".......... 171
THE MEANING OF THE GREEK WORD, "ELENCHO"....... 224
THE MEANING OF THE GREEK WORD, "GENNAO"........ 169
THE MEANING OF THE GREEK WORD, "HILASMOS"... 54, 146
THE MEANING OF THE GREEK WORD, "HOMOLOGEO" 42, 137
THE MEANING OF THE GREEK WORD, "KEIMAI"......... 194
THE MEANING OF THE GREEK WORD, "MENO"........... 61
THE MEANING OF THE GREEK WORD, "METABAINO". ... 122
THE MEANING OF THE GREEK WORD, "MISEO".......... 68
THE MEANING OF THE GREEK WORD, "NIKAO"....... 72, 139
THE MEANING OF THE GREEK WORD, "NIKE"........... 171
THE MEANING OF THE GREEK WORD, "OPHEILO"....... 147
THE MEANING OF THE GREEK WORD, "PARESIA"........ 160
THE MEANING OF THE GREEK WORD, "PARRESIA"........ 99
THE MEANING OF THE GREEK WORD, "PERIPATEO"28, 63, 212
THE MEANING OF THE GREEK WORD, "PHILUAREO"..... 253
THE MEANING OF THE GREEK WORD, "PLANAO"...... 40, 95
THE MEANING OF THE GREEK WORD, "PLANOS"......... 217
THE MEANING OF THE GREEK WORD, "PLANO".......... 112
THE MEANING OF THE GREEK WORD, "PLEROO"......... 17
THE MEANING OF THE GREEK WORD, "SKANDALON"..... 68
THE MEANING OF THE GREEK WORD, "SUNISTAO"...... 208
THE MEANING OF THE GREEK WORD, "TELEIOO"..... 61, 159
THE MEANING OF THE GREEK WORD, "TEREO".... 59, 61, 170
THE MEANING OF THE GREEK WORD, "THEAOMAI".... 2, 152
THE MEANING OF THE WORD, "AMEN".................. 230
THE MEANING OF "CONFESS" IS TO "AGREE"............ 114
THE MIRACLE OF THE VIRGIN BIRTH.................. 144, 196
THE NECESSITY OF CHRIST'S VIRGIN BIRTH............. 156
THE PERSON AND WORK OF CHRIST.................... 176
THE RIGHT BIBLE GIVES US LIGHT...................... 67
THE SAVIOUR WAS AND IS PERFECT AND SINLESS........ 111
THE SON CAME FROM THE FATHER AND RETURNED..... 90
THE SOURCE OF ETERNAL LIFE IS THE SON OF GOD...... 94
THE THOUSAND-YEAR REIGN OF CHRIST................ 97
THE TRINITY IS A TRI-UNITY—ONE IN THREE............. 89
THE TRINITY IS TAUGHT IN THESE VERSES............. 175
THE TRUTH CAN MAKE PEOPLE FREE................... 201
THE WORLD'S HATRED OF CHRISTIANS................ 121
THEAOMAI... 2, 152
THERE ARE MANY DECEIVERS AND ANTICHRISTS....... 217
There is BOLDNESS.................................. 36

There is CLEANSING. 35
There is FELLOWSHIP through the literal Blood of Christ. 34
There is FORGIVENESS through the literal Blood of Christ. 34
There is JUSTIFICATION through the literal Blood of Christ.. ... 34
There is PEACE through the literal Blood of Christ. 34
There is PROPITIATION through the literal Blood of Christ. ... 34
There is PUNISHMENT. 36
There is RECONCILIATION through the literal Blood of Christ.. 35
There is REDEMPTION. 33
There is REMEMBRANCE through the literal Blood of Christ. ... 35
There is SANCTIFICATION through the literal Blood of Christ.. 34
There is VICTORY (Over Satan) through the literal Blood. 37
THESE CHRISTIANS WERE WORLD COMPROMISERS. 78
THEY WHO DO GOD'S WILL ABIDE FOREVER.. 82
Thirteen Things About The Apostle John. 2
THIS CENTURION SAW CHRIST AS THE SON OF GOD. 156
THIS CHURCH ALLOWED DICTATOR DIOTREPHES. 254
THOMAS CALLED CHRIST HIS LORD AND HIS GOD. 196
Those Who Committed The Sin Unto Physical Death.. 187
THOSE WHO DISAGREE WITH THE BIBLE ARE LIARS. 49
TIMOTHY WAS NOT TO BE ASHAMED OF CHRIST. 100
Tis.. .... 51, 57
Titus. 31, 60, 78, 92, 98, 106, 108, 153,
164, 178, 181, 210, 235, 242,
243, 248
TITUS WAS A FELLOWHELPER IN PAUL'S MINISTRY. 248
Trinity. 6, 88, 89, 175, 176, 219
TRUE CHRISTIANS ARE TO LOVE AS CHRIST LOVED. 166
TRUE CHRISTIANS HAVE BOLDNESS AND ACCESS.. 161
TRUE CHRISTIANS HAVE BOTH FLESH AND SPIRIT.. 151
TRUE CHRISTIANS HAVE TWO NATURES. 80
TRUE CHRISTIANS MUST FORSAKE ALL IDOLS. 198
TRUE CHRISTIANS SHOULD GLORIFY GOD. 132
TRUE CHRISTIANS WILL BE LIKE CHRIST. 104
TRUE FAITH IN CHRIST BRINGS EVERLASTING LIFE. 146
true God. 9, 13, 94, 179, 182, 195, 196,
198
TRUE TRUST IN CHRIST BRINGS ETERNAL LIFE. 144
truth. .... iii, 1, 4, 6, 9, 16, 21, 23, 27,
30-32, 38, 40, 41, 44, 49, 52,
59, 60, 65, 67, 85-90, 95, 96,
101, 108, 111-113, 117, 123,
125, 126, 131, 133, 140, 142,

                                148, 151, 155, 167, 173-175,
                           178, 182, 191-193, 196, 199-204,
                              206, 209, 212, 214, 223, 225,
                              233, 237, 240, 245, 247, 255,
                                                   256, 258
TRUTH MUST BE KNOWN AND FOLLOWED. 200
trying. 118, 134
TURNING FROM SATAN'S POWER. 118
TWO JUDGMENTS FOR PEOPLE–FOR SAVED & LOST. 161
Two Of Aaron's Sons Committed The Sin Unto Death. 189
TWO PHASES OF CHRIST'S SECOND COMING. 98,
                                                        104
Two Verses On Love. 65
unclean. 3, 36, 135, 189, 225
unfeigned. 107, 108, 142, 148, 167, 202,
                                                        214
UNFEIGNED LOVE IS NECESSARY. 214
UNFEIGNED NON-HYPOCRITICAL LOVE. 142
Unlimited Atonement. 54, 55
UNRIGHTEOUSNESS DEFINED BY THE BIBLE. 191
USE AND PREACH ONLY THE WORDS OF TRUTH. 256
Verses About Joy. 237
Verses About The Truth. 199
Verses On Abiding. 62
Verses On Antichrist. 138, 219
Verses On Ashamed.. 99
Verses On Assurance. 126, 183
Verses On Being Born-Again. 115
Verses On Being Strong. 75
Verses On Bible Preservation.. 205
Verses On Boldness. 160
Verses On Cain. 119
Verses On Charity. 244
Verses On Christ As The Saviour. 152
Verses On Christian Love. 141, 166
Verses On Christ's Dying For Sins.. 109
Verses On Christ's "Whosoever Will". 55
Verses On Cleansing. 46
Verses On Confession. 42
Verses On Confidence. 99, 127
Verses On Darkness.. 23
Verses On Deceivers. 218
Verses On Deception.. . . . . 40, 113

Verses On Doctrine.	221
Verses On Elders.	233
Verses On Eternal Life..	93
Verses On Everlasting And Eternal Life.	145
Verses On Evil.	225
Verses On Faithfulness.	43, 239
Verses On False Prophets.	135
Verses On Fear.	162
Verses On Fellowship.	15, 27
Verses On Following.	254
Verses On Forgiveness.	45, 70
Verses On God The Father.	88
Verses On God's Sending His Son From Heaven..	143
Verses On Grace.	209
Verses On Hate..	121
Verses On Hope.	106
Verses On Idols.	197
Verses On Joy.	17, 228
Verses On Judgment.	161
Verses On Just.	44
Verses On Keeping Christ's Commandments..	59
Verses On Knowing.	86
Verses On Liars.	49
Verses On Light.	22, 66
Verses On Love..	65, 129
Verses On Loving Genuine Christian Brethren.	148
Verses On Lying.	31, 60
Verses On Malicious Words.	253
Verses On Mercy.	210
Verses On Murder.	123
Verses On Name's Sake.	246
Verses On Obedience To God's Words.	215
Verses On Overcoming.	73
Verses On Peace.	211
Verses On Pleasing..	129
Verses On Prayer.	186
Verses On Pride.	81
Verses On Promises.	91
Verses On Prosperity.	236
Verses On Purity.	107
Verses On Recognizing Christ As The Messiah.	137
Verses On Rewards.	220
Verses On Satan, The Wicked One.	74, 193

Verses On Sin. 39
Verses On The Antichrist And Antichrists. 84
Verses On The Deity Of Christ. 196
Verses On The Devil. 117
Verses On The Flesh. 79
Verses On The Indwelling Holy Spirit. 131, 140
Verses On The Indwelling Of The Holy Spirit. 151
Verses On The Last Time Or Last Days. 83
Verses On The Second Coming Of Christ. 97
Verses On The Sinlessness Of Christ.. 111
Verses On The Son Of God. 154
Verses On Those Who Partially Saw God. 149
Verses On Trying And Testing. 134
Verses On Unclean And Evil Spirits. 135
Verses On Walk. 28
Verses On Walking. 63, 212, 216
Verses On Wickedness. 194
Verses On Witness.. 14
Verses On Writing. 256
virgin birth. 6, 10, 13, 19, 62, 144,
156, 173, 174, 176, 178, 196,
223
Waite, Dr. D. A.. . . . . 1, i-iii
walk. 12, 16, 18, 21, 23-32, 35, 48, 61-
65, 67, 69, 80, 81, 84, 86, 112,
129, 198, 200, 212, 213, 215-
217, 224, 237, 251
walking. 2, 16, 21, 31, 63-65, 67-69, 80,
81, 84, 102, 154, 212, 213, 216,
227, 237
WALKING AFTER THE SPIRIT. 80
WALKING CIRCUMSPECTLY.. 64
WALKING IN GOOD WORKS AFTER SALVATION. 216
WALKING IN NEWNESS OF ETERNAL LIFE.. 216
WALKING IN THE LIGHT. 16, 67
WALKING IN THE LIGHT BRINGS FELLOWSHIP. 16
WALKING IN TRUTH BRINGS GREAT JOY. 21
WALKING IN TRUTH BY GOD'S WORDS. 31
Walls. 238
Website: www.BibleForToday.org.. i
whole world. 53, 54, 56-58, 79, 109-111,
124, 147, 152, 194, 218
WHY GOD SENT HIS SON FROM HEAVEN. 147

WHY WORDS OMITTED FROM THE GNOSTIC GREEK. 176
wicked. 23, 49, 66, 72-76, 79, 81, 103,
119, 121, 134, 135, 145, 146,
160, 171-173, 185, 192-195, 203,
213, 216, 221, 247, 251
wicked one. 72, 74, 75, 119, 192, 193
wickedness. 23, 26, 62, 77-79, 82, 194,
195, 202, 209, 254
WICKEDNESS LIES WITHIN THE HEARTS. 195
witness.. .... 1, 6, 8, 14, 15, 35, 44, 120,
144, 173-177, 201, 235, 240,
244
WOLVES LOOKING LIKE SHEEP. 135
Words of God. .... iii, 18, 21, 30, 31, 47,
97, 101, 143, 185, 197, 199,
203, 204, 206, 220, 234-237,
243
WORLD ENTANGLEMENT IS DEPLORABLE. 78
wounds. 240
write.. .... 6, 17, 21, 51, 65, 66, 69, 72,
100, 108, 142, 148, 166, 193,
214, 227, 230, 246, 256-260
writing. 6, 17, 21, 70, 75, 82, 87, 121,
131, 138, 150, 233, 254, 256-
258
"ANOTHER DISCIPLE" IS THE APOSTLE JOHN. 4
"JOY"--A FRUIT OF GOD THE HOLY SPIRIT. 20
"ON ME" REMOVED FROM JOHN 6:47 BY GNOSTICS. 145
"OU ME"–THE STRONGEST GREEK NEGATIVE.. 208
"OUR SINS" MEANS THE WHOLE WORLD'S SINS.. 110
"PAS" REFERS TO EVERY TRUE CHRISTIAN. 106
"THE FAITH" REFERS TO BIBLE DOCTRINES. 172
"THE PRINCE OF LIFE" IS A TITLE OF CHRIST. 9
"THE SON OF GOD" A TITLE FOR CHRIST.. 154

About The Author

The author of this book, Dr. D. A. Waite, received a BA (Bachelor of Arts) in classical Greek and Latin from the University of Michigan in 1948, a ThM (Master of Theology), with high honors, in New Testament Greek Literature and Exegesis from Dallas Theological Seminary in 1952, an MA (Master of Arts) in Speech from Southern Methodist University in 1953, a ThD (Doctor of Theology), with honors, in Bible Exposition from Dallas Theological Seminary in 1955, and a PhD in Speech from Purdue University in 1961. He held both New Jersey and Pennsylvania teacher certificates in Greek and Language Arts.

He has been a teacher in the areas of Greek, Hebrew, Bible, Speech, and English for over thirty-five years in ten schools, including one junior high, one senior high, four Bible institutes, two colleges, two universities, and one seminary. He served his country as a Navy Chaplain for five years on active duty; pastored three churches; was Chairman and Director of the Radio and Audio-Film Commission of the American Council of Christian Churches; since 1969, has been Founder, President, and Director of THE BIBLE FOR TODAY; since 1978, has been Founder and President of the DEAN BURGON SOCIETY; has produced over 700 other studies, books, cassettes, VHS's, CD's, or VCR's on various topics IN DEFENSE OF TRADITIONAL BIBLE TEXTS, on radio, shortwave, and streaming on the Internet at BibleForToday.org, 24/7/365 on the BROWN BOX.

Dr. and Mrs. Waite have been married since 1948; they have four sons, one daughter, and, at present, eight grandchildren, and fifteen great-grandchildren. Since October 4, 1998, he has been the Pastor of the Bible For Today Baptist Church in Collingswood, New Jersey. His sermons are heard both on radio and the Internet over www.BibleForToday.org on the BROWN BOX.

Order Blank (p. 1)

Name:_____
Address:_____
City & State:_____Zip:_____
*Credit Card #:*_____*Expires:*_____

Verse by Verse Preaching Books By Dr. D. A. Waite

[ ] Send 1, 2, & 3 John–Preaching Verse By Verse By Pastor D. A. Waite, 300 pages ($15.00 + $8.00 S&H) fully indexed

[ ] Send 2 Peter & Jude–Preaching Verse By Verse By Pastor D. A. Waite, 215 pages ($15.00 + $8.00 S&H) fully indexed.

[ ] Send *1 & 2 Thessalonians–Preaching Verse By Verse* By Pastor D. A. Waite, 327 pages ($15.00 + $8.00 S&H) fully indexed.

[ ] Send *Hebrews–Preaching Verse by Verse*, By Pastor D. A. Waite, 616 pages ($30.00 +$10.00 S&H) fully indexed.

[ ] Send *Revelation–Preaching Verse by Verse*, By Pastor D. A. Waite, 1032 pages ($50.00 + $10.00 S&H) fully indexed.

[ ] Send *1 Timothy--Preaching Verse by Verse*, by Pastor D. A. Waite, 288 pages, hardback ($11+$5 S&H) fully indexed.

[ ] Send *2 Timothy--Preaching Verse by Verse*, by Pastor D. A. Waite, 250 pages, hardback ($11+$5 S&H) fully indexed.

[ ] Send *Romans--Preaching Verse by Verse* by Pastor D. A. Waite 736 pp. Hardback ($25+$8 S&H) fully indexed

[ ] Send *Colossians & Philemon--Preaching Verse by Verse* by Pastor D. A. Waite ($12+$5 S&H) hardback, 240 pages.

[ ] Send *Philippians--Preaching Verse by Verse* by Pastor D. A. Waite ($10+$5 S&H) hardback, 176 pages. fully indexed.

[ ] Send *Ephesians--Preaching Verse by Verse* by Pastor D. A. Waite ($12+$5 S&H) hardback, 224 pages. fully indexed.

[ ] Send *Galatians--Preaching Verse By Verse* by Pastor D. A. Waite ($12+$5 S&H) hardback, 216 pages. fully indexed.

[ ] Send *1 Peter–Preaching Verse By Verse* by Pastor D. A. Waite ($10.00 + $5.00 S&H) hardback, 176 pages. fully indexed.

Send or Call Orders to:
THE BIBLE FOR TODAY
900 Park Ave., Collingswood, NJ 08108
Phone: 856-854-4452; FAX:--2464; Orders: 1-800 JOHN 10:9
E-Mail Orders: BFT@BibleForToday.org; Credit Cards OK

Order Blank (p. 2)

Name:_____
Address:_____
City & State:_____Zip:_____
Credit Card #:_____Expires:_____

Other Books By Dr. D. A. Waite

[ ] Send *A Critical Answer to God's Word Preserved* by Pastor D. A. Waite, 192 pp. perfect bound ($11.00+$4.00 S&H)
[ ] Send *Defending the King James Bible* by DAW ($12+$5 S&H) A hardback book, indexed with study questions.
[ ] Send *BJU's Errors on Bible Preservation* by Dr. D. A. Waite, 110 pages, paperback ($8+$4 S&H) fully indexed
[ ] Send *Fundamentalist Deception on Bible Preservation* by Dr. D. A. Waite, ($8+$4 S&H), paperback, fully indexed
[ ] Send *Fundamentalist MIS-INFORMATION on Bible Versions* by Dr. Waite ($7+$4 S&H) perfect bound, 136 pages
[ ] Send *Fundamentalist Distortions on Bible Versions* by Dr. Waite ($6+$3 S&H) A perfect bound book, 80 pages
[ ] Send *Fuzzy Facts From Fundamentalists* by Dr. D. A. Waite ($8.00 + $4.00) printed booklet
[ ] Send *Foes of the King James Bible Refuted* by DAW ($10 +$4 S&H) A perfect bound book, 164 pages in length.
[ ] Send *Central Seminary Refuted on Bible Versions* by Dr. Waite ($10+$4 S&H) A perfect bound book, 184 pages
[ ] Send *The Case for the King James Bible* by DAW ($7 +$3 S&H) A perfect bound book, 112 pages in length.
[ ] Send *Theological Heresies of Westcott and Hort* by Dr. D. A. Waite, ($7+$3 S&H) A printed booklet.
[ ] Send *Westcott's Denial of Resurrection*, Dr. Waite ($4+$3)
[ ] Send *Four Reasons for Defending KJB* by DAW ($3+$3)
[ ] Send *Holes in the Holman Christian Standard Bible* by Dr. Waite ($3+$2 S&H) A printed booklet, 40 pages
[ ] Send *Contemporary Eng. Version Exposed*, DAW ($3+$2)

Send or Call Orders to:
THE BIBLE FOR TODAY
900 Park Ave., Collingswood, NJ 08108
Phone: 856-854-4452; FAX:--2464; Orders: 1-800 JOHN 10:9
E-Mail Orders: BFT@BibleForToday.org; Credit Cards OK

Order Blank (p. 3)

Name:_____

Address:_____

City & State:_____Zip:_____

Credit Card #:_____Expires:_____

[ ] Send *NIV Inclusive Language Exposed* by DAW ($5+$3)

[ ] Send *26 Hours of KJB Seminar* (4 videos*)* by DAW($50.00*)*

[ ] Send *Making Marriage Melodious* by Pastor D. A. Waite ($7+$4 S&H), perfect bound, 112 pages.

[ ] Send *Burgon's Warnings on Revision* by DAW ($7+$4 S&H) A perfect bound book, 120 pages in length.

[ ] Send *The Superior Foundation of the KJB* By Dr. D. A. Waite ($10.00 + $7.00 S&H)

Other Books By Dr. D. A. Waite (Continued)

[ ] Send *Biblical Separation–1,896 Bible Verses About It* by Dr. D. A. Waite ($14.00 + $7.00 S&H)

[ ] Send *Westcott & Hort's Greek Text & Theory Refuted by Burgon's Revision Revised--Summarized* by Dr. D. A. Waite ($7.00+$4 S&H), 120 pages, perfect bound.

[ ] Send *Dean Burgon's Confidence in KJB* by DAW ($3+$3)

[ ] Send *Vindicating Mark 16:9-20* by Dr. Waite ($3+$3S&H)

[ ] Send *Summary of Traditional Text* by Dr. Waite ($3 +$3)

[ ] Send *Summary of Causes of Corruption*, DAW ($3+$3)

[ ] Send *Summary of Inspiration* by Dr. Waite ($3+$3 S&H)

[ ] Send *Soulwinning's Versions-Perversions* By Dr. D. A. Waite ($6.00 + $5.00 S&H)

Books By Dean John William Burgon

[ ] Send *The Revision Revised* by Dean Burgon ($25 + $5 S&H) A hardback book, 640 pages in length.

[ ] Send *The Last 12 verses of Mark* by Dean Burgon ($15+$5 S&H) A hardback book 400 pages.

Send or Call Orders to:
THE BIBLE FOR TODAY
900 Park Ave., Collingswood, NJ 08108
Phone: 856-854-4452; FAX:--2464; Orders: 1-800 JOHN 10:9
E-Mail Orders: BFT@BibleForToday.org; Credit Cards OK

Order Blank (p. 4)

Name:_____
Address:_____
City & State:_____ Zip:_____
Credit Card #:_____ Expires:_____

[ ] Send *The Traditional Text* hardback by Burgon ($16+$5 S&H) A hardback book, 384 pages in length.
[ ] Send *Causes of Corruption* by Burgon ($15+$5 S&H) A hardback book, 360 pages in length.
[ ] Send *Inspiration and Interpretation*, Dean Burgon ($25+$5 S&H) A hardback book, 610 pages in length.

Books By Dr. Jack Moorman

[ ] Send *Samuel P. Tregelles--The Man Who Made the Critical Text Acceptable to Bible Believers* by Dr. Moorman ($2+$1)
[ ] Send *8,000 Differences Between TR & CT* by Dr. Jack Moorman [$65 + $7.50 S&H] Over 500-large-pages of data
[ ] Send *356 Doctrinal Errors in the NIV & Other Modern Versions*, 100-large-pages, $10.00+$6 S&H.
[ ] Send *The Doctrinal Heart of the Bible--Removed from Modern Versions* by Dr. Jack Moorman, VCR, $15 +$4 S&H
[ ] Send *Modern Bibles--The Dark Secret* by Dr. Jack Moorman, $5+$3 S&H
[ ] Send *The Manuscript Digest of the N.T.* (721 pp.) By Dr. Jack Moorman, copy-machine bound ($50+$7 S&H)
[ ] *Early Manuscripts, Church Fathers, & the Authorized Version* by Dr. Jack Moorman, $18+$5 S&H. Hardback
[ ] Send *Forever Settled--Bible Documents & History Survey* by Dr. Jack Moorman, $20+$5 S&H. Hardback book.
[ ] Send *When the KJB Departs from the So-Called "Majority Text"* by Dr. Jack Moorman, $16+$5 S&H
[ ] Send *Missing in Modern Bibles--Nestle-Aland/NIV Errors* by Dr. Jack Moorman, $8+$4 S&H

Send or Call Orders to:
THE BIBLE FOR TODAY
900 Park Ave., Collingswood, NJ 08108
Phone: 856-854-4452; FAX:--2464; Orders: 1-800 JOHN 10:9
E-Mail Orders: BFT@BibleForToday.org; Credit Cards OK

Order Blank (p. 5)

Name:_____
Address:_____
City & State:_____ Zip:_____
Credit Card #:_____ Expires:_____

Books By Miscellaneous Authors

[ ] Send *Guide to Textual Criticism* by Edward Miller ($7+$4) Hardback book
[ ] Send *Scrivener's Greek New Testament Underlying the King James Bible,* hardback, ($14+$5 S&H)
[ ] Send *Scrivener's <u>Annotated</u> Greek New Testament,* by Dr. Frederick Scrivener: Hardback--($35+$5 S&H); Genuine Leather--($45+$5 S&H)
[ ] Send *Why Not the King James Bible?--An Answer to James White's KJVO Book* by Dr. K. D. DiVietro, $10+$5 S&H
[ ] Send Brochure #1: "*1000 Titles Defending the KJB/TR*" No Charge
[ ] Send *The LIE That Changed the Modern World* by Dr. H. D. Williams ($16+$5 S&H) Hardback book
[ ] Send *With Tears in My Heart* by Gertrude G. Sanborn. Hardback 414 pp. ($25+$5 S&H) 400 Christian Poems
[ ] Send *Dean Burgon's Defense of the Authorised Version* By Dr. David Bennett ($14.0 + 8.00 S&H)
[ ] Send *Drift in Baptist Missions, Churches & Schools* by Dr. David Bennett ($12.00 + $8.00 S&H)

More Books By Miscellaneous Authors

[ ] Send *Able To Bear It* By Gertrude Sanborn ($14.00 + $7.00 S&H)
[ ] Send *Visitation In Action* By Mr. R. O. Sanborn ($10.00 + $7.00 S&H)

Send or Call Orders to:
THE BIBLE FOR TODAY
900 Park Ave., Collingswood, NJ 08108
Phone: 856-854-4452; FAX:--2464; Orders: 1-800 JOHN 10:9
E-Mail Orders: BFT@BibleForToday.org; Credit Cards OK

Order Blank (p. 6)

Name:_____
Address:_____
City & State:_____Zip:_____
Credit Card #:_____Expires:_____

[ ] Send *Daily Bible Blessings From Daily Bible Readings* By Yvonne Sanborn Waite ($30.00 + $10.00 S&H)
[ ] Send *Husband-Loving Lessons* By Yvonne Sanborn Waite ($25.00 + $8.00 S&H)
[ ] Send *Gnosticism–The Doctrinal Foundation of New Bibles* by J. Moser ($20.00 + $8.00 S&H)
[ ] Send *God's Marvelous Book* By Dr. David Bennett ($15.00 + $8.00 S&H)
[ ] Send *CCM Not The Problem–Only A Symptom* By Dr. David Bennett ($12.00 + $7.00 S&H)
[ ] Send *English Standard Bible (ESV) Deficiencies* By several authors ($7.00 + $4.00 S&H)
[ ] Send *Strong's Micro-Print Concordance* By the Sherbornes ($21.00 + $8.00 S&H)

Books by D. A. Waite, Jr.

[ ] Send *The Doctored New Testament* by D. A. Waite, Jr. ($25+$5 S&H) Greek MSS differences shown, hardback
[ ] Send *Readability of A.V. (KJB)* by D. A. Waite, Jr. ($6+$3)
[ ] Send *4,114 Definitions from the Defined King James Bible* by D. A. Waite, Jr. ($7.00+$4.00 S&H)

Question And Answer Books By Dr. D. A. Waite

[ ] Send *The First 200 Questions Answered* By Dr. D. A. Waite ($15.00 + $7.00 S&H)
[ ] Send *The Second 200 Questions Answered* By Dr. D. A. Waite ($15.00 + $7.00 S&H)

Send or Call Orders to:
THE BIBLE FOR TODAY
900 Park Ave., Collingswood, NJ 08108
Phone: 856-854-4452; FAX:--2464; Orders: 1-800 JOHN 10:9
E-Mail Orders: BFT@BibleForToday.org; Credit Cards OK

Order Blank (p. 7)

Name:_____

Address:_____

City & State:_____ Zip:_____

Credit Card #:_____ Expires:_____

Question And Answer Books By Dr. D. A. Waite

[ ] Send *The Third 200 Questions Answered* By Dr. D. A. Waite ($15.00 + $7.00 S&H)

[ ] Send *The Fourth 200 Questions Answered* By Dr. D. A. Waite ($15.00 + $7.00 S&H)

[ ] Send *The Fifth 200 Questions Answered* By Dr. D. A. Waite ($15.00 + $7.00 S&H)

[ ] Send *The Sixth 200 Questions Answered* By Dr. D. A. Waite ($15.00 + $7.00 S&H)

Send or Call Orders to:
THE BIBLE FOR TODAY
900 Park Ave., Collingswood, NJ 08108
Phone: 856-854-4452; FAX:--2464; Orders: 1-800 JOHN 10:9
E-Mail Orders: BFT@BibleForToday.org; Credit Cards OK

The Defined
King James Bible
Uncommon Words Defined Accurately

I. Deluxe Genuine Leather
✦Large Print--Black or Burgundy✦
1 for $44.00+$12.00 S&H
✦Case of 12 for✦
$34.00 each+$50.00 S&H
✦Medium Print--Black or Burgundy✦
1 for $39.00+$8.00 S&H
✦Case of 12 for✦
$29.00 each+$40.00 S&H

II. Deluxe Hardback Editions
1 for $22.00+12.00 S&H (Large Print)
✦Case of 12 for✦
$17.00 each+$40.00 S&H (Large Print)
1 for $19.50+$8.00 S&H (Medium Print)
✦Case of 12 for✦
$12.50 each+$30.00 S&H (Medium Print)

Order Phone:1-800-JOHN 10:9

Pastor D. A. Waite, ThD, PhD

"Love Not The World"
(1 John 2:15-17)

The Meaning Of "The World." God mentions the phrase, "all that is in the world." In these three verses, there are three areas that make up "the world" as God defines it. (1) Area one: "the lust of the eyes." (2) Area two: "the lust of the flesh." (3) Area three: "the pride of life." The command given in verse 15 for every genuine Christian is to stop loving "the world"–any part of it. Their love should be fixed upon God the Father and on His Son, the Lord Jesus Christ.

The Result Of Loving "The World." The result of true Christians loving any one of the areas of the "world" is that "the love of the Father is not in them." If this is the case–no matter how they try to deny it--their "love" for their Heavenly Father "is not in them." absent from them. This is a very serious condition to be in!

The Destiny Of "The World." The lusts and pride of this "world" are fleeting and temporary. They pass away. Only they who do the "will of God" will abide forever. That "will" is found in an accurate Bible like the King James Bible. The first part of God's will is to truly trust the Lord Jesus Christ as Saviour and receive everlasting life, then, follow God's Words!

www.BibleForToday.org

BFT 4155   ISBN #978-1-56848112-8

www.ingramcontent.com/pod-product-compliance
Lightning Source LLC
Chambersburg PA
CBHW050129170426
43197CB00011B/1771